PORSCHE
WATER-COOLED TURBOS
1979–2019

TITLES IN THE CROWOOD AUTOCLASSICS SERIES

PORSCHE
WATER-COOLED TURBOS
1979–2019

Johnny Tipler

Foreword by Alois Ruf
With photos by Antony Fraser

THE CROWOOD PRESS

First published in 2020 by
The Crowood Press Ltd
Ramsbury, Marlborough
Wiltshire SN8 2HR

enquiries@crowood.com

www.crowood.com

British Library Cataloguing-in-Publication Data
A catalogue record for this book is available from the British Library.

ISBN 978 1 78500 693 7

Title page: An original artwork of a Porsche 991 GT2 RS, painted by
Caroline Llong, a Parisian artist based in Marseilles who specializes
in depicting cars, and Porsche and Ferrari in particular. As she says,
'All my paintings are resolutely modern, and characterized by brilliance
of colour, depth of light, dazzling reflections and an amazing energy.'
(www.e-motion-art.fr). CAROLINE LLONG

Contents page: Artwork of a Porsche 997 Turbo created specially
for the book by French watercolourist Laurence B. Henry
(www.laurencehenry@hautefort.com). LAURENCE B. HENRY

Typeset by Shane O'Dwyer, Swindon, Wiltshire

Printed and bound in India by Parksons Graphics

CONTENTS

ACKNOWLEDGEMENTS

This is my fifth book about Porsches, all written for Crowood, and like its predecessors, *Porsche Water-Cooled Turbos 1979–2019* is prolifically illustrated with photographs by Antony Fraser, my regular work colleague, so I'm indebted to him for providing shots taken on our forays into the countryside when we visit specialists in Britain and Europe, travelling in press cars provided by Porsche GB as well as our own vehicles.

I've received support from Porsche GB press office in respect of access to state-of-the-art 911 Turbos, while at the Porsche Museum in Zuffenhausen, Jessica Fritzsch ensured photoshoots happened; other helpful folk at the factory included Katja Leinweber, Tobias Hütter, Tony Hatter and Dieter Landenberger, as well as former design head Harm Lagaaij. I've also much appreciated assistance from Porsche photographic archivists Jens

Comrades in arms (or at least in cups): photographer Antony Fraser and author Johnny Tipler with 997 Turbo Cabriolet brave the snow beside the Falkirk Wheel.
ANTONY FRASER

Torner, Tobias Mauler and Amel Ghernati, who have unstintingly presented legions of pictures from their library over the years, and I've tried to use photos that have never been seen before, at least by me. Other photographers who have supplied images include Peter Meißner of Moment-fotodesign, Sarah Hall, Alex Denham, Kostas Sidiras, Carlie Thelwell, Christopher Ould and Peter Robain.

It's a real treat to feature paintings of Porsche by some terrific artists – Laurence B. Henry, Caroline Llong, Tanja Stadnic, Alina Knott, Anna-Louise Felstead and Sonja Verducci – who have all supplied images of their work, in some cases executed specially for the book.

In the course of my job as a freelance journalist I call on a lot of Porsche specialists in Britain and Europe, as well as interviewing racing drivers and personalities associated with the marque. I visit establishments such as the Porsche Museum at Zuffenhausen, and attend race meetings and historic rallies where there tend to be a preponderance of Porsches. In this context I'm particularly fond of the Nürburgring 24-Hours, Spa Six-Hours and Monte Carlo Rallye Historique. The point is, I meet a great many Porsche enthusiasts who've become friends and have been helpful one way or another in the compilation of this book. So, here they are, in no particular order: Johan Dirickx, Mike Van Dingenen, Hans Dekkers and Joe Pinter at 911Motorsport; John and Tanya Hawkins at Specialist Cars of Malton; Ian Heward at Porscheshop; Paul and Rebecca Stephens; Adrian Crawford, Richard Williams and Louise Tope at Williams Crawford; Steve Bennett, editor of *911 & Porsche World* magazine, from whom I get many of my commissions; Andy Moss and Stuart Manvell at SCS Porsche; Andrew Mearns at Gmund Cars; Ollie Preston at RPM Technic; Simon Cockram at Cameron Cars; Mark Sumpter at Paragon Porsche; Martin Pearse at MCP Motorsport; Jonny Royle and Jonathan Sturgess at Autostore; Joff Ward at Finlay Gorham; Phil Hindley at Tech9 Motorsport; Russ Rosenthal at JZM; Josh Sadler, Steve Woods and Mikey Wastie at Autofarm; Colin Belton at Ninemeister; Karl Chopra at Design911; Mike at Ashgood Porsche; James Turner of Sports Purpose; and not forgetting the guys at Kingsway Tyres Norwich who diligently swap tyres and balance wheels for me.

Then I must mention my continental friends, beginning with tuner and builder extraordinaire Alois Ruf and his team, including Estonia (Mrs Ruf), Claudia Müller, Marcel Groos, Marc Pfeiffer, Michaela Stapfer, Anja Bäurle and Anja Schropp, who have always made our trips to Bavaria a real pleasure. And, of course, a huge thank you to Alois for writing the Foreword. Next up,

the genial Willy Brombacher and his FVD operation, including his son and daughter, Max and Franziska; Ron Simons, proprietor of RSR Nürburg and RSR Spa, who has provided cars and instructors (Freddy Mayeur!) for laps of these great circuits, and an unforgettable Mosel wine road trip with Kostas Sidiras as attendant snapper. Then, Thomas Schnarr at Cargraphic, whose silencer adorns my Boxster. My colleague and I have also been entertained by Ande Votteler, Manon Borrius Broek, Tobias Sokoll and Marc Herdtle at TechArt, Björn Striening at speedART, Oliver Eigner at Gemballa, Thomas Schmitz at TJS German Sportscars, Michael Roock at Roock Racing, Jan Fatthauer at 9ff, Dirk Sadlowski at PS Automobile, Eberhard Baunach at Kremer Racing, Dmitry Ryzhak and Oleg Kucharov at Atomic Performance Parts and Motorsport Equipment, and Manfred Hering at Early911S. Thanks also to another old friend, Kobus Cantraine, for providing Porsches to have fun in. Likewise, Mark Wegh at Porsche Center Gelderland.

Constructive observations and encouragement from my PA, Emma Stuart, are much appreciated, and I want to mention a swathe of aficionados, colleagues and commissionaires with whom I spoke or drove, including Rachel Parkin, Verena Proebst, Claudio Roddaro, André Bezuidenhout, Brent Jones, Mauritz Lange, Peter Bergqvist, Jürgen Barth, Hans-Joachim Stuck, Jacky Ickx, Vic Elford, Mike Wilds, Mario Andretti, Jörg Bergmeister, Dirk Werner, Klaus Bachler, Mark Mullen, Lee Maxted-Page, James Lipman, Patrick O'Brien, Simon Jackson (editor of *GT Porsche* magazine), Alastair Iles, Mike Roberts, Lee Sibley (editor of *Total 911*), Timo Bernhard, Peter Dumbreck, Wolf Henzler, Olaf Manthey, Brendon Hartley, Angelica Grey, Walter Röhrl, Andrea Kerr, Steve Hall, Tim Havermans, Wayne Collins, Peter Offord, Carlie Thelwell, Fran Newman, Joachim von Beust, Kenny Schachter, Ash Soan, Nick Bailey and Els van der Meer at Elan PR, Angie Voluti at AV PR, Sarah Bennett-Baggs, Mike Lane, Angelica Fuentes and Keith Mainland, Keith Seume (editor of *Classic Porsche* magazine), Andy Prill and Bert Vanderbruggen – to name but a few.

Other benefactors who in no small way enabled the composition of the book include Chris Jones at Brittany Ferries, Frances Amissah at Stena Line, Michelle Ulyatt at DFDS Ferries, Natalie Benville at Eurotunnel, Charlotte Wright at Rooster PR, Natalie Hall at P&O Ferries, Simon and Jon Young at Phoenix Exhausts, Angie Voluti at Vredestein Tyres, Stefanie Olbertz and Kerstin Schneider at Falken Tyres, and Samara Amos at Continental Tyres. Many thanks to all concerned, and hopefully I haven't left too many people out.

FOREWORD

ALOIS RUF

CEO and owner of Ruf Automobile GmbH, Porsche concessionaire and doyen of turbocharging methodology

We began our first experiments with turbocharging at Ruf Automobile in 1974, fitting a turbo to a 2.7-litre 911 engine, and in 1977 we presented our first Ruf Turbo, developing 303bhp. The first car to bear a Ruf chassis number was the BTR of 1983, running a 3.4-litre Ruf turbo engine producing 374bhp, and our 'Yellowbird' CTR achieved international acclaim when it beat the world's fastest supercars in a media shoot-out at Ehra-Lessien test track in 1987, going at 340km/h (211mph).

The fact that you can utilize the velocity of the exhaust flow to drive a turbo compressor to pre-charge the intake air is fascinating, conceptually as well as in a practical sense, because it is free power that would otherwise go to waste.

The traditional ways of increasing the performance of an engine are by enlarging the displacement of the engine, raising the rpm, and raising the combustion pressure.

The last method works with turbocharging as the most efficient and elegant solution. When the boost 'sneaks up' on you, I call it the 'quiet storm' – like a ghost that suddenly pops up behind you. You check your speedometer, and the needle shows 50km/h (30mph) more than you expected – achieved in a split second. Instead of squeezing out the horsepower from a naturally aspirated engine, the turbocharger effortlessly elicits the power from a turbo engine, giving it a light-footed feel. All the years spent developing turbocharged engines bore fruit, and the infamous turbo flat spot was banished by balancing the plumbing of the intake and the exhaust side, as well as identifying the ideal initial compression ratio for the engine.

We had proved conclusively that turbocharging worked perfectly harmoniously with air-cooled engines, and so, following on from our experiences with turbocharged engines in the 1970s and 1980s, we were watching carefully to monitor how the transition went from air-cooled to water-cooled engines

Alois Ruf explains some of the CTR-4 Yellowbird's finer points to the author during a visit to the company's Pfaffenhausen headquarters.

ANTONY FRASER

A couple of Ruf Yellowbirds, separated in time by three decades: the latest CTR-4 (left) and original CTR-1.

ANTONY FRASER

in the Porsche flat-six racing cars. Le Mans has always been the yardstick for being the hardest endurance race in the world, challenging the race car builders. First, the 956 with water-cooled cylinder heads and 4-valve technology showed it was possible not only to go the distance, but to take the victory as well. Soon afterwards, the 962 followed on with all water-cooled engines. It was clear that future success for this high-performance flat-six engine, which was on its way to delivering 250bhp per litre, could only be achieved with water-cooling. That's because the cooling media can be brought to the hard-to-reach corners within the cylinder head water-jackets in order to avoid heat-nests or hot spots. Soon enough, digital engine management

perfected everything, protecting the engine and enabling economical fuel consumption.

Here, at Ruf Automobile, we celebrate eighty years in business in 2019, more than half of which have been, for us, 'turbo years'. So, we can say with some confidence that turbo is the future for your combustion engines. As a measure of how we have progressed in the last thirty years, you can read all about our latest CTR Yellowbird and its radically different chassis construction in Chapter 4 of this book.

I hope that all car connoisseurs and petrolheads thoroughly enjoy reading Johnny Tipler's book on water-cooled Porsche and Ruf Turbos.

TIMELINE

1979 The 924 Turbo is introduced.

1980 The 924 Carrera GT is launched.

1981 The 924 Carrera GTS and GTR are in action.

1985 The 944 Turbo goes on sale; it delivers 217bhp from the 2.5-litre straight-four engine.

1986 The 944 Turbo Cup race series heralds the Porsche Carrera Cup.

1988 The 944 Turbo S is introduced, which develops 250bhp.

1991 The 944 Turbo Cabriolet is unveiled.

1992 The 968 Turbo S is a limited edition model with racing intent.

1999 The 996 Turbo debuts at the Frankfurt Show.

2000 The 3.6-litre, twin-turbo, all-wheel-drive 996 Turbo goes on sale.

2002 The X50 tuning package becomes available, raising power from 415bhp to 444bhp.

2003 The 996 Turbo Cabriolet is launched.

2005 The 997 Turbo is unveiled at Geneva Salon, with 473bhp.

2007 The 997 Cabriolet is released.

2007 The 997 GT2 becomes available, featuring rear-wheel drive and capable of 523bhp.

2010 The 997 Turbo S is introduced, with a 3.8-litre engine, 523bhp and seven-speed PDK transmission. The 997 GT2 RS is launched, with 3.6 litres delivering 612bhp.

2013 The 991 Turbo and Turbo S released; the former develops 513bhp from a 3.8-litre flat-six, the latter 552bhp.

2013 The 991 Turbo and Turbo S Cabriolet versions become available.

2015 Facelifted 991 Turbo and Turbo S models go on sale.

2016 All 991 models except the Turbo and Turbo S are powered by new 3.0-litre turbocharged flat-six engines.

2016 The 718 series Boxster and Cayman models powered by 2.0- and 2.5-litre turbocharged flat-four engines appear.

2017 The 718 Boxster GTS and Cayman GTS 2.5-litre flat-four engines develop 361bhp. The 991 Turbo S Exclusive series is launched, comprising just 500 units with a power kit.

2018 The 991 GT2 RS released, developing 690bhp from a twin-turbo 3.8-litre flat-six.

2019 The 935 is launched, a pastiche of a slant-nose racing car from the late 1970s.

2020 The 992 Turbo is unveiled.

OPPOSITE PAGE:
Turbo trio: a striking line-up of 911 turbos composed specially for the book by Jonathan Sturgess at Cambridgeshire-based Autostore (www.autostore.co.uk), comprising a 996 Turbo, 997 Turbo and 991 Turbo Cabriolet. CHRISTOPHER OULD

INTRODUCTION

From 1973, when Porsche first applied forced induction to its 917 Spyders for use in the North American Can-Am series and the European Interserie championships, it was inevitable that the technology would transfer onto the 911 street car, and the earliest 911 Turbo was shown at the Paris Salon in 1973. The first racing 911s to receive turbochargers were the factory's Carrera RSR Turbo race cars, one of which finished second at Le Mans in 1974, driven by Gijs van Lennep and Herbert Müller. Porsche's racing 911s evolved into the 934, hugely successful as a Group 4 car in the GT category of the World Sportscar Championship (Le Mans etc) and US-based IMSA (International Motor Sports Association) series. By 1976, the turbocharged Porsche of choice for international GT racing was the more extreme Group 5 935, which was good enough to win Le Mans outright in 1979. Both the 934 and 935 could have twin turbos rather than single units, depending on in which category or race series they participated.

Porsche's first road-going application, the 930, or 911 Turbo as it was originally known, appeared in 1974, and remained in production until 1989, to be superseded in 1991 by the 964 Turbo. The high-tech twin-turbo 959 featured as a Group B Paris–Dakar Rally weapon and road-going supercar, produced in very limited numbers between 1983 and 1993. The final incarnation of the air-cooled 911 Turbo was the 993 Turbo, built between 1995 and 1998. Anyone interested in these models might like to look out for my book *Porsche Air-Cooled Turbos (1973–1998),* also published by The Crowood Press.

Meanwhile, a model line of turbocharged, water-cooled, front-engined Porsches evolved, which I've covered in this book, as they are, well, turbos obviously, and they are sports cars

ABOVE: **The 924 Carrera GTS was a derivative of the 924 Carrera GT, introduced in 1981, created predominantly for rallying and similar competition purposes.** ANTONY FRASER

RIGHT: **Finished in Velvet Red Metallic, this 944 Turbo is a rare Club Sport version, originally delivered in Finland in 1988 and now resident in Belgium.** ANTONY FRASER

Another rare car developed at Weissach by Jürgen Barth, the 968 RS Turbo Club Sport is one of four RS-Ts, campaigned in South Africa in 1993 before being imported into Great Britain.

ANTONY FRASER

bearing the Porsche badge. I wondered whether they commanded a separate book all to themselves, but on balance I elected to bring the total water-cooled oeuvre together here. The front-engined cars were manufactured in parallel with the air-cooled 911s, starting with the 924 Turbo, which was in production between 1979 and 1982. This model spawned the 924 Carrera GT, followed chronologically by the 944 Turbo (1985–91), Turbo S and Turbo Cup derivative. The final example of the front-engined Turbos was the 968 Turbo (1992–3) and its Turbo S and RS offshoots. Then, with the dawning of the new millennium, came the first of the water-cooled 911 Turbos, the 996 Turbo, followed in 2005 by the 997 Turbo and in 2013 by the 991 Turbo. These mainstream models begat 'S' versions as well as GT2 and GT2 RS derivatives, the main difference being that the mainstream cars were four-wheel drive and the competition-oriented GT2s were rear-drive only. Minor facelifts were introduced in 2017, and the 992 will inevitably usher in a Turbo version in late 2019 or 2020. Meanwhile, advances in environmental legislation and turbocharging efficiency meant that, from 2016, all petrol-engined Porsche cars, bar the GT3, were turbocharged, not just the Turbos, allowing us to consider the forced-induction 991 GTS and 718 Boxster and Cayman models in the book's last two chapters.

First of the water-cooled turbocharged 911s, the 996 Turbo was introduced in 2000. The intakes in the front panel feed cooling air to brakes and radiators, while ducts in the rear three-quarter panels ahead of the wheel arches serve the intercoolers. JOHNNY TIPLER

Launched in 2005, the 911 Turbo's shape was rationalized with the 997 model, with air intakes and light housings better co-ordinated than on its predecessor. JOHNNY TIPLER

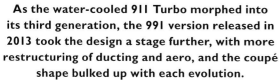

As the water-cooled 911 Turbo morphed into its third generation, the 991 version released in 2013 took the design a stage further, with more restructuring of ducting and aero, and the coupé shape bulked up with each evolution. JOHNNY TIPLER

The 991 GTS is a great result of Porsche's move to turbocharge the majority of their petrol-engined models. This is FVD Brombacher's interpretation, parked at Holzschläger Matten-Kurve on the Schauinslandstrasse near Freiburg. JOHNNY TIPLER

TURBOCHARGING

Open up the engine lid on modern Porsches and you're mainly confronted by plastic covers concealing the mechanicals that lie beneath. Up on a ramp it's easier to see what goes on, and it's while looking upwards from down below that you perceive the turbochargers and their integral positioning within the exhaust system. We've come to take them for granted because they have become an almost standard piece of equipment – certainly there have been turbocharged models consistently in the Porsche range since 1974.

While most readers will know what a turbo does, this is a book about cars that specifically use them and are designated as such, so it would be remiss not to start with a basic overview of how a turbocharger functions. The turbo is basically an air pump that takes air at ambient atmospheric pressure and compresses it to a higher pressure, feeding the compressed air into the engine's cylinders via the inlet valves. Engines are dependent on air and fuel, and an increase in either will increase power output. So, to augment airflow, compressed air is blown into the engine, mixing with the injected fuel and enabling the fuel to burn more efficiently, thereby increasing power output.

The turbocharger harnesses the engine's exhaust gases to drive a turbine wheel that's connected by a shaft to a compressor wheel. Instead of discharging down the exhaust pipe, hot gases produced during combustion flow to the turbocharger. The exhaust gases spin the turbine blades up to a mind-boggling 150,000rpm. The compressor sucks air in through the air filters and passes it into the engine. As the exhaust gases are expelled from the engine via the exhaust valves, they are passed to the turbine fan within the turbo, and so the cycle continues. The additional oxygen consumed enables a turbocharged engine to generate around 30 per cent more power than a non-turbo unit of the same cubic capacity.

The turbocharged engine ideally needs an intercooler to moderate the temperature of the incoming air. That's because, in passing through the turbo blades and being thus boosted, it gets exceedingly hot, and this is not good news for the engine. Most turbocharged engines, certainly in a competition context, employ an intercooler. This is basically an air-to-air radiator, usually mounted prominently in the car's airstream – for example, at the front of the engine bay in the case of the 924 Carrera GT and in the rear wing of the 930. Hot air from the turbo goes in at one end and is cooled as it passes through the intercooler, just like a water-cooled car's radiator, before entering the engine at a much lower temperature and thus denser.

The alternative means of applying forced induction is supercharging, which was more widely used to boost engine

From 2017, all Porsche 911s – bar the GT3 – were turbocharged, though not identified as such. This is the 991 GTS, revealing twin turbos installed within the exhaust systems on either side of the engine.
ANTONY FRASER

performance in the 1930s. The difference between the two units, supercharger and turbocharger, is that the supercharger derives its power from the crankshaft, whence it's driven by a belt (in the same way as the water pump and alternator), whereas the turbo draws power from the engine's exhaust gases. Superchargers spin at up to 50,000rpm while the turbocharger can spin much faster. Emissions wise, the supercharger doesn't have a wastegate, whereas turbos have catalytic converters to lower carbon emissions. Turbochargers run extremely hot and need to be well insulated. Superchargers deliver boost at lower revs than a turbocharger whereas the turbo works best at high engine speeds. In practical terms, the supercharger is easier to install, though it takes a small portion of the engine's power in its operation. Turbochargers are quieter in operation, and fuel economy is affected less adversely with a turbo'd engine, while superchargers are more reliable and easier to maintain than the more complex turbocharger. The turbo mutes the exhaust note, so if, like me, you derive a certain ecstasy from the raw rasp of a Porsche flat-six, air- or water-cooled, you'll know that the gruff boom emitted by a turbocharged car is slightly anticlimactic by comparison. There are fairly clear advantages and disadvantages to both forms of forced induction, but since turbos work better with high-performance applications and, at the same time, are more efficient in dealing with emissions, Porsche took the turbo option.

ABOVE: **The 924 Carrera GTS's 1984cc slant-four engine achieved a maximum 1.0 bar turbo boost to produce 245bhp via its 40 per cent limited-slip differential, enabling a 0–100km/h time of 6.2sec and a top speed of 249km/h (155mph).** ANTONY FRASER

LEFT: **Cutaway of a KKK turbocharger, conveniently left in my hotel room at Breidscheid beside the Nordschleife, revealing the component's internals, which basically consist of the compressor casing at top left and compressor wheel that's connected by a shaft to the turbine wheel, which is accommodated in the turbine casing. For a full description of forced induction, I recommend getting hold of a copy of Alan Allard's *Turbocharging and Supercharging*.**

JOHNNY TIPLER

CHAPTER ONE

THE FRONT-ENGINED TURBOS: 924, 944 AND 968

THE 924 TURBO

Four decades ago, the 924 was the entry-level Porsche. In 1979, the model took a major leap up market in the shape of the 924 Turbo. The 924 Turbo went out of production in 1982, and was superseded in the forced-induction stakes by the 944 Turbo and subsequent 968 Turbo. In recent years I've been lent a few by Andrew Mearns of Gmund Cars, Knaresborough, and driven them over the Yorkshire Dales, where their competent handling provided compelling evidence that their time has come again. Andrew has a soft spot for the 924 Turbo himself:

It's a nice car to drive. People are looking at them again, thinking, 'Hang on a minute, a 924 Turbo for £18 grand,' and this is entry-level money for any decent classic car. In that context, I think the 924 Turbo is still slightly undervalued, and in practical terms, as a sports car it's very well put together, though it is quite quirky because the turbocharging is old school, with a certain amount of lag as it's a relatively big turbo.

Social media is a fair barometer for what's vexing and sexing people – from the hysterical to the merely eye-popping – but I was surprised that there were over twice as many 'likes' for the pic I posted of a 924 compared with a hunky 911 backdate. The comments on the 924 revealed much greater fondness, whimsy even, for the front-engined cars. They're not exactly comfortable bed-fellows with the 911 Turbos that constitute the greater

OPPOSITE PAGE:
Cheddar gorgeous: the 924 Turbo was available in quite sophisticated livery combinations including two-tone and pinstriping in the early 1980s. ANTONY FRASER

THIS PAGE:
As the cut-off eligibility year marches into the 1980s, more 924 Turbos are entered in the Monte Carlo Rallye Historique. Here, the French car of Glasgow-starters the Grangeons rounds a hairpin descending the Col de Perty in the Rhône-Alpes in 2018. Snapper Alex Denham is the figure at first right. JOHNNY TIPLER

part of this tome, but they are nevertheless bona fide Porsche sports cars and thus they have a chapter dedicated to them. So, my task is to take a run out onto the bleak, sheep-frequented moorland byways of the Yorkshire Dales National Park and see how the 924 Turbo has stood the test of time.

Encapsulating Porsche's expertise with turbocharging, the 924 Turbo bridged the performance gap between regular 924 with 125bhp and the 204bhp 911 SC. Launched for the 1979 model year with 170bhp, power rose in 1981 to 177bhp. The 924 Turbo was also designated the 931/932, and production totalled 11,616 units. The 924 Turbo shown here was recently acquired by Richard Kirk, who is Andrew's right-hand man and has a long history with the model. It's a second-generation car and has the large lift-out sunroof panel too. The 2.0-litre straight-four was modified to better handle the extra turbo boost, including lowering the standard 924 compression ratio and fitting a new cylinder head with better flow characteristics, plus an oil cooler.

The Turbo has a five-speed transaxle gearbox, with dog-leg first, and I find the slots are much closer than in the four-speed. The steering feel and feedback is also different, and it's weighted subtly differently. Among the noteworthy details are the NACA cooling duct in the bonnet and the slatted bonnet front and the slotted valance, which provide airflow to the oil cooler. The Turbo's multi-spoke forged alloy wheels reference

contemporary BBS lattice centres and have five bolts, as opposed to the standard 924's four studs, and are shod with Falcon Azenis 195/35 × 16 tyres all round. The Turbo has a flap over the fuel cap – advocating 98 octane on the label – superseding the regular 924's lockable finger-grip cap.

The colour of this one is called Mocha Black, a deep brown hue that's become quite fashionable recently. The sticker in the back window is that of the supplying dealer, Dingle Garages, Colwyn Bay, and quite avant-garde for 1981. Richard explains:

> There's a few things that aren't practical in modern use, like the radio, which is quite crackly, but it is the original radio so I wouldn't want to change it. In the service history there's a handbook for a CB radio so I assume that's what the antenna mount is for on the rear three-quarter panel. It's all the little clues like this that tell you the history of the car.

Mileage is quite low at 72,000km (45,000 miles), and though the speedo shows just 24,000km (15,000 miles), that's because the speedo was replaced at circa 48,000km (30,000 miles), attested by the stamps in the service book. Apart from the Turbo graphic on the sill there's nothing that shouts turbo, not even a boost gauge. The upholstery is Berber check, a nice combination

In the Yorkshire Dales, a 924 Turbo and its standard 924 stablemate both provided entertaining drives over the moorland byways.
ANTONY FRASER

ABOVE: **The 924 Turbo's slant-four was based on the Audi 100 block with single overhead camshaft head and 7.5:1 compression ratio (later 8.5:1), to improve low-speed throttle response and better handle the extra turbo boost. Power output was 180bhp at 5,500rpm.**
ANTONY FRASER

ABOVE RIGHT: **Cabin interior of the 924 Turbo, showing fabric-upholstered seats, handbrake to the right of the driver, and generic 1980s Porsche four-spoke steering wheel.** ANTONY FRASER

RIGHT: **Driving the 924 Turbo on the Yorkshire Dales hill roads, the driver has to get acclimatized to its dog-leg first gear and pedal position, but finds it a willing and compliant car on the undulating terrain.** ANTONY FRASER

of two-tone brown and beige, which looks like a luxury option compared with the pinstripe in the standard 924. Richard's Turbo history goes back more than three decades.

If you had a child seat fitted in your car, once the child outgrew it they would give you your money back when you returned it. It was a safety incentive, so I took my Turbo along and said, 'Right, put a child seat in the back,' and they mounted it on top of the transmission tunnel between the rear seats. My daughter remembers those days fondly, and she's in her thirties now! And, yes, I did get my money back.

We motor out onto the upland wilderness of Nidderdale fells. The first thing to get acclimatized to is the seating position, which, although the seat is low-slung in the cab, means I am sitting quite close to the top of the windscreen so that my hat is bumping on the sun visor. Personally, I would welcome more seat adjustment and to be sitting slightly lower in the driving position. The pedal position also takes some getting used to, being oriented slightly differently in the pedal box from what I'm used to (which is currently a 986 Boxster S).

The 924 Turbo is an eager car; there are one or two controls to get used to, such as the dog-leg first gear and the handbrake being to the right of the (RHD) driver's seat. The view ahead is interrupted by the pop-up headlights that seem somewhat comical today, though you might recall that the much-vaunted Ferrari Daytona and various Lotuses also had a similar lighting arrangement, and we also have to remind ourselves that when stylist Harm Lagaaij drew the 924 in 1973, the Daytona was very much the car of the moment.

Performance wise, there's no comparison, of course. The 924 Turbo's acceleration is reasonably swift, though not spectacularly rapid. There's plenty of torque, pulling from quite low down in third gear, and once it's warmed up there's a nice burr... from the exhaust. It's fluent enough through the bends, and I drop from fourth to third to get around quicker corners. The brakes are a bit spongy and not so convincing, though again I tell myself it's a forty-year old car. It's swishing and swaying along quite nicely, and through the twistier sections turn-in is easy-over progressive, the steering is accurate and the handling neutral, and there's no inclination towards oversteer or understeer. It's a decent ride, if a bit on the bouncy side. Winding through undulating hill country I'm using third for the most part, and for the corners I'm mostly leaving

it in third as well, as it's torquey enough for that to work for most bends, with some sharper turns and steep hills above the cattle grid zones requiring second. The car is also stable in a straight line, and I've wound it up to 115km/h (70mph) on a B-road – and, as luck would have it, I'm blocked by a horsebox at the very point where we pass a speed camera van: here, in the middle of nowhere, in God's own country. My colleague is less fortunate, however, having already passed the horsebox.

The 924 Turbo is a sprightly performer, edging the standard 924 in that regard, with firm ride and nice turn-in to corners, where I can balance it neatly on the throttle. The steering is a bit of a battle when turning around in a tight spot, as I do for the moorland photoshoot, but easy enough when in motion, and there's a pleasing delicacy about the gearshift on the move as well. There is a little bit of lag but, really, it's just a question of being in the right gear at the right time and looking for the turbo spooling up, and then you get the power surge. Does it feel much faster than the standard 924? It's meant to be 2.5sec quicker to 60mph, but I'm not sure there's that much in it in practice.

It's evaluation time. I'm burning up the back road from Lofthouse to Pateley Bridge, and it's one third-gear bend after another, holding 3,500rpm, and it's more entertaining than it's got any right to be. It's not a stiff chassis exactly, and I should think that, torsionally, it's quite flexible, but nevertheless it does go exactly where I want it to. One of the most outstanding plus points is that it's driver-friendly: you can do virtually anything you want with it. It's not over-powered, and handling is adequately compliant. The 924 Turbo is an easy-going car, once you've got used to the seating position, pedals and so on. It's biddable, has no tricks up its sleeve, goes the way you point it, and, in the context of a car from the mid-1970s, it may lack the panache of a 911 but nonetheless is a character in its own right.

924 CARRERA GT

The 924 Carrera GT is probably the most desirable of all Porsche's front-engined water-cooled models, being a limited production run as well as having a racing pedigree. Launched in the white heat of the Turbo era, it recalls the marque's remarkable performance at Le Mans in 1980, when three Carrera GTs that bore close resemblance to cars you could buy in the showroom finished sixth, twelfth and thirteenth overall.

Unveiled as a styling exercise at the Frankfurt Show in September 1979, the 924 Carrera GT was an evolution of the 924 Turbo – and designated factory type number 937. The bodykit is unpretentious, as the car was intended for competition work, produced in sufficient numbers for homologation into Group 4, leading into the Group B supercars that would take over in 1982. According to Porsche's chief race car tester, Jürgen Barth, there was initially no factory interest in racing its front-engined cars, but he and co-engineer Roland Kussmaul were allowed to do their own thing with some 924 Turbo prototypes. The Le Mans cars of 1980 stemmed from there.

Visually, the 924 Carrera GT stands out because of its plastic front wings and wheel spats – and that distinctive bonnet air

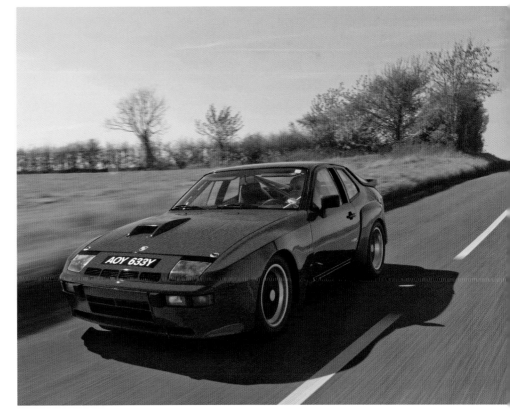

The 924 Carrera GTS and its GTR sibling are evolutions of the 924 Carrera GT, introduced in March 1981. Headlights are mounted behind Plexiglass fairings, rather than the parent car's pop-up type. This particular car was owned by the late racing driver Richard Lloyd, who drove a 924 GTR at Le Mans in 1982 and was known to the author through his motorsport PR business, but was killed in a light plane crash in 2008. ANTONY FRASER

924 CARRERA GT 1980–1982

Layout and chassis

Steel body, composite wings, two aluminium seats, hot-dip galvanized shell, polyurethane extremities, top-mounted air scoop for intercooler

Engine

Type	Front-mounted, in-line slant-four
Block material	Cast iron
Head material	Aluminium
Cylinders	4
Cooling	Water-cooled
Bore and stroke	86.5 × 84.4
Capacity	1984cc
Valves	SOHC, 2 valves per cylinder
Compression ratio	8.0:1
Carburettor	Electric pump, Bosch K-Jetronic injection, KKK turbo, Langener & Reich intercooler
Max. power (DIN)	210bhp at 6,000rpm
Max. torque	303lb ft at 6,000rpm
Fuel capacity	80ltr (17.6gal)

Transmission

Gearbox	Getrag manual 5-speed, transaxle rear drive, limited-slip differential optional
Clutch	911-type single dry plate
Ratios	1st 3.671
	2nd 1.778
	3rd 1.217
	4th 0.931
	5th 0.706
	Reverse 2.909
Final drive	4.125

Suspension and Steering

Front	MacPherson struts, coil springs, anti-roll bar
Rear	Trailing arms, torsion bars
Steering	Rack and pinion
Tyres	205/55VR × 16 front, 225/50VR × 16 rear
Wheels	16in Fuchs alloys
Rim width	7 J × 16 front, 8 J × 16 rear

Brakes

Type	Front and rear ventilated and drilled discs
Size	30mm all round

Dimensions

Track	1,420mm (55.9in) front, 1,389mm (54.7in) rear
Wheelbase	2,402mm (94.6in)
Overall length	4,200mm (165in)
Overall width	1,685mm (66in)
Overall height	1,270mm (50in)
Unladen weight	1,080kg (2,380lb)

Performance

Top speed	241km/h (150mph)
0–60mph	6.9sec

scoop. Under the skin, what makes it special is the intercooler that the ordinary 924 Turbo didn't have, riding on a stiffened and lightened platform to provide handling at the raw edge. We know that Porsche are past masters at creating these race-derived special editions – and the 924 Carrera GT is worthy of the same degree of respect as the revered 911 Carrera 2.7 RS from 1972, as the resulting sports car is something of a technical tour de force that's evolved from the series production model.

The Frankfurt show car was developed into the limited-production 924 Carrera GT released in June 1980, coinciding neatly with the success at Le Mans – Jürgen Barth and Manfred Schurti came sixth overall in an era when the slant-nose 935 and (winning) mid-engined 936 were dominant. Two versions were available: the road-legal production run of 406 units of the standard GT, which enabled the homologation process – of which six were prototypes; and the GTR, based more closely on the

The 924 Carrera GTS's broad-shouldered polyurethane and glass-fibre composite wheel arches replaced the standard 924 Turbo's narrow steel panels, and the steel doors and bonnet were exchanged for aluminium skins. The front spoiler and outer sills were also in flexible polyurethane, reinforced with glass-fibre. ANTONY FRASER

works Le Mans machines, which would metamorphose into the full-on GTR and GTS Rally competition cars the following year.

The street car was equipped with the 924 Turbo engine, augmented by an air-to-air intercooler lying flat on top of the engine's cam cover and served by the dedicated air scoop. It developed 210bhp at 6,000rpm, which may not be a wildly increased output, but the car derived its punch and its raw character from a good power-to-weight ratio. This was achieved by omitting superfluous sound-deadening and swapping narrow steel front wings for broad-shouldered polyurethane and glass-fibre composite panels, and trading the steel doors and bonnet for aluminium skins. The front spoiler, outer sills and rear wheel-arch extensions were also in flexible polyurethane, reinforced with glass-fibre. Although the characteristic 924 Turbo vents in the front of the bonnet were retained, the Carrera GT had a single long horizontal slot at the base of the front spoiler. There was also a larger rear spoiler on the outer rim of the tailgate. It also used an aluminium transaxle tube and lightweight suspension components in a firm-riding recipe that included Bilstein dampers and stiffer springs.

In the cabin, still recognizably that of the 924 with its two-plus-two ergonomics, there are lightweight 911 SC sports seats, upholstered in black cloth with a red pinstripe (although one customer specified a full-leather interior). The Carrera GT tips the scales at just over 1,000kg (2,200lb), undercutting the normal 924 Turbo by 181kg (399lb). This, combined with the punch from the intercooled turbo engine, enables a top speed of 240km/h (150mph) and a 0–100km/h time of 6.9sec. By comparison, the normal 924 Turbo produces 177bhp and makes 204km/h (127mph) tops, with 0–60mph coming up in 9.2sec.

The 924 Carrera GTS and GTR

The evolution of the 924 Carrera GT logically encompasses its two derivatives: the GTS and GTR. In March 1981, the two offshoots came out once the construction of the road-going Carrera GT run was complete for homologation purposes. Although the GTR and GTS are primarily competition cars, with headlights lurking behind Plexiglass fairings rather than the parent car's pop-up type, a number were adapted for road use and finished with full cabin furnishings and wind-up windows instead of the sliding Plexiglass type. Glazing is thinner than standard-issue 924 panes. In addition, they have 911 seats instead of the racer's 935-style racing buckets.

The Carrera GTS delivers better low-speed torque than the GT by deploying a maximum 1.0 bar turbo boost to produce 245bhp via a 40 per cent limited-slip differential, easing ahead of the Carrera GT with a 0–100km/h time of 6.2sec and a top speed of 249km/h (155mph). Being a race and rally machine, its suspension is uprated with lighter front wishbones and coil-sprung rear suspension, enhanced by cast aluminium trailing arms. In rally trim, the GTS features yet tougher suspension – with higher ground clearance, plus a sump guard and underbody shield and a built-in roll-cage. Brakes are ventilated cross-bored discs all round, allied to 911 Turbo hubs. It's 59kg (130lb) lighter than the Carrera GT by virtue of glass-fibre wings, air dam and rear bumper, as well as doors and bonnet. Wings and rear arches are also more prominent than the Carrera GT's. The rear greenhouse panel is in Plexiglass, although roadable versions have the normal glass tailgate with a wiper.

A 280bhp version, described as the GTS Rally or Club Sport, became available from January 1981 – stripped for action, with no protection below the floorpan and an aluminium roll-cage and fire extinguisher inside. Famous owners of this beast over the years include Derek Bell, Lord Mexborough, the Earl of March and George Harrison.

Lighter still, the GTR model – R for Rennsport (racing) – was intended for use in the FIA Group 4 category, where it was eligible for the 1982 World Endurance Championship. It's no surprise that it was directly descended from the 1980 Le Mans car, weighing in at 945kg (2,084lb). But the output is quite staggering. The much-modified 2.0-litre 924 Turbo power unit delivers a serious 375bhp, thanks to Kugelfischer mechanical fuel injection and a larger KKK turbocharger, now housed on the left-hand side of the engine block instead of below and to the right front. It could hit 291km/h (181mph) and top 100km/h in 4.7sec. Brakes were sourced from the 935 race car, having originated in the 917. When new, you could specify any colour you liked for the GTR, provided it was white. Relative to the basic 924 Turbo's £13,998 – and even the Carrera GT's £19,211 – the £34,630 price tag in 1981 was stratospheric. By comparison, the (red only) GTS would set you back a not unreasonable £23,950, relatively speaking.

Contrast this with the showroom sticker of £18,180 for a Sport Equipment 911 SC at the time, and the status of the 924 Carrera GT in the marque's hierarchy becomes a little clearer. Of the 406 units of the 924 Carrera GT, just seventy-five were in right-hand drive, with UK deliveries starting in January 1981. There were just forty units of the GTS and nineteen of the GTR, all of which were left-hand drive.

Bodywork and Chassis

The GTS and GTR panels were of glass-fibre rather than polyurethane. These more extreme cars were fitted with a one-piece nose section with integral lights and rubber overriders – and no front bumper. The contours of the front wheel arches are slightly wider in the GTS/GTR than the Carrera GT, and the back ones are a tad taller, as well as wider. Their glass-fibre tailgate spoilers are slightly different to the GT's, with a built-in Gurney flap lip and a moulded GTS logo beneath.

The Porsche badge is a decal glued on the bonnet, although some owners opt to site the number plate there instead. In all cases, the windscreen is bonded to the shell, rather than rubbered in place, improving the airflow over the cabin top. If you're looking at a car with a big 'step' between the frame and the glass, its screen isn't bonded, so it may not be genuine. There are fundamental changes in the rear chassis as well, to do with the use of coil springs requiring variable ride-height platforms. The boot floor is also raised to make provision for a 120-litre (26.4gal) fuel tank to provide suitable range for endurance racing, so there are no rear seats. In addition, the Carrera GT has a slightly extended rear bumper, projecting further than the 924 Turbo's, and a larger-lipped wrap-around tailgate spoiler with a rougher surface finish. It comes in just three body colours: Diamond Silver metallic (twenty-two UK cars), Black (twenty) or Guards Red (thirty).

Here's how the chassis numbering works. The factory's model designation is 937, so the VIN number stamped on the left of the false bulkhead should read WPOZZZ93ZBN7... and so on. The 93 serves to indicate 937; the letter B is the factory code for 1981, and the N identifies it as a car built at the Audi plant at Neckarsulm, north of Stuttgart. The numerology should be followed by two zeros and a three-digit number corresponding to its positioning in the 406-unit production run. The first chassis number was 066 and the last 449. By comparison, a 924 Turbo is type number 931 and will have a VIN containing 93ZBN1. The GTS VIN should read WPOZZZ93ZBS7..., the S referring to its Stuttgart construction, then 10001 to 10059 depending on its place in the production chart. As a separate production run, the GTR chassis identification ran from 93ZBS720001 to 0022, with numbers 13 and 18–21 omitted.

In all cases, the swirling Carrera script is emblazoned on the top of the right-hand front wing, with the Carrera GT identification to the right of the rear panel. The cursive turbo label appears on the inner door sills. When checking out a car, examine it closely for ill-fitting panels and odd gaps suggesting poor accident repairs. Check for over-spray on hard-to-mask areas such as the suspension. The plastic panels will almost certainly have ripples, which is not a concern, but look underneath to see if the underbody protection has been compromised.

The Interior

Creature comforts and amenities in UK-spec cars include 911 SC sports seats, deep-pile carpet, electric windows, Panasonic radio/cassette player (model number CQ863) with electric aerial, tinted glass, driver's door electric/heated mirror, rear wiper, headlamp washers and four-spoke sports steering wheel. Again, the GTS is in a different league: it has the three-spoke 911 SC wheel, racing bucket seats and four-point harnesses. Door trims are unique, with grab handles instead of door-pulls and flimsy catches. Bonnet cables have been known to fail. Only the principal moulding remains of the original 924 dashboard, its binnacle containing the 300km/h (186mph) speedo and rev-counter with integral boost gauge, while other dials are mounted in a centre console ahead of the gear lever. Apart from a thin veneer of black carpet, all other trim is absent. The downside is that none of the specialized interior trim is available any more.

The Engine

The 924 Carrera GT uses the 924 Turbo engine, with the same Porsche-designed aluminium cylinder head (and cast-iron block) but modified combustion chambers, 3mm larger exhaust valves and repositioned spark plugs relative to the standard car. The electronic ignition system is more refined, and it's fitted with forged pistons and an air-to-air intercooler mounted over the rocker cover. The KKK (type K26-2660 GA 6.10) turbo has a slightly larger body – and its maximum boost pressure is 0.75 bar, so output is up to 210bhp at 6,000rpm. It runs two auxiliary cooling fans instead of just one, although the water radiator is identical. The oil cooler is relocated ahead of the radiator, and the larger-bore exhaust is more of a straight-through system.

The weakest link is the turbocharger – it has a startlingly short 40,000- to 64,000km (25,000- to 40,000-mile) life expectancy. The engine should always be allowed to run for a couple of minutes before switching it off, to allow the oil to circulate and the

ABOVE: **Being a competition-oriented machine, the 924 Carrera GTS cockpit harbours a comprehensive roll-cage and fire extinguisher, while the author is belted into the bucket seat with a full Autoflug harness.** ANTONY FRASER

RIGHT: **Despite its competition tendencies, the 924 Carrera GTS cabin is also a comfortable environment, offering carpeted floorpan, padded bucket seats and the normal range of early 1980s controls and instrumentation.** ANTONY FRASER

compressor to cool off. Otherwise, oil cooks in the turbo and there's none available for the bearings on start-up. The engine should also be allowed to warm up for a few minutes before pulling away, to let the lubricant coat the bearings effectively.

Just when you think you've got the hang of the Carrera GT, you discover the GTS is quite different in many ways. For instance, instead of the intercooler, pride of place under the bonnet goes to the cast-alloy inlet manifold, fronted by the modified injection system from the Porsche 928, which supplies the injectors via an eight-into-four adaptor stack. The massive intercooler is tucked up in the front of the car, and there's an unconnected safety cutout switch on the inner wing in front of the VIN plate. The battery is positioned in the boot for optimum weight distribution – and there's a hand-made light-alloy expansion tank for the cooling system.

Suspension, Gearbox and Brakes

The most noticeable difference between the 924 Turbo and the Carrera GT is the dog-leg first gear, located to the left of the gate, so the main four ratios are selected in an H-pattern and convenient for competition use. Reverse is ahead of first. The G31/03 five-speed gearbox is of the transaxle type, in unit with the rear axle for optimum weight distribution. Compared with the 924 Turbo, it has a stronger final drive, and case-hardened crown wheel and pinion in third, fourth and fifth gears. The actual ratios are the same as for the 924 Turbo, although first gear

synchro is out of the 911 for easier shifts when cold, along with a 911 clutch. The limited-slip differential is optional. On the GTS the finned transaxle has its own minimalist oil cooler beside it. Check that the casing isn't leaking on prospective cars.

The Carrera GT sits 10mm (0.4in) lower than the 924 Turbo, and uses Bilstein gas dampers. The steering joints are beefed up, as are the anti-roll bars and rear trailing arms. Brakes are ventilated discs measuring 392mm (11.5in) up front and 290mm (11.4in) at the rear, with dual brake circuits front and rear, allied to a stepped tandem master cylinder. There are two ducts within the front valance to cool the front discs. The brake circuit is split front/rear, while that of the 924 Turbo is a diagonally split twin-circuit system.

Wider wheels give the 924 Carrera GT a broader track than the 924 Turbo, which accounts for the bulbous wings and wheel arches in the first place. Track, both front and rear, measures 1,477mm (58in), including 21mm spacers at the rear. Wheels are forged five-spoke Fuchs, 7J × 15in shod with 215/60 VR15 tyres front and rear, while 7 and 8J × 16in wheels with 225/50 VR16 rear tyres were an optional fitment – and standard on the GTS Rally or Club Sport model.

Performance

On the road, the Carrera GT offers a vivid driving experience. When the turbo kicks in it's creamy smooth – and after 3,000rpm it pulls like a train. Up to a point, there's so much

Although the characteristic 924 Turbo vents in the front of the bonnet were retained, the Carrera GTS also had a large intake where the standard model's NACA duct would have been, plus a single long horizontal slot at the base of the front spoiler. ANTONY FRASER

torque available that you can (almost) get away with treating it like a four-speed gearbox and forget about first, although second is frequently difficult to find. Handling is neutral, with a hint of understeer, and the car drifts rather than the back end coming out at speed. The brakes are the weakest link – they feel like early 1980s brakes and, although they do the job, they don't match the car's performance. The steering is high-geared, as well, which makes over-correcting a temptation. It's a fast, well-balanced driver's car – reliable, economical (returning 9.4ltr/100km or 30mpg) and easy on tyres.

Alongside the 260km/h (160mph) speedometer, the rev-counter is oriented to provide an unrestricted view of the dial from 3,000rpm to 6,000rpm beneath the rim of the non-adjustable steering wheel. The turbo emits a characteristic whistle just below 2,000rpm and the boost gauge in the base of the rev-counter starts to register at 2,500rpm with 0.5 bar, rising to 1.2 bar around 3,000rpm when torque peaks – and there it stays. Lag is minimal. There's a surge of power at 3,500rpm, complemented by a change in the exhaust note as it comes on full song.

It's a fast A-road car, provided it's not too crowded, and highly entertaining on smooth-surfaced B-roads and back doubles, when an incautious right foot makes you conscious of its depths of power. Handling is spot on, as you would expect from such a well-honed package, incorporating positive scrub-radius front-suspension geometry that provides all the front-end grip you need to tackle fast corners. Track-day buffs say it's as fast as a Boxster on the straights, but loses out on the bends. Put that down to the march of time. It's a racer for the road, yet at the same time it's kitted out like its more civilized siblings. The only thing it doesn't do well is town-centre parking, as it hasn't got power steering.

Le Mans Legends

The inspiration for the 924 Carrera GT came from the factory's Le Mans entries in 1980, when the three cars developed under Norbert Singer by Jurgen Barth and Roland Kussmaul completed the marathon event, vindicating the decision to go racing with the front-engined water-cooled model.

Financed by the Porsche concessionaires in Germany, USA and the UK, Barth and Manfred Schurti drove the German car to finish sixth overall and third in the GTP class, averaging 179.6km/h (111.60mph) over 4,310km (2,678 miles). Al Holbert and Peter Gregg drove the American car to thirteenth place, despite a dropped exhaust valve, and Derek Bell, Tony Dron and Andy Rouse handled the British car to twelfth, requiring just a change of spark plugs but experiencing the major drama of losing its one-piece nose cone at night in the turbulence of a passing 935 on the Mulsanne Straight. The following year, Barth/Röhrl came seventh in their 924 GTR and Schurti/Rouse were eleventh, but the Alméras/Sivel car retired with transmission failure. In the rally arena, Walter Röhrl won the 1981 German Rally championship in a 924 Carrera GTS, with the Hessen Rallye, Rallye Vorderpfalz and the Serengeti Safari Rallye to his credit.

Walter Röhrl discusses a seat fitting with Jürgen Barth and Roland Kussmaul at Weissach during the construction of the 924 Carrera GTRs in 1979–80.
PORSCHE PHOTO ARCHIVE

DEREK BELL INTERVIEW

Derek Bell has never really stopped racing. His frontline competition career spanned more than two decades, including an F1 stint at Ferrari and five Le Mans wins, culminating twice in the World Sportscar Championship title. He can be relied upon to drive any front-line car at any major historic meeting, from vintage Bentley to classic Mustang, Classic Le Mans and Copenhagen Historic GP. Derek is a legend, and certainly one of the most successful drivers in history. And much of that was achieved in Porsches. We chatted with him in a rare downtime moment when he wasn't gunning some supercar up the Hill at the Goodwood Festival of Speed.

Johnny Tipler: I believe you have a modern 991 at the moment?
Derek Bell: Yes, I do; I'm part owner of the Bentley and Porsche dealership in Naples, Florida, so I have to cross the Alligator Alley on a weekly basis, and I'm always there if I'm in America. And I can't afford to buy a Bentley but I can afford to buy a 991, so I bought a 991. Plus, the 991 is the sort of fun car that, when you're driving on a dead straight bit of road like Everglades Parkway it's not as boring as it might be in a bigger car, which cruises very beautifully at 80mph (130km/h); a 911 has a bit more character to it at that point.
JT: You raced a 924 Carrera GTR, a 934 and a 935, but did you ever get to race a 911 RSR?
DB: I once raced a 934 and a RSR for the same team in the same race at the Nürburgring in 1976, which was rather exciting because I got out of one and they stuck me in the other – that was Max Moritz Racing – and I was happy enough in the 934, which was turbocharged. Then they put me in a regular Group 5 RSR, and a normally aspirated 911 is much more fun to drive than the 934 turbo because it's such a handful when all the power comes in. The following year I drove a 935 for Georg Loos (GELO Racing) and also with that the power doesn't come in gently, one might say!
JT: Even though you've got those massive wheels and tyres on the back?
DB: Yep, at the Nürburgring, with 160 corners, you spend so much time leaping and jumping over the crests, and when you touch the ground you want it to be progressive and not suddenly go up from 350 to 550 horsepower during that split second you're in the air. And also the 934 was never built to be a proper race car, though you'll think it was, but it's not like a 935 that

Having enjoyed a long and successful association with Porsche, Derek Bell owns a 924 Carrera GTS, while his daily drive is a 991.
ANTONY FRASER

was built from the ground up as a race car and really was a proper car for the job. Oh yes, it was certainly a racing car, the 935. It's a car you get in and get hold of the gear lever, which sticks up like a mast, and you say to the car, 'It's either you or me, but today it's me,' and you would have to convince yourself that you're going to beat the hell out of it, or it will beat the hell out of you. You are actually fighting it and you're saying, 'I'm in charge today, not you,' and that has to be your attitude, you have to be ahead of it the whole time. It wasn't scary, it was just magnificent.
JT: To go back slightly, your first race in any Porsche was in a 917 at the 1971 Buenos Aires 1,000km with Jo Siffert.
DB: Which I won!
JT: That's quite incredible. But you were trying out long-tail bodywork on the 917 for them at Hockenheim during the preceding winter.
DB: That came about after John Wyer Automotive tested at Goodwood with me, Ronnie Peterson and Pete Gethin in the 917, and for some reason I got the contract to drive for them, probably because Ronnie had his eyes on Formula 1 and that's where he should have been, and I'd had my couple of years in Formula 1 with Ferrari. Of course Pete Gethin was also getting in there as well, but I always thought I was as good as Peter, though I thought Ronnie was a star, which of course he was. So, I got the drive and then I did the test at Hockenheim in the pissing rain at Christmas in the dark, nearly, which was actually really very unfunny, and from there of course we went straight to Buenos Aires in January.

JT: Wasn't there an incident involving a cyclist on the track?

DB: That was unbelievable! There were two other German drivers there as well, Hans Herrmann and Herbie Muller, and I was driving all afternoon, and of course at 4 o'clock in late December it's nearly pitch black. We weren't using the infield as such, we were coming straight down into the stadium and on the back straight and out onto the long circuit again so we missed out all the squiggles in the middle because we were purely there just to do aerodynamic high-speed testing. And when you think about it, to do any testing in the pouring rain is really rather pointless, but being Porsche, you carry on, because I'm sure they were getting some details back from it. I had this contraption on the passenger seat and I went through two points on the track where I had to flick the switch as I went in and press the button as I came out, and the beam told them what speeds I was going through at as I came down into the stadium. By 5 o'clock I couldn't see the bloody marker point because it was so foggy and so dark, so they went out and put spotlights on the two places, and I had to flick the switch and five seconds later switch it off. Certainly in normal testing people wouldn't be out there, apart from Porsche. Anyway, I came flying down the back straight into what we called the East Curve and then headed back towards the stadium, and just before I got to what we now call the Senna Curves, which was just a very fast kink then, I was hammering along at 160mph (257km/h) in the wet in the long-tail 917 and as I came flying up there, in that split second I suddenly saw this guy on a bicycle pedalling like hell, looking at me with the biggest eyes I've ever seen in my life, and my thought was, 'I'm going to take him off the road!' It was so quick that I couldn't even swerve, but I never hit him, and he must have got home for tea and said to his wife, 'You know, I don't think I'll go that way any more!' It was an amazing experience, but we survived, thank God.

JT: Absolutely, but a lot of your contemporaries from that year in particular didn't.

DB: Well, I lost both my team mates that one year (1971). Pedro died at the Norisring, and I replaced him as number one in his car. Jackie Oliver had left because he had a bit of a falling out with David Yorke, and I didn't know Olly that well though we'd raced in Formula 3 together. So he sort of disappeared from Pedro's car, which left Jo, me and Pedro, and of course when Pedro died, which was an absolute tragedy, they put me as number 1 in his car with Dickie Attwood, and Jo was number 1 in our car, which he

had been all year anyway, and he was joined by Gijs van Lennep. And I'll tell you for what it's worth, when you are the new boy in the team, if anything goes wrong people say it's the new guy's fault, and there were problems with one of my gearboxes in the 917, so they pulled me to one side and said, 'Bell, you'll have to be easier on the gearbox,' but at Watkins Glen, which was the first race I replaced Pedro, Jo was running his car with Van Lennep and they had gearbox wear, so I said to Porsche, 'I don't think that was my fault, I guess it must have been Jo who was a bit hard on the gearbox.' That's just a small story from that era, and then of course Jo died in October at the Brands Hatch Victory race. That was a tragic year when you look back on it, but at the time you didn't think it was out of the ordinary; in Formula 3 or Formula 2 people got killed all the time, so although you didn't take it for granted – you couldn't – you didn't get too worked up about it; I mean, today if three or four people got killed in a year we would all retire, wouldn't we, because it's too dangerous, but in those days it was like going to war.

JT: Later on, in 1985, you lost another team mate, Stefan Bellof.

DB: He was an amazing talent, and I adored the boy, but I don't think he was managed correctly, that's my feeling; I didn't think he was guided enough. I always thought Ken (Tyrrell) would guide him more, and then he was driving for Walter Brun and I imagine they were encouraging him to use his incredible skills to the full, but they should have said, 'You've got to get yourself together, get steady before you go so fast.'

JT: To go back to Porsches, you drove the 924 Carrera GTR at Le Mans in 1980.

DB: With Al Holbert, yes; we qualified thirty-fifth, and we ran as high as fifth overall, but then it burned a piston going down Mulsanne, though we still managed thirteenth overall. We'd have been best placed 924 if it wasn't for that.

JT: Let me steer you to the 936 that you drove in 1981; it's a mid-engined car, and it must have been nice to drive after a 935?

DB: I sat in the car for the first time at Le Mans and in my first practice session I did the fastest lap I'd ever done in my life; it wasn't the quickest overall, but certainly the quickest that I'd ever done and, in the race, we never had to lift a body panel up at all; we just drove the whole way in the lead. It's so easy to drive, it's beautiful, you just go faster and faster.

JT: Moving on to 1982, you were successful with the 956 at Brands Hatch, so what was the transition like from the 936? Clearly, you've got a ground effect chassis…

(continued overleaf)

DEREK BELL INTERVIEW *(continued from previous page)*

DB: Yeah, that's it; I remember it was a hell of a lot better, and we went a lot, lot faster. It was the same basic engine as the 936: it was the Indycar engine that was configured to run on petrol rather than the methanol that we used in 1981, and that engine we then used in 1982 and 1983. The ground effect during braking and cornering makes such an immense difference.

JT: Was the 962 an especially different car from the 956?

DB: Yes, it was a little different, because it was 65 or 75mm (2.5 or 3in) longer in the wheelbase, but it did make a difference. It was for safety reasons, so the driver's feet were behind the front axle, and the difference between the two cars used in the WSC and IMSA was that the Group C car was twin turbo and that made a totally different sound to what we had in America, which was the big raw 911-type turbo engine in the back, which looked like it had a windmill stuck on top of it, and we had up to 800+ horsepower. The IMSA 962 was a little higher off the ground for American regulations so it didn't have quite as much ground effect, but it was an amazing car.

JT: Your first World Sportscar Championship title was in 1985.

DB: I would have been American (IMSA) champion too, but I couldn't compete on both sides of the Atlantic at the same time because some of the races clashed, so I never became American champion because obviously it was more important that I won the World Sportscar Championship.

JT: Your co-driver in 1985 was Hans Stuck, and you jointly won the world title. In 1986, you had Al Holbert with you as well as Stucky.

DB: Yes, in 1986 I was world champion on my own without Stucky because of Porsche trying to play a trick on us and leaving me out of a couple of races, so I didn't get the points, and actually I thought I'd lost the title to Jaguar and Derek Warwick, but in the last race at the Norisring somehow they didn't do as many laps as they had recorded. John Fitzpatrick lent me his old 962, because he spotted that Porsche were entering just one car as it was only two one-hour race heats; he said, 'It is pretty obvious they want Stuck to be world champion on his own.' It was the only round that had just one driver, and he was doing it in a

rocket ship of a car – everything was lightweight rather than being doubled up to be reliable. Of course, he had problems and came thirteenth, while I was driving around slowly in eleventh or twelfth place, so I beat him to the title by one position, which was rather poetic justice.

JT: So, was that mid-1980s period the halcyon years as far as you're concerned?

DB: Absolutely, yeah, from 1981 on, once I got the 936, right through to 1990, that was the most amazing period of anybody's life, but we all have great periods, and I'm sure it was really for Stucky, to be honest. And don't forget that Al (Holbert) and I won Daytona and Le Mans, both in 1986 and 1987. I think I won thirty-seven races in the WSC and IMSA, and Professor Bott said I was the winningest driver in the history of Porsche during the Group C era. I won more races than any other factory driver, and that includes the races I drove with Jacky Ickx and Hans Stuck.

JT: Do you have a particular event that stands out as the best?

DB: There is. We had some phenomenal races, but the 1985 Miami Grand Prix at Bayfront Park in IMSA stands out. I was leading the race with Al Holbert and we had twelve laps to go. I was in the Löwenbräu 962 and David Hobbs and Darren Bradfield were in the Budweiser car, which was a Lola-Chevy, which of course is perfect on a street circuit with that immediate power, and the organizers wanted the American muscle cars to win. There was a full course yellow and when I went to restart it was firing on four cylinders instead of eight,

Derek Bell is always up for a demonstration run, as here in a 956 at the Ennstal Classic Rally stopover at Gröbming, Austria. He tends to attract those of a glamourous persuasion, too. JOHNNY TIPLER

Three titans of the World Endurance Championship – as well as being Rothmans-Porsche team mates and Le Mans winners: Derek Bell, Jochen Mass and Jacky Ickx share a chuckle over Mass's biographical notes. PORSCHE PHOTO ARCHIVE

In a competition career spanning more than two decades, Derek Bell drove in F1 for Tecno, Surtees, McLaren and Ferrari. He won Le Mans five times – in 1975, 1981, 1982, 1986 and 1987, and was World Sportscar Champion in 1985 and 1986. ANTONY FRASER

and I got overtaken by the works Jaguar and also the Budweiser car and it took me two laps for the engine to clear. When it cleared I went after them and I shot by on the inside at the last corner and went through to win the race. You could really drive the 962 hard, and these were three- to four-hour races as opposed to five or six hours, so you could drive the pants off it because of the sort of tracks you were on, like around the streets of San Antonio, where we also won, where you're drifting it through the corners and just missing the walls by inches. Whereas tracks like Silverstone are wonderful, but they didn't have the same drama to them because, if you spin you might get it back eventually, but on a street track there was nothing but kerbs and walls. I think the most memorable WSC race that I didn't win was coming second at Le Mans in 1983 with Jacky [Ickx]. He got hit on the first lap, and there was big pressure on fuel economy so we had to really economize, yet we managed to take a lap off the whole field to get back into the lead without more fuel, which was pretty remarkable. Then at 6 in the morning we had a fusebox problem so I had to change the electronics at Mulsanne, and then Jacky took over and we had to work our way back up through the field; we finished second by about 26 seconds, and I think that was my best race at Le Mans even though we didn't win it.
JT: Who's been your favourite co-driver?

DB: I always think of Jacky as being the ultimate team mate, the ultimate racing driver, and I have the greatest respect for him – his vitality, his speed, the way he got everything right – and of course that's why I always wanted him as team mate because if he got it right then he got it right for me too. Hans Stuck has to come next because of his amazing speed and the humour he brought to the team and to me. He told me a couple of years ago, 'You know, the reason I was put with you was because you were going to straighten me out,' so I probably had the best time with him because of our relationship, and he's always been a great friend. And Al Holbert, because you can't do 24-hour racing with somebody and not get on with them. Al was an amazing engineer and very good at building and developing a car, running the team and driving the car, when his race strategy was second to none. The rest of us were just drivers but Al actually was a technical guy. It was a tragedy he got killed in a plane crash in 1988; he'd just shown me the scale model of a car he hoped to build for Porsche to replace the 962, and afterwards Norbert Singer asked me to pick up the reins, but I said no as I'm based in Florida now.

And with that he was gone, off to blast another Porsche 962 through the Goodwood scenery. They should probably call it Bell's Hill as he drives it more than anyone else.

The 924 Carrera GT on the Rallye Monte Carlo Historique

Spawn of Jürgen Barth and Roland Kussmaul, the 924 Carrera GTS heralded Porsche's competition future – or, at least, one strand of it – back in 1979. The pair relived those halcyon days in the 2018 Rallye Monte Carlo Historique, and photographer Alex Denham and I tracked their progress through France, over the Alps and down to the principality.

Actually, it's not a genuine Carrera GTS, but a carbon copy of the pair's original Monte Carlo Rally 924 Turbo, with which they finished twentieth in 1979 and nineteenth in 1980. The WRC version of the Monte is shadowed by the Rallye Historique, staged a week or so later and running over mostly the same stages. In some villages, the flags and bunting are still draped over walls and across the road, and my guess is they probably stay put all year. The main difference is that the Old Timer rally is fundamentally a regularity-based event, a minutely timed handicap rather than a flat-out blinder, though try following it, and you'll find it does proceed at a frenetic pace nevertheless.

Inaugurated in 1998, the Historique regularly attracts well over 300 entries, an amazing array of classic cars built between 1950 and 1979 – from Alpine and Alfetta to Wartburg and Volvo. That permits a great repertoire of Porsches, and there are, annually, at least thirty or forty in the running, from 356s, 914s and 912s to 911s, going up to the SC, plus a growing number of 924 Turbos. In 2018, then, it's a thrill to find these two Porsche gods crewing this perfect replica of their 1980 924 Turbo – effectively the prototype Carrera GTS – on the Historic Monte. After all, these are the guys that created the

original model. 'This is a copy of our 924 GTS rally car from 1980 and 1981,' affirms Jürgen. Although the Porsche factory was completely behind the construction and development of the original 924 Carrera GT and its evolutions, Jürgen and Roland's replica was built a couple of years ago by Swiss driver and entrepreneur Franco Lupi, and funded by shipping magnate and co-owner of Aston Martin, Peter Livanos.

My snapping companion, Alex, and I join their party ahead of the Reims start. They explain that the replica 924 Carrera GTS was constructed on a donor 924 Turbo and created over the course of a year in the workshops of Gstaad-based specialist Franco Lupi. It was a straightforward metamorphosis. The donor 924 Turbo was stripped and the shell seam-welded, with additional supports around the shock turrets. A new engine was built up, and after testing at Paul Ricard, fresh brakes were fitted. Why, though, would Mr Livanos be motivated to back the construction of a rally rep such as this?

Well, it is an iconic car that did pretty well in 1979 and 1980, helmed by two of Porsche's top people, sufficiently so for the original car to be displayed in the Porsche Museum, and it comes right at the end of the eligible age span to qualify for an entry.

If that's not enough to inspire its creation, as Jürgen says, 'the simple answer is that it is not so expensive to produce as some cars.'

Having covered this fascinating event eight or nine times, I've noticed 924s appearing more and more, and I can see how a 924 Turbo could be a leading contender. Barth and Kussmaul advised Lupi and Livanos during the build process. Jürgen says:

We gave them all the information, ex-Porsche mechanics helped build the engine and gearbox, and Roland personally supervised the construction. You'd have to ask Peter why he chose the 924, but I think it's the case that the Monaco Automobile Club is probably not accepting any more 911s because there are already too many. So that was the reason why he chose the 924

Turbo, and also because they are limiting the final eligible build-year to 1979.

A cut-off date that Jürgen finds irrational.

In my opinion, that is stupid, sorry to say, for the FIA to stop all the historic cars at 1979. It's crazy! I mean, we're losing cars, and they get modified too radically so that you never can recover the original. It's worked perfectly until now, but the FIA doesn't understand Historics, and they justify it by saying, 'Oh, well, after 1979 the cars have too much electronics.' Yes, but we also have much bigger homologation numbers, so it's very difficult to understand their thinking.

This is the second time that Jürgen and Roland have done the historic Monte. In 2017, they came 133rd in the 924 GTS rep, so finishing 105th a year on has to be seen as progress. I refer Jürgen to last year:

Well, after the first stage, out of 322 cars we'd moved up to 299th, and then by the end we managed to understand a little bit of the regularity stuff because we hadn't done that before, and you need a lot of instruments to cope with it. And now the high-tech instruments and things like this Blunik are complicated. But it's good fun, and we developed a technique for

The cabin interior of the Barth-Kussmaul 924 Carrera GTS is a combination of laboratory and rally car; here, Roland does the paperwork ahead of the final stages above Monte Carlo, 2018. ALEX DENHAM

it, so that normally, on a clear stage, we go slowly, but if it's snow you have to really attack to achieve the average speed. It's paradoxical, because you think everybody would be taking it easy under those circumstances. But you have to keep checking your speed, and the instruments tell you if you are plus or minus the ideal speed. I'm not relying on Roland to tell me; it's even better now as I have an instrument on the dashboard that shows us some lines, and if the lines are matching then you are ideal, if the lines are off then you have to brake or accelerate. This system even tells you the ideal line through the corners; it is very sophisticated, and that makes it complicated for the co-driver because he needs to be constantly looking at the instrument checking the lines and recalculating. The GPS system is up to us, but we don't know which measurements the organization is using, because at certain points on the stages they're calculating our speed and location and we don't know where those points are being monitored. So, we constantly have to aim for the average kilometres per hour, but in the hairpins, you have to accelerate before the hairpin, then go slowly around the hairpin, then accelerate until you've got up to speed again. And of course, this isn't normally how I would be driving. If it's snow, its different, because then you have to go fast anyway.

There's another angle to regularity rallies, thinks Jürgen.

I think it's a way of keeping motor sport alive, so that historic cars survive and people can have fun driving them on the roads, because the stages are not closed, so you can meet something else coming on a single-track road, but if you are only going at regularity speed there's less danger. Plus, these older cars are rare and quite fragile now.

We get into the fine detail.

The car was prepared in Würzburg by an old friend, Armin Knüpfing, who has run a Carrera Cup team since 1992 and is an ex-factory mechanic who's worked on Indycars, Group C 962s and the Paris–Dakar. Roland and I picked up the car on the trailer and we drove to France.

So, how does it drive?

It's a nice, neutral-handling car, and you can drive it really smoothly without any big problems, and that's perfect. OK, you have to work with the lag of the turbo, which is a little bit of a handicap when coming out of the hairpins, but no, for me it's not a problem. Comparing this car, the GTS, and the race car, the GTR, the GTS is the better car, because in rallying you need a little bit of elasticity and a softer car; the 924 GTR has more power and a better gearbox and better uprights, but for rallying it's a different set of values.

As well as a substantial roll-cage, the rear luggage bay of the Barth-Kussmaul 924 Carrera GTS houses a rally tyre-shod spare wheel and compartmentalized fuel tank. ALEX DENHAM

Fronted by the battery of Cibié spotlamps and topped by its intercooler, the 2.0-litre Turbo slant four in the Jürgen Barth/Roland Kussmaul 924 Carrera GTS develops approximately 210bhp at 6,000rpm.

ALEX DENHAM

Inside the cabin there's a bolted-in steel Heigo roll-cage, and co-pilot Kussmaul faces a profusion of navigation equipment. The Fuchs wheels are clad with 185/65 R15 SESS Nokian Hakkapeliitta Sisteron tyres that have an amazing tread pattern, with one half of the tread more deeply and prominently incised than the other. The spare is handily housed in the rear luggage deck, as well as the 70-litre (15gal) safety tank. The car is fronted by a phalanx of four Cibie spotlamps and a pair of fog lights. The bonnet is hinged but secured at the front by Dzus fasteners, just as it was in 1979. The four characteristic 924 Turbo ducts ahead of the spotlamps play an even more vital role. Atop the engine, the oblong aluminium panel that first catches the eye replicates the air intake system installed in the 1980 car, as Jürgen explains, because the car was only homologated as a 924 Turbo at the time: 'this intake air cooler was for the 924 Carrera GT, but the GT had an opening on the hood (bonnet), and you couldn't use that because it was a modification and the car was only homologated as a 924 Turbo, so we had to find a way of cooling it.'

When they tackled the Monte Carlo Rally for the first time in 1979 the team had originally prepared the 924 Turbo like this, and then it turned out they couldn't run it as a Turbo because there weren't enough cars built by then. 'So, for 1979, we had to change it into a normally aspirated car, which meant we had to close the ducts and vents, which we did with sponsor stickers and the metal rally plaque, so nobody knew!'

The GT prototype was running in 1980, but it wasn't yet homologated so they still couldn't use the characteristic Carrera wheel arches on the rally car, hence the milder riveted flares fitted here. Actually, I think they are more aesthetically pleasing than the more macho versions that followed on the 924 Carrera GT. Jürgen recalls those days fondly:

You have to always remember that originally it was not a factory project, it was a private project that Roland and I started, with the blessing from the top management; in this way, we showed the factory that it could be a good car, so the decision was then taken that we build the Carrera GT and the GTS, and go to Le Mans with the GTR.

We catch up with Jürgen and Roland again on the stages out of Valence. We queue behind their 924 GTS to follow them onto the notorious Col de l'Echarasson stage. It's obviously pretty snowy – it always is – but the stewards check out our Boxster's winter Vredesteins and shake their heads: only studded tyres will do here, they say, because there's only one line in the snow, with no run off to left or right. And no one wants to be a mobile chicane. We can walk in and snap, though, which is just fine under the circumstances. We observe Jürgen's immaculate car control in the snow and ice, but Alex isn't so lucky: panning the 924 GTS, she slips into a snowdrift, but I haul her out none the worse for wear. Anyway, there are plenty more stages where the snow's either been ploughed off the road or simply melted, which we can drive on, stopping every so often when Alex spots a suitable vantage point to take pictures from.

On day four we meet up with our quarry in the *parc fermé* at Èze, a picturesque, if busy, village high on the bluffs west of Monaco. 'We're having fun,' beams Jürgen. 'Roland a bit less than me, because he is fighting with the Blunik System.' That's part of the navigator's kit that he was referring to back in Reims, and if, like me, you're unfamiliar with Blunik, here's how this very latest in in-car navigational equipment works. It's a compact system for maintaining stage segment and transit section times accurately, specifically in regularity rallies. It consists of a clock, chronometer, speedometer, odometer, speed table, calculator and calibrator, all packed into a single rectangular box. It enables the navigator to view total and partial distance, average and instantaneous speed, time and distance remaining to finish the sector, with a constant display of the sensor readings. Significantly, it displays the regularity maintenance numerically, so that, if it shows a negative number, the driver needs to accelerate, and conversely, if it's a positive number, then he must slow down. If it shows

00, he's going perfectly. It allows the crew to schedule regularity segments, with or without changes of average, and connection sections, and memorizes different calibrations. So, as far as the 924 GTS is concerned, and indeed all historic rally cars, it's an anachronism, given that the much less sophisticated Halda, Terratrip or Brantz devices were the norm back in 1980. State of the art Blunik may be, but Roland is less than enamoured.

We have some slight problems with the Blunik. Sometimes it's doing what I want, but sometimes it's not, because it wouldn't start itself, so we got penalized a little bit this morning. But yesterday on the last stage in the snow we did one of the best times, with least penalties.

So, not all bad then. 'We are keeping up with the top cars now, so I think we are below 100th. But we didn't start out with an ambition to win or anything, we're just having fun. The car has been running well, with no problems.' Unlike many entries who have a dedicated pair of mechanics following them, Jürgen and Roland's communal service crew is looking after five cars, operating out of four vans and four 4×4 SUVs. Are they prepped for the evening's run up to Sospel and Lantosque via the notorious Col de Turini and Col de la Couillole? 'Yeah, we are all set up for the night,' confirms Jürgen, a picture of calm. Surely this will be the most demanding of all, though? 'No, I think it will be easy, because there's not so much snow, and it's wet and quite warm now – it's 8 degrees – so road conditions could really be much worse. Now it's important we have fun!' Midnight up on Turini: the white 924 Carrera GTS purrs blithely by. It's Jürgen and Roland, reprising their Monte Carlo outing of four decades ago, and there's so little in the way of snow and ice this year that it's almost a walk in the park.

Next day, in warm sunshine, we meet up in the Quai Albert 1er *parc fermé*. Save for road grime, their 924 GTS is unblemished. Of all the stages that they've done this year, which have been the trickiest?

The long one where you wanted to come in, l'Echarasson, that was quite demanding, where we did quite well, and then on the second stage where it was a bit snowy. It was a long stage with 45km (28 miles), but we didn't get too many penalties. Last night was not so difficult.

Will they do the Historic Monte again? 'Peter (Livanos) has invited us for next year, which is nice. The Historique is a fantastic mixture of classic cars, and good fun for us.' I'll drink to that! At this point, we bid them *auf Wiedersehen* and head for the Tip-Top.

ABOVE: **The 924 Carrera GTS of Jürgen Barth and Roland Kussmaul on the snowy Col de l'Echarasson stage in the Vercors (1,146m/3,760ft) during the Rallye Monte Carlo Historique, 2018.** ALEX DENHAM

RIGHT: **The 924 Carrera GTS of Jürgen Barth and Roland Kussmaul on a transit section out of Valence during the 2018 Rallye Monte Carlo Historique.** JOHNNY TIPLER

**Jürgen Barth and Roland Kussmaul speed through Chaudon in the Alpes de Provence
in their 924 Carrera GTS during the 2018 Rallye Monte Carlo Historique. Actually,
'speed' is relative, as this is a regularity stage so they aren't going that quickly.**

JOHNNY TIPLER

THE 944 TURBO CUP CAR

The Porsche Supercup is rooted in the 944 Turbo Cup series that ran from 1986 to 1989. I sampled two of the original contenders, driving them around Abbeville Circuit's tight little twists and turns, getting a taste of a proper factory-built racing car. Chuck it in, aim for the apex, oversteer, apply some opposite lock and power out, gradually unwinding the steering. Remarkably, it's not that different from any of the faster road-going front-engined Porsches. From the 924 Carrera GTS to the 968 Club Sport, this is familiar territory, nice and easy to drive fast and have fun with. And that was precisely Porsche's thinking in 1986 when they launched the dedicated 944 Turbo Cup championship.

The forerunner of the multi-national Carrera Cup and Supercup series was Porsche's calculated contribution to recreational motor sport. Anyone could have a crack at it (given the wherewithal, of course). In the inaugural seven-race series, hobby drivers went head to head with professionals in virtually bog-standard 944 Turbos, the forty contestants sharing a DM45,000 purse at each race. The higher you finished, the more you earned. Initially

the curtain-raiser for the ADAC Supercup Group C races, the Turbo Cup blossomed into the 964-based Carrera Cup in 1990, and by 1993 the Supercup was tagged onto F1's coat-tails.

A decade earlier, the bandwagon had started rolling. The 944 Turbo Cup was born into an era of heady international motor sport where Porsche were dominant. As if you needed reminding, the Group C endurance racing epoch was reaching its zenith, with Porsche's all-conquering 935, 956B and 962C rampant, handsomely winning the World Sportscar Championship six years running from 1981 to 1986. The 911 SC RS was a leading light in the European Rally Championship, and the 959-derived 4×4 won the Paris–Dakar Rally. In Formula 1, TAG-Porsche V6 turbos powered McLaren to the 1985 and 1986 world titles. Porsche could do no wrong. On the road, the front-engined range – 924, 944 and 928 – were flavour of the moment, while the 911 was yesterday's papers. In production from 1981 to 1991, the 944 epitomized the line-up's middle ground in the showroom, and was considered the obvious model to use to promote the brand. The flagship 217bhp '951' Turbo variant came on the scene in 1985, and that was chosen as the basis for the Turbo Cup race cars.

ABOVE: **The forerunner of the multi-national Carrera Cup and Supercup series was Porsche's 944 Turbo Cup. In the inaugural seven race series, hobby drivers went head to head with professionals in virtually bog-standard 944 Turbos, of which these are two.** ANTONY FRASER

BELOW: **The cutaway illustration of the early 944 Turbo reveals the transaxle driveline with gearbox in-unit with the rear axle, and the turbocharger to the left-hand side of the slant-four engine manifolding, with intercooler to the front.** PORSCHE PHOTO ARCHIVE

The 944 Turbo was announced in July 1984, powered by a 2479cc slant-four engine, incorporating twin balancer shafts, Bosch Motronic engine management and KKK K26 turbocharger, and developing 217bhp. ANTONY FRASER

Under the bonnet of the 944 Turbo Cup car, there's a strut brace, and the in-line four-pot slant-mounted engine is the 2479cc 8-valve 944 Turbo unit featuring single KKK K26 turbo with separate wastegate and front-mounted intercooler. Porsche have fitted KKK turbochargers from the outset, the manufacturers, Kühnle, Kopp and Kausch, having started up in 1962 making turbos under licence from the US Schwitzer Corporation. They took over Eberspächer in 1972, and started producing their own range of KKK-branded turbos from 1974. ANTONY FRASER

It's all very well blitzing Le Mans or duneing in the Sahara in extreme machines like the 962 and 959, but to maintain relevance for the regular customer, the Turbo Cup racers were very little modified from stock. The transition from leaded to unleaded fuel was in the offing, so Porsche insisted the Turbo Cup cars ran with catalytic converters, a technology very much in its infancy at the time. So, as well as ensuring the cars were environmentally acceptable, the objective was also to assess the performance of a catalysed exhaust at full race temperatures. The few changes to the standard car that first year included harder rubber suspension bushes, thicker (27mm and 21mm) anti-roll bars, stiffer spring and damper settings, with 8in Fuchs wheels and 245/45 × 16 on the front and 9in with 255/40 VR16s on the back. To ensure a level playing field – bearing in mind there were some very experienced players in the game as well as arrant amateurs – the Motronic control units, knock sensor and boost pressure wastegate were sealed, and Porsche stewards carried out spot checks on three cars chosen randomly after every race.

Cabin interior of a 944 Turbo Cup car: you would hardly know the difference from the standard car, apart from the roll-cage and red line at steering wheel top.
ANTONY FRASER

At Weissach, as we've observed, Jürgen Barth and Roland Kussmaul had enjoyed success with the front-engined 924 Rally, the Carrera GT and 944 GTP between 1979 and 1982, but now they were busy with other ventures including the 961 Le Mans car and customer 962s, so another project leader was needed. Welcome aboard Dieter Glemser, former Porsche 906 racer, 1972 ETC champ and veteran of the legendary Köln Capri 2600RS versus BMW 3.0 CSL battles of the early 1970s: no stranger to powerful front-engined GT cars, then. In the hot seats, the key players in the inaugural seven race series were Jo Winkelhock, Jörg van Ommen, Roland Asch and Harald Gröhs, with tin-top expert Winkelhock emerging victorious at the last round. The earnings were shared out so that the winner banked DM5K, the second-placed driver DM4.5K, all the way down to the racer in twenty-fifth place, who received DM100.

With close and dramatic racing, the series was a hit. (Just like many of the protagonists were to each other!) The recipe was spot on, and for 1987 Porsche elected to run five rounds in Germany and five at other European tracks: Zolder, Spa, the Nürburgring, Brno and Monza. Once established on the scene, the 1988 and 1989 Turbo Cup grids served as curtain-raisers for the higher-profile DTM rounds, and the ten-race series ran at Zolder, Hockenheim, Nürburgring, Avus, Mainz-Finthen, Norisring, Hungaroring, Salzburgring, Spa-Francorchamps, and the Nürburgring again. Blaupunkt became title sponsors in 1987, prize money rose by DM10K, and the engines were re-chipped to make 250bhp, along with concessions to stiffer suspension. The 944 Turbo became more of a race car, with lighter fibreglass panels and the shell seam-welded in places, and the traditional Fuchs wheels were replaced with cast magnesium 'telephone dials'. The technical tweak this time was switchable ABS, so that the manufacturer could assess the benefits of assisted braking under race stresses. Lessons were passed on to the customer pretty quickly: despite its relatively lavish spec, the 944 Turbo S introduced in 1988 is a road-going manifestation of the 1987 Turbo Cup car.

Across the border in France, things were rather different: the Turbo Cup got under way under the auspices of concessionaires Sonauto, and competitors were given much freer rein with spec and set up. Straight-through exhausts with no cats were allowed as unleaded petrol was hard to find there, and they had a larger sump, made of lightweight magnesium like the intake manifold. Drilled discs and race pads were sourced from the 928 S4, and a strut brace was fitted between front shock turrets. The cabin was stripped of rear seats, replaced by a Matter roll cage, and Recaro race seats and five-point harness on the driver's side. Unlike the German Turbo Cup cars that served to promote a road-going race car ethic, all leisure equipment, including air-con, hi-fi, central locking, electric windows and power steering, were deleted from the French cars in the interests of reducing weight. Outside, smaller Cup mirrors were fitted, and air intakes replaced the fog lamps. Winner of the French Cup championship that year was René Metge (hot from winning the Paris–Dakar too), while the German series victor in 1987, 1988 and 1989 was Roland Asch, who went on to star in the 964 Carrera Cup in 1991.

Detective Work Required: Two Historic 944s

So, let's have a look at the two examples I'm sampling at Abbeville. The red car is from the original 1986 season. Owner Kristof van Hoof talks us through the spec. 'The 944 Turbo Cup was a standard Turbo, but with a very basic 944 interior, with no options like a normal Turbo would have: no power steering, no air conditioning, no electric mirrors, but they kept the carpets, passenger seat and the back seat, and raced like that.' During the 1986 season this car was run by VW Schultz, now Porsche Centre Essen, and driven by Annette Meeuvissen. From Düsseldorf, this blonde bombshell's race career began in the Fiesta Challenge, winning the Ladies' Cup in 1982. After a season in the 944 Turbo Cup in 1986, she drove BMW M3s for Schnitzer and Zakspeed in the DTM from 1987 to 1991, teamed with the likes of Altfrid Heger, Dieter Quester and Roland Ratzenburger. She retired from racing in 1992 and worked as a performance driving instructor for BMW.

Kristof bought this Turbo Cup 944 in 2013, and thereby hangs a detective saga worthy of Hercule Poirot.

I found it a year ago, advertised in Belgium as a 944 Turbo, nothing more. It looked just like a standard 944

The few changes made to the standard 944 Turbo to turn it into a Turbo Cup Car included harder rubber suspension bushes, thicker anti-roll bars, stiffer spring and damper settings, with 8in Fuchs and 245/45 × 16 tyres on the front and 9in with 255/40 VR16 tyres on the back. This is the ex-Annette Meeuvissen car from 1986; possibly twelve out of the original forty 944 Turbo Cup cars were painted red. ANTONY FRASER

Turbo. Although they didn't do much to them to turn them into racing cars, someone had converted it back into a street car, so it was missing the roll-cage, it had Konis instead of Bilsteins, a normal driver's seat, and because they put in new carpets you couldn't see where the cage had been.

The irony was that Kristof was intent on buying the car to create a pastiche Cup car like his friend Hans's genuine 944 Turbo Cup car. Little did he know that in fact he'd bought the real deal. First of all, he spotted some things that didn't tally with a normal 944 Turbo, such as the wind-up windows and ignition cutout switch beside the battery, which the vendor seemed oblivious of. As far as the seller was concerned, it was simply a 944 Turbo, but by now Kristof was almost certain it was a Turbo Cup car, so he offered to buy it in spite of a broken water pump. Back home, he lifted up the carpets, revealing the points where the cage had been. Despite incorrect 'elephant's ears' mirrors instead of smaller 'flag' mirrors, Kristof donned his Poirot outfit and began playing detective. You would start with the chassis number – or so you might think – but back in 1986 the Cup cars didn't have a special racing designation, just an option code – and that sticker was missing.

I sent the chassis number to Porsche and their archives confirmed that it was indeed a Cup car, and it has matching engine and gearbox numbers. But they can't, or won't, give any information about who raced the car in 1986; they just say they don't know, so I had to search in another way.

Kristof already had a pair of Turbo Cup 'flag' mirrors, and when he took off the 'elephant's ears' mirrors to fit them, lo and behold, he discovered yellow paint.

That was the first clue regarding the original paint scheme. So, then I bought all the old magazines from 1986 containing reports of the Turbo Cup races, and there were about twelve red cars out of the original forty. But luckily there were only a few with red and yellow paintwork, so I felt I was getting close.

Scanning eBay one day he came across a Porsche promo video of the whole 1986 Cup series. The identity of the car would soon be revealed! 'I don't know why they made the promotional film, maybe for the press, but on there I saw a red 944 with stylized yellow flames painted along the side and roof of the car, and a completely black rear end.' Excitedly, Kristof began removing small test areas of red paint and, sure enough, there was more of the yellow and black in the right places. 'It still has its original paint scheme intact,' he explained. 'Underneath the red was a primer coat, and then the black or yellow, and then underneath that, again the red.' Kristof shows me a snapshot of 1986 driver Annette Meeuvissen leaning against the car along with maestro Hans Stuck. Sadly there was no chance of an interview, as she had died of cancer, aged forty-two, in 2004. There is no justice.

The Meeuvissen 944 was registered as a road car in Belgium in 1989, having been superseded by the upgraded Turbo S-spec Cup Cars at the end of the 1988 season. It had reached that point where old racing cars were just that, and of no use to anybody, so they took out the roll-cage and made it a street car. Kristof for one has found a use for it, though, and is glad its identity was concealed for a quarter of a century. 'What are the chances of finding a race car with this provenance, still with its original engine and the 8- and 9in Fuchs wheels all sitting on the car?' He started sourcing the rest of the equipment to resurrect its Turbo Cup identity. A set of correct, rebuilt 944 Turbo cup dampers came from Bilstein USA, a legacy that Kristof believes stems from the model's longevity Stateside. 'In the US and Canada, they raced those cars a bit longer than we did in Europe, in that Rothman's series, so they used them a couple of years longer and also more intensively.' Kristof's ongoing plans for the car's restoration to its Turbo Cup appearance stop short of reapplying the flames that bedecked the bodywork in its Annette Meeuvissen days. He'll have it repainted red, sure, but it will be presented like Porsche's promotional Turbo Cup press car with rather less ostentatious graphics, just a few title sponsor decals.

Kristof's pal Hans Goosens had originally been hunting for a 964 Cup car, but soon found they were out of his budget.

So I started looking for another proprietary-built Porsche racing car, and the 944 Turbo Cup came on the radar. It's more affordable, a lot cheaper to run, and if you hit the barriers you can find a front wing for a 944 far cheaper than a 964: one is €50, the other €1,000.

Having scoured the market in Germany and even discovered one in South Africa, Hans eventually found a 1988 car at the Belgian classic Porsche specialists August Porsche Addiction at Ohain, just south of Brussels (home to one Jacky Ickx). 'It wasn't really for sale, but the owner had bought it for his daughter to

go racing with, but she found the steering was too heavy for her and she couldn't turn the wheel, so he put it up for sale.' He was still tempted by the South African car, but the thought of shipping costs and the swingeing 30 per cent Belgian import tax and VAT focused his attentions on the Brussels car. 'It was fully original, needed no work, the guy gave me a very good price, and I drove it home through the snow on slicks, which was simply frightening!'

There was some history, including photos of it racing at different circuits, but Hans craved more.

I knew who the drivers were, so I started contacting them. The first guy to respond said he'd driven the car with that serial number during the 1989 season, having bought it from a German team with Swiss drivers. That was Autohaus Friedrich Scholz, and the first driver in 1988 was Nicky Leutwiler, who's a famous name because he also drove a Porsche 956 and 962 and he's still active in motor sport. He finished the season seventh in the charts.

The car passed into the hands of Swiss driver Fredi Briedl, who joined the well-known Strähle Autosport team (Paul-Ernst

Hans Goosens' 944 Turbo Cup race car is a little more austere than Kristof van Hoof's red one here at Abbeville Circuit, because it had a longer and more intense competition history and was adapted accordingly. ANTONY FRASER

Strähle was a long-time Porsche racer and rallyist), and soon afterwards the team bought the car and ran it for the 1989 season. After Briedl had an accident in the early part of the season it was taken over by Rudiger Schmidt, who finished third in the Turbo Cup series with this very car. In fact, Strähle Autosport was extremely successful, having won the 944 Turbo Cup with Jo Winkelhock in 1986 and Roland Asch in 1987, 1988 and 1989, as well as the Porsche Turbo World Cup in Kyalami during one of the Championship's occasional flyaway races. Strähle sold the car in 1990 to an Italian doctor who drove it for a couple of years, then it relocated to Berlin in 2007, where engine and bodywork were completely refurbished and its racing identity restored. It passed on to Berlin-based classic specialists Springbok, from whom the Belgian dealer bought it for his daughter.

There's a time and a place for everything. I've driven Kristof's car on the road, but we're at a race track and these are racing cars, so let's get stuck in. I belt up in the Recaro race seat in Hans's white charger, and instantly it feels like home. It's a little more austere than the red car, but hardly any different to how you'd render any 944 track-day dicer these days. The 944 Turbo Cup car has a great driving position, and it's very easy to get comfortable with the right relationship of feet to pedals to wheel. It's a lot like the 924 Carrera GTS in that respect, which is traceable in the 968 Club Sport too. The 944's unassisted steering is heavy, but I don't actually find that to be so when I'm out on the circuit, it's just when I'm stationary or turning around in the paddock that the wheel needs hauling.

The gearshift is positive, though not especially sensitive through the gate; I'm anticipating turbo lag, but really, it's imperceptible, smothered to a great extent by enormous torque. To get the most out of a car at Abbeville you need to be in the lower gears at high revs, and though there is a bit of lag out of a couple of corners, the torque of the blown 2.5-litre straight-four does most of the work. I can almost get round the whole track in third gear, dropping to second for some corners while feeling the limits; but in third gear I can certainly get away from a lot of other cars. Having the luxury of ABS brakes, it's no great effort slowing for corners either.

The 944 Turbo's handling is more stable and predictable than the 911's, but when it breaks away it's a more sudden occurrence; at speed with the 911 you're engaged in a balancing act, delicately swishing round the dancefloor, but in the 944 it's a less involving experience – till it snaps – and it's like a mid-engined car in that respect. Fine if you're provoking it deliberately. So, to bring out the beast, I'm having a fling into the corners, setting up a drift like an old-school racer. I learned to do that pedalling an Alfa Romeo GTV6 in the AROC championship years ago, and when you find that swaying rhythm it's almost dreamlike.

This would be a very interesting way to own a 944 Turbo. It's a practical road car too, if a little hard-edged. The Turbo Cup was Porsche's opening gambit in the single-marque racing stakes, making a factory racing car available to amateur drivers, and it's also my opening gambit in the budget Porsche stakes. Finding one might require a bit of sleuthing though.

Even given its race seat and harness, the author finds the 944 Turbo Cup car has a great driving position, and it's very easy to get comfortable with the right relationship of feet to pedals to wheel.
ANTONY FRASER

Finnish Line: the 944 Turbo Club Sport

In the land of Nokia and Nokian, Häkkinen and Räikönnen, the Finns have a penchant for extremes: like yumping spectacular distances on the 1,000 Lakes Rally – and insisting on US-spec safety bumpers on their 944 Turbo Club Sports.

It's a rare one, this 944 Turbo Club Sport. Our friend Bert Vanderbruggen recently imported it from Finland to Belgium and invited us to have a go on the local back roads near his Kalmthout home. Though the journey was convoluted, there was a certain logic to the purchase. 'I found the car thanks to a Scandinavian journalist,' says Bert, 'and he told me about the Finnish collector who wanted to sell it. You know I like rarities, and this one is in absolutely fantastic condition, and it's also a very rare opportunity to have a 944 Turbo Club Sport.'

One reason that classic cars are particularly well preserved in Finland is because of the climate. This may sound strange in a land known for its snow and ice and mosquitoes. That's the point: from October till June, cars are cocooned away, leaving just a three-month window to enjoy them. Bert provides the meteorological lowdown:

> Most of the old-timer cars are very well kept, because they only drive their classics during the summertime. Winter's already started at the beginning of October and lasts until April, and it can be minus 30 degrees, with snow, ice and salted roads, so the summer period is very short.

In fact, there are virtually separate worlds in Finland: one operating in almost perpetual daylight and unexpectedly high temperatures, the other distinguished by pitilessly cold winters and near twilight during the day. 'It's a very big contrast between summer and winter, so these cars are only used a few months every year, and that's the reason why most Scandinavian cars are in better condition than those in Belgium or England.' An interesting hypothesis, but Bert's 944 Turbo CS is the physical proof.

Bert's not sure how many 944 Turbo Club Sports were produced – and I checked with Porsche HQ but they didn't seem to know either. 'There were only a few,' says Bert; 'I think about 230 cars, so not that many at all. But the car is completely original, it's fully documented, and the first owner even kept the original pictures from the moment he got the keys from the garage, so I have everything.' The logbook clearly states it's a Turbo Club Sport model, yet, puzzlingly, there's no logo to demonstrate its identity as such, like the emblem bedecking the front left-hand wing top of the 3.2 Carrera CS, 968 CS and 928 CSs. As well as the scarcity of Club Sport variants, this one is endowed with something extra in the posterior, namely, a US-market impact bumper. It seems that's down to Finnish safety rules back in the 1980s, when all 944s, 928s and 924s were obliged to bear the extra protrusion of the lumpen bumper. Still, it wears it not too badly and isn't a serious aesthetic detractor. It's rather mitigated by the diffuser bodykit below the rear apron.

The invoice file and service record are pleasingly full, endorsing the car's provenance… if only I could read Finnish. What I can discern is that the chassis number is WPOZZZ95Z-KN100114, and the car was invoiced to Jarno Anttila by the Sports Car Centre, Helsinki, at DM60,000 (£22,700) on 3 August 1988. A second invoice dated 5 October 1989 is presumably when it was passed on to Jyrki Luukkonen, whom Bert bought it from in April 2015.

Owner Bert Vanderbruggen thinks that Porsche released perhaps 250 units of the 944 Turbo Club Sport. The logbook clearly identifies this as a Turbo Club Sport model, though it doesn't have the requisite decal on its left-front wing.
ANTONY FRASER

Great rear tracking shot of the 944 Turbo Club Sport on a Belgian back road. This car was imported from Finland, hence the US-spec rear bumper overriders where they were a mandatory part of the spec.
ANTONY FRASER

Side-on panning shot shows the 944 Turbo Club Sport to be little different to the regular 944 Turbo, though the rear oversize rubber overriders and diffuser beneath the rear valance are exceptions.
ANTONY FRASER

All the documents are here; you can read everything about it, all the history from invoices, transport documents and original service books, which is nice. When Jyrki bought the car, he asked for the documentation from the dealership, including the letters they exchanged with the first owner. You can see his order documents and the old invoice.

The body hue is Velvet Red Metallic, U6, a special order on the Porsche colour chart, and the internal upholstery majors in pinstripe black-and-white velour with leather bolsters, a great period look though somewhat at odds with the car's Club Sport identity. What else? Bert talks us through the equipment sheet:

It has no catalytic converter, it has a heavy-duty battery, washers for the headlights, heated sports seats, air-con, the second oil cooler, sports steering wheel, alloy wheels and locking wheel nuts. Both rear mirrors are electrically adjustable, the back seat is a single

bench instead of two parts; it has a sports exhaust, limited-slip diff, spoiler kit on the underside of the car, a rear wiper, and a space-saver spare, plus additional fog lights in front. So you can see the first owner ticked all the option boxes.

And there's the paradox: Club Sports generally have most of the creature comforts deleted, while Bert's car is fully loaded.

Here's what we know about the 944 Turbo Club Sport variant, according to 944 expert Jon Mitchell of JMG Porsche at Wimborne:

The 944 Turbo Club Sport is a car of myth and legend! Despite the people on the internet who say there is no such thing, the reality is that they were an option, not advertised, but available nevertheless. Typical option code for them is M637, and Porsche also sell the front wing decal with 'CS' (like the 3.2 Carrera and 968) as its logo. Usually the car was made for

45

someone of interest, and the value will go up if the first owner was someone of interest, such as a race driver connected to Porsche.

This car's first paint is totally original, as it's an unrestored car, with every invoice and a complete dossier. The Porsche blurb in the file says that the 944 Turbo is virtually identical to the cars that compete in the 944 Turbo Cup, with 250bhp, a 0–100km/h time of 5.9sec and a maximum speed of 261km/h (162mph). Under the bonnet the in-line four-pot engine and its ancillaries appears the same as a regular 2479cc 8-valve 944 Turbo. It's all shiny paint and metal, and the engine is one of those 'eat your dinner off it' specimens. It has four-piston fixed caliper disc brakes with ABS, sports suspension, limited-slip differential, and the underside is flat-bottomed to create ground-effect downforce as the air passes underneath the car.

The unit-construction sunroof shell is all in galvanized steel, and the 944 Turbo drag coefficient is cd0.33. The removable sunroof is equipped with an electric tilt facility and built-in safety lock. It's operated by a rocker switch mounted on the centre console and the panel can be removed entirely and stowed in the luggage compartment, which we did for the photoshoot, and it is fiddly to take out and relocate. A deflector on the leading edge of the sunroof aperture helps reduce wind noise. Amongst the normal 944 gauges on the dashboard there's a turbo boost gauge.

The front suspension is by coil springs and dampers, wishbones, anti-roll bar and ventilated discs, and at the rear light-alloy semi-trailing arms, transverse torsion bar and light-alloy transverse axle. Wheels are earlier forged Design-90 style, regular 944 Turbo issue, 7J × 16in at the front, shod with 225/50 ZR16 tyres, and 9J × 16in at the rear, with 245/45 ZR16 tyres. The rim of the seven-spoke forged D90 wheel projects slightly, which makes it appear more like a dished wheel, while the spokes join the rim with a shield-like reinforcement at the point of contact with the rim (the cast version doesn't do this).

Further research reveals that the 944 Turbo's Club Sport suffix was based on the factory's M637 options spec sheet and was available for the 1988 Turbo S and 1989–91 Turbo, but only in countries that hosted the 944 Turbo Cup series, which meant Germany, France, Belgium, Canada and the USA. The M637 optioned cars were imported into the USA between 1986 and 1991 by racer Al Holbert, who ran Porsche Motorsport North America. They were a mix of 944 Turbos, 16-valve S and S2 Club Sports, destined for Stateside race careers. The package included components from the broader-based M030 options list, such as upgraded suspension and brakes from the earlier 1985–88 Turbo.

In point of fact, the 944 Turbo Cup cars were relatively lightly modified compared with later iterations of Cup Cars: the few changes to the standard 1986 944 Turbo included harder rubber suspension bushes, thicker 27mm and 21mm anti-roll bars front and rear, stiffer spring and damper settings, and 8in D90s or Fuchs wheels with 245/45 × 16 tyres on the front and 9in with 255/40 VR16s on the back. The package option that became available later included 30mm front and 25.5mm rear

The super-clean engine bay of the slant-four 944 Turbo engine is rather surprisingly lacking a strut brace. The 2479cc 8-valve slant-four unit develops 250bhp, and it goes from 0 to 100km/h in 5.9sec with a maximum speed of 261km/h (162mph). ANTONY FRASER

The 944 Turbo Club Sport provides competent handling, manifest in agility and stability during cornering. ANTONY FRASER

Motoring in the 944 Turbo Club Sport, the author finds it's an easy-to-drive, no-frills car, deploying full-on straight-line acceleration when the turbo kicks in. ANTONY FRASER

anti-roll bars, height-adjustable Koni dampers, plus upgraded inner and outer front drop-link bushes and front castor mounts. Brakes consisted of larger 32mm discs, four pot Brembo calipers with 36mm and 44mm pistons, working with asbestos-free pads and vibration dampers and ABS. The limited-slip differential from option M220 was also fitted as standard on the 1988 944 Turbo S and 1989 Turbo. For the 1987 Turbo Cup series, engines were re-chipped to 250bhp, along with stiffer suspension. The 944 Turbo became more of a race car, with seam-welded shell and lighter fibreglass panels, and the Fuchs

wheels were replaced with similarly sized pearl white cast magnesium 'Telephone Dials'. The new technical tweak was switchable ABS, installed so that Porsche could assess the benefits of assisted braking under race stresses. All of which found its way onto the Turbo Club Sport road car.

In France, however, 944 Turbo Cup competitors were given much more leeway with spec and set up. Straight-through exhausts with no cats were permitted because unleaded petrol was hard to find there, and the cars had a larger sump made of lightweight magnesium like the intake manifold. Drilled discs and race pads were sourced from the 928 S4, and a strut brace was fitted between the front shock turrets. The cabin was stripped of its rear seats and fitted with a Matter roll-cage, and Recaro race seats and five-point harness on the driver's side. Unlike the German Turbo Cup cars, whose original purpose was to promote a road-going race car ethic, all leisure equipment, including air-con, hi-fi, central locking, electric windows and power steering, were removed from the French cars in the interests of lighter weight, while smaller Cup mirrors were fitted and the fog lamps made way for air intakes. Of course, we don't see any trace of these deprivations in Bert's car. By comparison it's an all-singing, all-dancing luxury package.

Bert is a man on the turn. That's to say, he's a dyed-in-the-wool 911 connoisseur, but he has become a front-engined Porsche convert. That's partly due to hanging out (the tail) at Abbeville racetrack in northern France with his 968 CS, which has persuaded him of the ease with which it's possible to have a great time on a circuit without too much exertion, or, as things stand, without vast financial outlay. Cars like this are greatly underappreciated, he believes, and he earnestly imagines that the day of the front-engined Porsche has arrived. That was another motivating factor in acquiring this oddity of a 944.

Of course, I love the noise from a 6-cylinder 911 and all the rest of it, but the 944 is the same quality as a contemporary 911 or perhaps even better. It gives me more pleasure than a 911, and it's time that people understand that. You know that my passion for Porsches started off with classic 911s, but this 944 is here because I started having so much fun with my 968

He's preaching to the converted in a lot of cases, but there's no supressing the messianic tendency of someone who's just seen the light: 'When you drive a 944 or 968, even a 928, you see what a great driving car they are, and even though the prices are going up you can still afford them for normal money.' Perhaps another case of 'buy now while stocks last'?

We motor out of Bert's village into the flat, largely arable Belgian countryside. Sweetcorn currently dominates. Initially my head's touching the sun visor so I juggle with the driving position for a few minutes to get the angles and distances of arms to non-adjustable steering wheel, legs and feet to pedals and angle of backrest sorted out. The electric seat adjuster buttons are on the side of the driver's seat but they're masked by the handbrake being down there as well, and I discover very quickly that I've got the heated seat switched on, which explains why I'm experiencing a Lapland-style sauna.

At the risk of damning with faint praise, the 944 Turbo Club Sport is indeed, as Bert says, such an easy car to drive. No fuss, nothing obstructive, just full-on lusty urge and extremely competent handling, and it's agile and stable in the bends. When the turbo kicks in it really does take off in a very agreeable way; it's fast and uncomplicated on these Belgian back roads. Any turbo lag is imperceptible since it's overcome by great reserves of torque. The ride's hard, but it's what you want in a sports GT. The steering is firm but equally responsive, the gears slot into place perfectly well in the five-speed gate. In general, the power assistance is nicely weighted, though I do have to haul on the steering wheel a little bit to get it to turn in. On a longish straight I glance at the clocks and note 5,000rpm in fourth gear, but I'm not sure what speed I registered there – 160km/h (99mph) perhaps. There's no getting away from it: the straight-four engine is a sweet unit at low revs, but it's pretty raucous at high revs and, yes, it does lack the acoustic delights of the air-cooled flat-six. However, it makes up for that by sashaying beautifully through the chicane-like corners and, having ABS brakes, there's no drama about slowing down for the turns either. It is a good car to drive fast easily.

The other face of the 944 Turbo CS is that it's a very functional car; I'm not sure that you would be able to guess its exotic nature, because on the face of it, it's not any different to a 944 Turbo. It's worn well, as they do, belying its 85,702km (53,253 miles), and it's like it has just left the showroom.

There's a bonus or two holed up in the luggage boot and the centre console. The little lock-up cubby box between the seats is full of the entire Abba song collection on CDs, testimony – if more were required – to its Scandinavian provenance. Better still, in the unmolested tool roll lurks a glasses case, and lo and behold, a pair of mid-1980s official Porsche accessory sunglasses! I spend the next half-hour acting out Michael J. Fox in *Back to the Future*. As far as Bert's concerned, the 944 is the future, along with the rest of the front-engined brigade. And, given the decent finish, they don't come much rarer than this Turbo Club Sport.

ROAD RACER: THE 968 RS TURBO

Porsche's Weissach works produced some of the most amazing competition cars over the years, and was particularly adept at recycling redundant componentry to build cars like the twenty-two examples of the 964 C4 Leichtbau (Lightweight), and the 924 Carrera GTRs that raced at Le Mans in 1980. A decade later, between late 1992 and early 1994, the Weissach boffins were creating a similar racing evolution from the 968 Turbo S homologation special. There were two versions, both powered by the 3.0-litre turbocharged 4-cylinder engine, one for Porsche's customer teams to contest the German ADAC GT Cup and the other to meet 1993's Le Mans GT regulations. It was extraordinary by any standards: there were fourteen units of the 968 Turbo S and just the four RS/Ts.

Who better to speak to than the maestro himself, Jürgen Barth:

> Yes, these cars were built in my Customer Sports department in Weissach at the same time as the 964 RSR 3.8 for the ADAC GT and other GT Series like BPR, but only four cars were built because the 911 was demanded more. I personally like it very much, but in the end, it was the customer's decision – not enough people wanted it.

Well, more fool them, as far as I'm concerned, having ripped up the Yorkshire Dales with the car shown here. It is a staggeringly fast and capable machine, possibly quicker and more poised than the equivalent 911, and you wonder whether perhaps there was some lingering prejudice against it because of that. It's more likely the project was canned due to the economic recession rather than being potentially superior to the 911 in competition.

You can tell it's been touched by the hand of God, or Porsche's customer racing manager, at least. 'There were weight differences between the Le Mans GT and the ADAC GT versions,' says Jürgen. 'The ADAC cars were ballasted by 150kg (330lb) over the basic 1,200kg (2,645lb), and their fifth and sixth gears were also shorter. The endurance cars had a larger fuel tank with fast-acting refuelling valves and air jacks.'

This particular car is on sale at Gmund Cars, Knaresborough, imported recently by Andrew Mearns from South Africa, where it lived in the Apex museum at Weltevreden near Stellenbosch. This is No. 2, the only one that's road-registered. Speed Yellow is about right, because it is jolly fast. Contemplating the stance and guise of the 968 RS Turbo, it's impossible not to believe

ABOVE: **This yellow peril is one of just four 968 RS Turbos – #02 – built in early 1993 in the Customer Sports department at Weissach and subsequently raced in South Africa.** ANTONY FRASER

ABOVE RIGHT: **The 3.0-litre slant-four motor of the 968 RS Turbo is more sophisticated than its mass-produced siblings: the intake system and top end are derived from the 944 Turbo mounted on a 968 crankcase, there's no restrictor on the engine, and it develops 337bhp, against 350bhp with restrictor.** ANTONY FRASER

RIGHT: **The garish cabin interior of the 968 RS Turbo includes matching Speed Yellow painted floor, roll-cage tubes and Momo steering wheel rim. The sophisticated aura is challenged by the hose at left supplying cooling air in a sweat-inducing racing environment.** ANTONY FRASER

49

that you're looking at a full-on racing car. It's positively bristling with amendments and additions: the fairing over the windscreen wipers to assist aero, the aggressive front splitter, the absent headlamps, duct on the bonnet for dissipating heat from the intercooler, the pair of inlet ducts, tow-eye, rear wing spoiler, special catches for rear hatch lid and bonnet, and mighty split-rim, three-piece, centre-lock 10 × 18in and 11 × 18in Speedline wheels, shod with Pirelli P-Zeros that almost scrape the bodywork. It sits 20mm (0.75in) lower than the 968 Club Sport. Try to rock the body, and it is locked solid. The driving lights have been converted to headlights – complete with plastic lens protectors, and the original headlights are kept in a cardboard box. The sills and side skirts are unique to the Turbo S and RS too.

Under the bonnet, the turbo is set at a different angle to that of the 924 progenitor, and there's a huge intercooler in the front of the engine bay. The engine's straddled by a carbon strut brace, flat of profile to clear the bonnet lid. A comprehensive assemblage of poles within the cabin constitutes the Matter roll-cage, probably constructed within the shell and then the roof welded in place over the top of it. The plumbed-in fire extinguisher system emanates from cylinders in the rear footwells, and the pipes run reassuringly around the interior of the cabin. Investigate more minutely, and the fasteners that run around the body panels also have waterproof washers; you don't get them on a conventional road car. The modules of the Bosch Motronic engine management system sit at the front of the passenger footwell. A crude plastic tube emerges beside the driver's side A-pillar delivering cool air, rather like one of those speaker tubes on the bridge of a ship. The gearshift is topped neatly by the knob from a 962.

The intake system and top end are derived from the 944 Turbo mounted on a 968 crankcase. There is no restrictor on the engine – which two of the four were obliged to fit when contesting the ADAC GT Cup – and it developed 337bhp in this format, against 350bhp with restrictor. Our feature car has been modified to give 420bhp and 620Nm (457lb ft) of torque. It's got a single-nozzle Sorbek water spray system to help cool the intercooler and oil cooler that are mounted within the front air intake. The water tank that feeds it is mounted at the back of the rear boot and operated by a press button on the centre console on an ad hoc basis as if you were washing the windscreen – it's not thermostatically controlled, so a bit primitive, and none of the other RS/Ts have it installed. It's even still got South African water in it. 'We've a range of different rear spoilers with the car,' says Andrew, 'and you could decide how radical you needed the downforce to be.'

The exhaust system consists of two pipes, one from the manifold and the other going straight to the turbocharger, and then from the end of the torque tube back it's as if a black anaconda has attached itself to the underside of the car. There is no silencer and no cat, just a single 76mm (3in) pipe and a large void where the silencer would live in the 968 road car.

BELOW LEFT: **Tracking shot of the 968 RS Turbo blatting along a Yorkshire Dales B-road. The original owner was able to specify his desired paint colour and request water-cooling for the frontal intercooler, as well as the wiper blade fairing below the windscreen, plus central bonnet duct and bigger rear wing.** ANTONY FRASER

BELOW RIGHT: **Rear tracking shot reveals the specific RS Turbo badging and the larger than normal adjustable rear wing.** ANTONY FRASER

Head-turner? Sure, though I'm mainly greeted with frowns by the good village folk up on the moors because of the fearful racket I'm making; if they only knew the significance of the yellow peril on their doorstep!

Here's the history. In April 1993, RS/Turbo No. 2 was sold to Bruce Joelson, a South African motorsport aficionado and friend of Gerd Schmid, Jürgen Barth's colleague in the Customer Racing department. Joelson was able to specify the colour and commission the water cooling for the frontal intercooler, as well as the wiper blade fairing, central bonnet duct and a bigger rear wing. The body modifications were carried out by TechArt in collaboration with the Customer Racing department, and thereafter applied to the 968 Turbo S road-going model. Joelson then raced the car in South Africa along with Peter Gough. After its first season he dispatched it to Weissach for servicing via Lufthansa, anticipating it would be delivered in Germany a day later. Alarmed that it hadn't arrived after a few days, he tracked it to Saudi Arabia where it had ended up, having been taken off the aircraft at Nairobi in favour of perishable goods. Needless to say, it was eventually returned to him in perfect order.

Ownership then passed to former factory test driver Robert Reister, who competed in the South African Porsche Challenge series, and he had the car till 2001. Latterly it was housed in the Apex collection of Porsche GTs on the Weltevreden Estate near Stellenbosch.

Accessing the 968 cockpit requires the dexterity of a contortionist, but after a few goes I've got the wriggle down to a fine art as I squeeze past the diagonal door bar and snuggle down into the Recaro bucket seat. There's no carpet or headlining; the armrests/door-pulls are bisected by the roll-cage diagonal down tubes, and there's a steel plate in the driver's footwell – plain rather than diamond or chequer pattern, but pretty uncompromising. It's unquestionably race-oriented, with its bare yellow interior and matching yellow leather Momo wheel, but surprisingly comfortable and not especially austere for all that. There's a passenger seat too, which it probably wouldn't have had fitted when it was raced. Both Recaros have Kevlar backs and are enmeshed with four-point OMP harnesses, while the handbrake is where it should be, to the left of the driver's seat. Ahead of the passenger, the glove locker is a façade concealing a section of roll-over tubing. It reads 15,442km (9,595 miles) on the odometer; tick over is just over 1,000rpm and on the move it whizzes around to 4,500rpm as a matter of course, when the boost gauge is registering 1.5 bar. There's an overboost control on the steering column stalk.

So, off we go! It's loud and it's raw and as we set off from Gmund heading for the Yorkshire Dales I'm feeling the tiniest undulation in the road surface through my backside. This sensation becomes less all-encompassing as other factors come into play: the directness of the power-assisted steering, the slickness of the six-speed shift, the powerful muscle-building clutch, the wheelspin in first gear, the eagerness of the engine to rev right round to 6,000rpm. Sure, I'm bouncing up and down due to the rock hardness of the suspension and the bumpiness of some of the Dales' moorland roads, with consequent inadvertent modulation of the throttle. Each surge of acceleration evokes a blare from the exhaust, accompanied by the rasping, popping and banging on the overrun.

This is an extreme road-going racing car that relishes forward progress and abhors any kind of interruption. Stones rattle on the underside of the un-sound-deadened wheel arches. The six-speed gearshift is slick, and under braking it's totally assured, though with each downshift the four-piece racing clutch grabs on the transmission. It's a wonderful linear power delivery, sweet as a pussycat at low revs, then at 4,000rpm the turbo comes in and it's on the cam and really takes off, with staggering acceleration out of bends and on the long, undulating straights. It's got its own aural repertoire: there's a deep, sonorous baritone boom echoing off the dry-stone walls, with

Behind the wheel of the 968 RS Turbo, the motorist feels the tiniest undulations in the road surface, remarking on the directness of the power-assisted steering, the muscle-building clutch and slick six-speed shift – and wheelspin in first gear. ANTONY FRASER

THE FAB FOUR

No. 1 chassis 968 RS Turbo was the prototype and development car built in 1992 and the one that has the most significant race history. Originally painted red, it is the car that was used for the factory promotional photos. The car was entered by Reinhold Jöst's Joest Racing in two rounds of the German ADAC GT series in 1993 and was a stopgap while the team waited for the factory to build RS Turbo chassis No. 4, which they'd already ordered.

The car was then painted yellow and prepped to race at Le Mans in 1994. It's the only 968 ever to compete at La Sarthe, #58, driven by owner Thomas Bscher, Lindsay Owen-Jones and John Neilson; it ran in the GT2 class but was eliminated after eighty-four laps in an accident. In December 1994, Lloyd Hawkins and Dennis Boada purchased it and it ran in the Sebring 12-Hours in March 1995 and Road Atlanta in April 1995, still in its Le Mans yellow. It was then returned to its original red, competing in USA Porsche Club events, and went under the hammer at Amelia Island auctions five years ago for $346,500.

No. 2 chassis is our feature car.

No. 3 chassis is black with pink and purple blobs and hence known as Bubbles. It employs all the endurance mods, including 120-litre (26gal) fuel tank, air jacks, and lightweight parts, and was raced by owner Erik Hendriksen and Justin Bell in five rounds of the 1994 BPR GT Championship, most notably finishing the Dijon 4-Hours in sixth place overall and Jarama in eighth. It's possibly the last of the four 968 Turbo RSs built, making it the last front-engined, 4-cylinder race car built by Porsche.

No. 4 chassis was originally bought by Joest Racing to compete in the 1993 German ADAC GT series. At its Nürburgring debut, Manuel Reuter qualified on pole, but in the Esses after the start was bumped out of contention by a 911 RS 3.8. It returned to Weissach for repair, and was then acquired by Michael Roock's Roock Racing Team. With the original Grand Prix White paint scheme enhanced with a blue front end and Mobil 1 graphics, the car was driven by Dieter Koll in the 1994 ADAC GT series. Thereafter it was on display in a German Volkswagen dealership, and in 1999 new owner Bruce Corwin shipped it to the USA. After competing in a few autocross and track days, he sold it in 2003 to Jason Burkett of Paragon Products in Texas. Unlike its three siblings, its bodyshell contained a sophisticated roll-cage tied to all four suspension points, and it also had a Halon fire extinguisher system, air jacks, adjustable rear wing, front air splitter and 43-litre (9gal) fuel cell.

The factory's Customer Racing department also made several spare 968 Turbo RS chassis in anticipation of further commissions, and indeed some have been used as the basis for non-factory built 968 Turbo RS cars by teams including Hendrick, Paragon, Freisinger, Fitzgerald, Autohaus and Milledge.

The first 968 RS Turbo was the only 968 ever to compete at Le Mans, #58, driven by owner Thomas Bscher, Lindsay Owen-Jones and John Neilson in the 1994 24-Hours. This is an exact copy of that car, driven here at Donington Park by Roberto Giordanelli. ANTONY FRASER

Pictured in the Donington Park circuit's pit lane, the original version of this replica ran in the GT2 class at Le Mans in 1994, but was eliminated in an accident after eighty-four laps. ANTONY FRASER

machine-gun backfire. I've never heard anything quite like the snarl on the overrun – more a deep, mournful bellow.

There's no need for wrestling with the wheel because of the power-assisted steering, though there's a certain amount of torque steer under full power, drawing it slightly to the right. But it's actually very compliant, civilized even, with sharp turn-in into the corners where it tracks absolutely true. Brakes are extremely efficient – they don't grab and there's no drama as they haul the car up. It's a hard ride but not horrendous, though it does bang on the bumps and I'm bounced around like hell. But this is one fun ride, and it's an extremely nice car to drive. A lovely one to race as well, I imagine.

Andrew Mearns sums up:

> It's like a 968 Club Sport that's been given surgery to turn it into a track monster. It's got all the race car components, and it's got all the aggression, though once it's in motion it's nice to drive. In spite of all the racing modifications it's amazing how tastefully it's been done. It's built as a race car yet it's poised, purposeful, functional and aesthetically pleasing; even the rear wing isn't too big or dynamically insane – it's still an attractive-looking car. It's comparable with a 964 RSR in terms of its rawness. And it's the rarest RS that Porsche ever made.

So, there we have it: amazing spec, looks and performance, factory-built race car provenance. But what are you going to do with it now? It's too amazing to be a mere track-day warrior – and you'd need to clamp on a can to avoid cocking the decibel meter. It's not quite old enough to go out in historics, though you could get into one of the Porsche Club GB Championships and do quite well, or, if you were sufficiently committed yet not necessarily chasing success, try the Britcar series. Or, indeed, the German VLN and, in the USA, C-production class in VARA, SCCA, NASA and SVRA. Just hammering it across the moors is fun but there's way more to it than that. It's so inspirational I could even see myself in a 968 CS.

968 TURBO S

When the scion of one car company drives a vehicle created by its chief rival, it must be something really special. A quantum leap, you could say. Herbert Quandt revitalized BMW in the 1950s, and his son Sven (from his second marriage) was sufficiently inspired by the 968 RS/Turbo race car from 1992 that he decided to order one for himself, albeit the road-going version. I sampled this particular 968 Turbo S, one of just fourteen produced, making it one of the rarest of Porsche model lines, even if it is a derivative.

This 968 Turbo S is effectively the prototype of the 968 RS Turbo competition car, of which the Porsche Customer Racing department built just four units, with fourteen of the Turbo S road-going version as well as this one. The pop-up headlight treatment of the 968 is quite different to the previous 944, with exposed lenses rather than encased niches.

ANTONY FRASER

53

Travelling with Antony and Ingrid Fraser, I visited Porsche aficionado Kim Koehler, who had displayed this Speed Yellow 968 Turbo S, formerly belonging to Sven Quandt, at Tecno Classica 2019. Kim owns an intriguing selection of middle-aged 911s and a coterie of elderly 912s scheduled for rehab, which we discover in his Klassık Kontor garage in Düsseldorf, in western Germany. We hit it off straight away: his street car is a Chiffon White 911 SC, and he keeps it looking period with a few copies of *Playboy* and other amusing mid-1970s paraphernalia tossed in the back.

Unique History

Let's backtrack for a moment, just to take stock of the origins and absolute rarity of this particular 968. Porsche's Weissach skunkworks produced some of the most amazing competition cars over the years, adapting redundant machinery and road-going models to create pioneering race cars like the 924 Carrera GTRs that ran at Le Mans in 1980, and lost causes like the 964 C4 Leichtbau (Lightweight). Between late 1992 and early 1994, they created a similar racing evolution from the 968 CS, namely the 968 Turbo S homologation special. There were two versions, both powered by the 3.0-litre turbocharged 4-cylinder engine, one for Porsche's customer teams to contest the German ADAC GT Cup and to meet 1993's Le Mans GT regulations, the other the road-going 968 Turbo S. They ended up making just fourteen units of the 968 Turbo S and four 968 RS/Turbos. Colours included Silver, Speed Yellow, Grand Prix White, Midnight Blue, Blood Orange and Guards Red. Why so few built? As the head of Porsche's Customer Racing department, Jürgen Barth, explained, there was simply less customer demand for them than the 911s. Another reason was that the series as a whole was not an outstanding success, and Porsche itself was in fiscal and managerial turmoil at the time. 'They were trying everything,' observes Kim Koehler, 'leaving no stone unturned to see where they could make money, and that's why they approved Jürgen Barth's project.'

Kim expounds on its rarity:

> The 968 RS Turbo was based on an idea Gerd Schmid had with Jürgen Barth in 1992, to take a 968 off the production line, use the engine from the 944 Turbo S and the contemporary KKK turbo, and they manufactured exactly this car – what we have here, the prototype. It still has the series number of a 968 Club Sport, but its specification confirms it is really a prototype.

Kim believes that there were in fact two prototypes, and that one was modified into an RS at Weissach. All series cars have #8900XX VIN numbers, while this Speed Yellow prototype is #800412.

Jürgen's colleague Gerd Schmid was in the process of setting up the 968 RS Turbo race programme at the time, and sought customers. Among the likely lads he wrote to was Sven Quandt, who was sufficiently captivated to take a closer look. Kim does the numbers:

> They built three 968 RS Turbos in 1993, and one prototype, plus ten Turbo S street cars; then they built another white one for the 1994 Geneva Show to promote the series again and sell more cars. They subsequently sold three more Turbo S street cars, and that was that. They stopped the race series, and that's when Sven came back and said, 'Can we negotiate the price?' And he got this one.

In the meantime, it served as a press car, registration number BB PW 221 – a Böblingen registration – and by 1994, it had clocked barely 64,000km (39,700 miles).

Sven Quandt is a racer at heart, who today runs X-raid, a Mini squad in the Dakar and other off-road rallies. Kim affirms:

> He's an absolute car nut. So, for a time, he was sufficiently excited about the concept of the car that he put in the order for one. He was in very close contact with Gerd Schmid. He's an engineer, Sven, building prototypes, and many of his rally cars are effectively prototypes.

He was head of Mitsubishi's motor sport programme between 2002 and 2004, but it's still a little ironic that the son of the BMW patriarch drove a Porsche. Kim adds:

> He was really interested in the details of its specification and construction. While he owned it, he was only driving it long distances, like to Varta board meetings in Hanover, so it's still immaculate. It was de-registered for several years, and he just had it standing in the entrance hall of his home.

Mechanically, the intake system and top end are derived from the 944 Turbo and mounted on a 968 crankcase. The exhaust system consists of two pipes, one from the manifold and the other going straight to the single KKK compressor, and driving

ABOVE LEFT: **Built in the Weissach Customer Racing department, the 968 Turbo S engine is based on that of the 944 Turbo S and fitted with the KKK turbocharger.** ANTONY FRASER

ABOVE RIGHT: **Modifications to the bodywork of the 968 Turbo S and RS Turbo were carried out by past masters in the field, Leonberg-based TechArt, while wheels and brakes come from the 993 Turbo S. Its owner, Kim Koehler, believes this is the prototype, stamped in the engine bay with chassis number #800412.** ANTONY FRASER

through a conventional six-speed manual with longer ratios and limited-slip differential. Wheels and brakes come from the 911 Turbo S, plus ABS and power steering. The bodywork modifications were carried out by TechArt at Leonberg, in collaboration with Weissach, and applied to both 968 RS/Turbo and the road-going 968 Turbo S.

Kim expands:

> It had amazing driving values from the beginning, and after three months of testing they homologated the series. So, after a very short period of testing they had the perfect set-up, and they offered it for DM175,000 (€90,900). That was an incredible amount of money at the time. Gerd Schmid thought it might be a bit too expensive, because he was still constantly in contact with potential customers, but they sold ten cars in the first official model year, 1993. They were very ambitious, because they built the prototype without the permission of the board, but then they got board approval on condition that they somehow sold up to 100 cars.

Obviously, that never happened.

In late 2018, Kim heard on the grapevine that the car could be available: 'A friend told me his father might have a Porsche he wanted to sell, though he didn't actually know precisely what it was. It sounded intriguing, so we had to dig out the history and then we found the delivery paperwork, which confirmed that it's the prototype.' Verifying the car's provenance wasn't straightforward, however.

> Official documentation of the series is scant. All the hand-written notes of Jürgen Barth and Gerd Schmid went into the archives, and they're still in a box somewhere because they did not digitize them; so, when I called Porsche and asked for the series numbers they told me, 'Yes, it's a 968 CS.' I said, 'Well, I have the delivery paperwork from Gerd Schmid confirming it's a Turbo S prototype,' and they replied, 'Well, yes, then it is probably the Turbo S prototype, but all documentation from those years is still in storage, and a bit weak.'

Even then, there was, potentially, quite some competition to acquire it. 'The Americans are super-interested in this 968 series now, and they are buying up all the cars. They were all hunting this car – people knew it existed, but it was like a mystery car because nobody knew where it was.'

Sporty Specifications

This is a car that looks like it means business. It differs from a 968 Club Sport in that the adjustable spoiler of the rear wing is exclusive to the Turbo S, and the Turbo S script on the boot is stock, like lettering on the 911 and the S is from the 924. It also has pop-up headlights, which the racing cars lacked. Apart from the TechArt aerodynamic refinements, the bodywork is in steel, and the doors do shut with a firm clunk. The wheels are 18in three-piece Speedlines with Turbo centre caps, and there's also a spare unused set that Sven Quandt bought just to be on the safe side. They're shod with Pirelli P-Zeros, 265/35 ZR18 on the back, and 235/40 ZR18 on the front.

There were two different bonnets as well: the Turbo S is steel with those distinctive arrowhead ducts in carbon-fibre, bonded in situ, while the RS/T has bigger inlets to cope with higher exhaust temperatures. There were problems with the turbos overheating to such an extent that a number were destroyed. As Kim puts it, 'It was getting pretty damn hot under the hood, so this car needs to be driven slowly until it has reached temperature otherwise the turbo will bust.' Indeed, this car received a replacement engine at Weissach under warranty at 70,000km (43,500 miles), though there's no record of exactly why.

Under the bonnet, the substantial Porsche-branded strut brace is prominent as it straddles the crowded engine bay, as is the deep, turbo S-labelled intercooler. It's obvious that the heat build-up is having a detrimental effect on the inlet

ducting as cracks are showing where the two materials abut one another: one expands and contracts, the other remains static. The front of the car is sensitive aerodynamically, because the bulk of its weight is to the fore. Kim recounts that Sven Quandt told him of an incident on the autobahn (motorway) where pieces of a shredded truck tyre became jammed under the splitter, cracking it, and causing the car to become unstable because of the airflow being disrupted under the car, making it seem to dance. So not only does this car have a new splitter – and it is relatively prominent – Mr Quandt also bought a second one as a spare. 'It's very important for the stability of the car, apparently,' says Kim.

The cabin interior presents as a well-coordinated environment, somewhat on the dark side, and dominated by the colour-coded seat backs. But wind-up windows? A legacy of its racing background, surely? Kim plays the cynical card:

It's still what they do with the sporty models. Take the 968 Club Sport – the last edition of the 968 in 1995; they really emptied out the whole car to get it cheaper, because it was too expensive for those times. It was a pretty old car in 1995, so to get it sold they needed to make it cheaper, and they took a lot of stuff out and called it the Club Sport so it sounded fast and sporty, and they sold pretty well. But many people were putting all the stuff back in because they actually wanted the comfort. Just imagine buying a car for more than DM100,000 and you don't have electric windows. Porsches from 1969 had electric windows, and this is a road-going Porsche from 1992, twenty-five years later, and it has manual windows.

Panning profile of the 968 Turbo S shows off a sleeker line than that of its predecessor, the 944 Turbo. ANTONY FRASER

And, of course, no back seats, though it doesn't have a roll-cage because it's the street version.

We need to find some picturesque countryside to photograph the 968. First thing I notice is that the ignition key slots into the right of the column rather than the left, which was allegedly a legacy of the traditional Le Mans start where drivers sprinted across the track, jumped on board and turned the key almost as one motion. The snazzy Recaro sports seats prove more comfortable than they suggest: firmly padded, supportive bucket seat skeletons. The four-spoke, air-bag steering wheel is the same as a contemporary 964, and in true RS fashion the doors have wind-up windows. The gearshift lever seems to be set higher because of the raised centre console, while the shift movement is slightly recalcitrant, but we'll see how it improves once warmed up.

On the move, the ride is more like that of a competition car, projecting all the little nuances of the road surface into the vibe of the car. But then you would hardly expect anything else. It's docile in traffic, and then the turbo comes in at 3,000rpm, uncompromisingly delivering a steady stream of power, which I enjoy – tentatively as it's a busy Saturday – on some smoothly surfaced A-roads out in the undulating arable countryside surrounding Düsseldorf. It's *Spargel* season – and, appropriately, an asparagus farm provides a great location for our shoot. Back on the road, the Turbo S's steering is nicely weighted, so it's responsive in bends and tight corners, where accurate turn-in is crucial. The weight balance is really good, and I'd place it in the touring car category, even though it is a very sporty set-up, but it's not as lively as a 964 RS in serving up its driving thrills. Damned by faint praise? Not by Sven

Quandt. He retains an upbeat view of the 968 Turbo S: 'It's one of the best cars I ever drove in my life,' he recalls, 'and for me, one of the best Porsches I've ever driven as well. It's most exciting in all disciplines – suspension, engine and feeling.'

The 968 – any 968 – is a superbly well balanced and competent chassis propelled by unburstable mechanicals. It simply lacks the ebullient character of its rear- (and mid-) engined stablemates. This one, though, has an intriguing pedigree, and was, after all, the progeny of Weissach wizards Jürgen Barth and Gerd Schmid: it doesn't get more inspirational than that.

CHAPTER TWO

THE 996 TURBO

First of the new breed of water-cooled turbocharged 911s, the 996 Turbo was launched in 2000, replacing the air-cooled 993 version, and was related to its 996 GT3 sibling by virtue of its 'Mezger' dry-sump engine. This revered powerplant, which is, by common consent, a stronger unit than the normally aspirated 996 flat-six, originated in the aluminium-cased flat-sixes powering the 930 Turbo, 3.0 SC and the partly water-cooled 962 4-valve engine, with cylinder heads derived from the 959 supercar. It was then engineered, no expenses spared, to debut as a 3.2 chain-cam twin-turbo in the Le Mans winning 1998 GT1.

Some legacy: and it was a bold, if rather pragmatic move to shoehorn it into the rear quarters of the 996. The 996 Turbo can deliver 420bhp at 6,000rpm, enabling genuine 305km/h (190mph) performance and acceleration to 100km/h in 4.2sec. Only the rear-drive 462bhp 996 GT2 and run-out Turbo S with the 450bhp X51 performance upgrade kit are more powerful examples of the 996, and so worth investigating if you seek a greater surge factor, and of course the Turbo Cabriolet if you're a sun worshipper.

The 996 Turbo was the fastest road-going, series-production Porsche, sharing the same engine as the GT2 and GT3. Unlike the standard car's water-cooled, Lokasil-linered flat-six, the Turbo used Nikasil, a more expensive race-proved surface treatment. The dry sump flat-six was controlled by specifically mapped Bosch Motronic ME 7.8 engine management. The six-speed gearbox was descended from the 993 Turbo, with the no-extra-cost option of the Tiptronic S gearbox, available for the first time on a turbocharged Porsche. Drivers could operate it as a fully automatic five-speed or use the sequential shift buttons on the steering wheel.

The 996 family resemblance is retained in so far as the Turbo sports an evolution of the 996 fried-egg headlights, which the second-generation Carrera 2 and Carrera 4 subsequently inherited, but in all other respects it looks more aggressive than the standard car. The 996 Turbo is fronted by gaping ducts that feed cooling air to the front-mounted radiator and brakes, while the gills in the sides of the rear valance aid engine cooling, and the pair of scoops in the rear wings supply fresh air to the intercoolers. The tail fin mounted on the engine lid is an electronically adjustable bi-plane that rises into the airstream at 120km/h (75mph). Maximum power output of 420bhp at 6,000rpm and 562Nm (415lb ft) torque from 2,700 to 4,600rpm enables the 996 Turbo to rush up to 60mph in 4.2sec and achieve 0–100mph in 9.4sec. But, surprisingly, the

OPPOSITE PAGE:

The 996 Turbo, pictured here at Harewood House, Yorkshire, displays large cooling air intakes in the front panel while one of its characteristic intake ducts can be seen in the rear three-quarter panel just ahead of the rear wheel arch. JOHNNY TIPLER

THIS PAGE:

The 911 GT1 of 1996 was based on the front chassis components of the contemporary 993 and the rear elements of the 962 along with its water-cooled, twin-turbo and intercooled 4-valves-per-cylinder 3164cc flat-six engine. It also shared the front and rear lights of the production 996. JOHNNY TIPLER

ABOVE: **The Tiptronic S gearbox was a no-extra-cost option, available for the first time on a turbocharged Porsche. Drivers could use the shift lever to operate it as a fully automatic five-speed, or press the sequential shift buttons on the steering wheel to go up or down the ratios.** ANTONY FRASER

ABOVE RIGHT: **The 996 Turbo was the first of the new water-cooled turbocharged 911s, launched in 2000, two years after its normally aspirated Carrera 2 and Carrera 4 entered production. The Turbo bodyshell was 60mm (2in) wider than its stablemates in order to accommodate wider wheels and tyres.** ANTONY FRASER

RIGHT: **The wide-open spaces of the North York Moors provide a fine environment in which to give the 996 Turbo its head.** ANTONY FRASER

air-cooled 993 Turbo is actually quicker on both counts. The accent is on drivability rather than kick-in-the-backside performance with the 996 Turbo.

It employs a pair of KKK K16 turbochargers and a mild 9.4:1 compression ratio, allied to permanent four-wheel drive to achieve the elusive feel of a turbocharged car, where you can't really discern the turbo at work. Its control system ensures that, in a straight line, the 996 Turbo is mostly in rear-wheel-drive mode, with a mere 5 per cent of motive power transmitted to the front wheels. But when the system detects a decrease in traction due to yaw or surface conditions, it dispenses up to 40 per cent of power at the front axle. Its forte is the provision of masses of effortless power in every gear from 1,800rpm.

TOP LEFT: **Not so much to see here, then. The 996 Turbo engine bay reveals air intake duct, air filter, oil filler, cooling fan and coolant filler cap, so, really, it's providing access to the filler modules.** ANTONY FRASER

TOP RIGHT: **Compact and neat, all ancillaries are huddled around the 996 Turbo's water-cooled 3.6-litre flat-six engine. The turbos are just visible behind the silencer on either side of the unit.** PORSCHE PHOTO ARCHIVE

ABOVE: **The cabin interior of the 996 Turbo is upholstered in grey leather and carpeting, with a later wheel fitted. Other than its white-faced dials and Turbo badge, it could be a standard 996 C2 or C4.** ANTONY FRASER

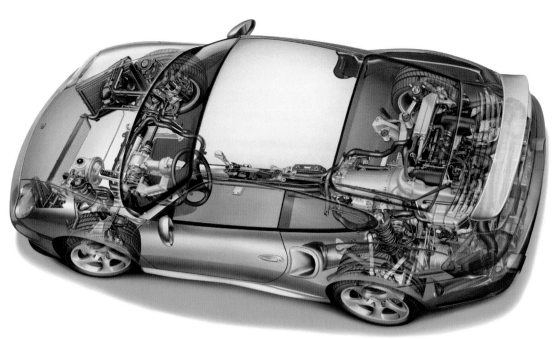

A magnificent cutaway
illustration of the 996
Turbo, showing the
car's four-wheel-drive
transmission set-up,
steering, suspension and
powertrain installation.
PORSCHE PHOTO ARCHIVE

The 996 Turbo Cabriolet was available from October
2003, a month after its debut at the Frankfurt Show.
PORSCHE PHOTO ARCHIVE

The Turbo's cabin interior is similar to the 996 Carrera 4, with
just a few minor detail changes to the instrumentation, plus a
more sophisticated trip computer. The 996 Turbo Cabriolet
went on sale in October 2003, a month after release at the
Frankfurt Show, with a showroom sticker price 12 per cent
more than the Coupé, justified by the additional engineering
required to stiffen the topless shell with reinforced sills and B-
pillars that add 70kg (154lb) to its overall weight. In terms of
performance, top speed is virtually identical at 304km/h
(189mph), and 0–60mph a tenth of a second slower at 4.3sec,
making it one of the fastest cabriolets ever built.

From 2002, a factory upgrade known as X50, consisting of
minor revisions to the turbos and engine management software, raised power to 450hp. By this time, sophistications
such as sat-nav, sunroof, BOSE hi-fi, rain sensor and electrically dimming rear-view mirrors were standard. The Turbo S
was unveiled at the NEC and went on sale in 2004, including
the X50 engine modifications and ceramic brakes, which were
previously optional, as standard equipment. The 996 Turbo
was discontinued on 12 January 2006, when 22,062 units had
been built, to make way for its 997 successor.

Over the years I've forged a sterling rapport with Oxford-
shire-based Porsche specialists Autofarm, going back to the
mid-1980s when I attempted to buy a 2.2 S from them, to
more recently when PR Nick Bailey regularly provided stories
on cars passing through their workshop or for sale. Take the

Suspension consists of MacPherson struts, coil springs, gas-
charged twin-tube dampers and anti-roll bar at the front, with
a five-link system at the rear supported by coil springs, single-
tube dampers and anti-roll bar, all allied to the Porsche Stability Management (PSM) set-up.

996 TURBO (2000–2005)

Layout and chassis

Two-plus-two coupé, unit-construction steel body/chassis

Engine

Type	M96/72 'Mezger' dry sump, horizontally opposed, rear-mounted 6-cylinder
Block material	Aluminium
Head material	Aluminium
Cylinders	6
Cooling	Water-cooled
Bore and stroke	100 × 76.4
Capacity	3600cc
Valves	4 valves per cylinder
Compression ratio	9.4:1
Fuel system	Multi-point injection, two KKK K16 turbochargers
Max. power (DIN)	420bhp at 6,000rpm
Max. torque	413lb ft at 4,250rpm
Fuel capacity	64ltr (19.5gal)

Transmission

Gearbox	Getrag G96/00 rear drive 6-speed; ZF 5HP19 automatic; M-B 5G Tiptronic; all-wheel drive
Clutch	Hydraulic single dry plate
Ratios	1st 3.82
	2nd 2.20
	3rd 1.52
	4th 1.22
	5th 1.02
	6th 0.84
	Reverse 3.44
Final drive	3.89

Suspension and Steering

Front	Independent suspension with MacPherson struts, aluminium links, longitudinal and transverse links, coil springs, gas dampers, anti-roll bar
Rear	Independent suspension with MacPherson struts, aluminium links, lateral and transverse links, coil springs, gas dampers, anti-roll bar
Steering	Rack and pinion
Tyres	225/40 × R18 front, 295/30 × R18 rear
Wheels	Aluminium alloy
Rim width	7.5 J front, 10 J rear

Brakes

Type	Front and rear vented discs with four-piston calipers
Size	350mm × 24mm front; 330mm × 20mm rear

Dimensions

Track	1,455mm (57.3in) front, 1,500mm (59in) rear
Wheelbase	2,350mm (92.5in)
Overall length	4,430mm (174.4in)
Overall width	1,765mm (69.5in)
Overall height	1,305mm (51.3in)
Unladen weight	1,540kg (3,395lb)

Performance

Top speed	305km/h (190mph)
0–60mph	4.2sec

transcontinental express shown here, a 996 Turbo finished in Seal Grey, which makes a change from the more often seen Polar or Arctic Silver, and is quite fetching in the metal: grey is the new black. Or silver. The cabin is upholstered in dark grey leather as well, and though I prefer black – certainly a black wheel – this complements the general hue of the car rather well. It's endowed with the fully loaded original factory spec that

adorns the majority of the new water-cooled generation, both 996 and 986 Boxster, and that includes Recaro sports seats, electric sunroof in this case, PSM (Porsche Stability Management), front and side airbags, bi-xenon headlights, the on-board computer that computes fuel range, oil level, outside temperature and so on, plus inertia belts for the rear seats and standard extras such as air-con.

This 996 Turbo at Porsche specialists Autofarm shows off its trademark Turbo wheels, sometimes known as 'ninja throwing star' wheels. The Turbo also has a permanent rear wing with a second retractable tier deployed at 120km/h (75mph). Porsche claim the rear spoiler generates 9kg (20lb) of downforce at the car's 306km/h (190mph) top speed. ELS VAN DER MEER

Full frontal of the 996 Turbo, featuring those Gen2 fried-egg headlights that were thought controversial when the model was launched – though popular opinion now prefers them to the original 996 C2 headlamps, which were also deemed to look like cooked eggs. More relevant is the characteristic trio of air intakes that occupy most of the front panel. ANTONY FRASER

For the last ten years it's covered its most recent 100,000km (60,000 miles) in the hands of a long-standing Autofarm customer who is, needless to say, a Porsche enthusiast; you don't go to a specialist like Autofarm unless you know what's what. Chassis number is 99Z1S6 81148, engine number is 641 02270, and there's a fully documented service history, evidenced by a large fiche of invoices and summarized as suspension overhaul, including fitment of Bilstein B6 shock absorbers in 2012 (at 88,000km/55,000 miles); a brake overhaul that included new discs in 2013 (at 103,000km/64,000 miles); and in 2014 an air-con system overhaul and new radiators. Finally, in 2018, the Turbo-twist 'throwing star' wheels were refurbished and a set of Michelin Pilot Sport tyres fitted, with mileage logged at 124,000km (77,000 miles). And it's had some detailing work done, specifically to the front-end coachwork, which has been refinished to eliminate stone chips.

I'm a relatively new convert to the world of kettles – those curiously liquid-cooled Porsches – having been enamoured of air-cooled 911s to the exclusion of all others for decades, but since espousing Boxsters and swapping my 964 C2 for a 996 C2, I've come to admire the purposeful on-road stance of the broad-beamed 996 Turbo as much as those of its 930 predecessor. My trial run with our subject car whisks me off onto the back roads adjacent to rustic Oddington, which is not ideal Turbo country in the grand scheme of things – ideally you need an unrestricted autobahn to really light up the blue touch-paper and head like a rocketship for the vanishing point – but they're good enough for a scenic point and squirt (as it were).

Sliding into the cabin, the electrically adjustable seats quickly locate a favourable driving position. It has only done just shy of 130,000km (80,000 miles), so all the mechanisms – steering, six-speed shift, switchgear, levers – are precise and in excellent shape. The steering feels nicely weighted, the six-speed stick moves slickly through the gate, and it delivers awesome acceleration along an undulating B-road east of Autofarm – possibly too quick in a picturesquely agricultural landscape. The chassis is hugely competent, reassuring and confidence inspiring. It handles very nicely, and I'm not conscious that the Turbo's front powertrain is as prominent as it can be in a C4 driveline. On these back roads its towering pace isn't as evident as its multifaceted ability. The compliant ride, fluent steering, easy shift, confidence-inspiring brakes, and sure-footed 4×4 traction and grip around the corners combine to provide an easy, almost languid ride. It may be a 420bhp twin-turbo salvo-server, but its schizophrenic personality is well concealed on these sinuous lanes.

But ask it for a slug of grunt and it delivers with aplomb, prompting a glorious sensation of indomitability. As I head back to Autofarm's pastoral base I hit the dualled A34 for a short distance, where I can floor the throttle with impunity: instantaneous Turbo kick-in, and the 996 squares its shoulders and hurls itself forward with the velocity of a howitzer shell. Enough! Haul it down with those ultra-efficient brakes. Point made; it's the all-round competence of the car that's the making of it – surfeits of power, finely honed handling and

all-wheel drive competence, governed from the supremely comfortable and efficient 996 cockpit.

Not that long ago, you'd have paid £20 grand less than Autofarm is currently asking for this car. That's a large amount of money, but it's a fair reflection of how the market for Porsche 911 Turbos has escalated during the past few years, and, actually, the 996 Turbo remains relatively inexpensive compared with its GT3 sibling, let alone all those air-cooled ancestors – the bestial 930 included. And yet, as a refined powerhouse, the 996 Turbo is without peers; it's extremely competent in performance terms, yet utterly civilised as a sportscar, and it's also the same amount (£20K or so) cheaper than a 997 Turbo.

Autofarm founder Josh Sadler runs a 996 that he's bored up to 3.9 litres so he knows a thing or two about souping up the model. Of the Turbo, he tells us, 'it goes as it should; basically, this is a correct, unmolested example of the 996 Turbo.' This car has all the boxes ticked: it's not so low mileage that you worry that there could be a snagging list from its original spec to attend to – cars are meant to be driven, and this one has been – and it's been very well looked after by one of the country's (the world's?) leading Porsche specialists. It's finished in a subtle and slightly more unusual colour as well. It is, however, twice the price of a wide-bodied 996 C4 or turbo-fronted 50th Anniversary model. So, does the Turbo's extra power and Mezger engine justify that? First of the modern Porsche supercars with sublime mile-munching capability, this is probably as good a 996 Turbo as you'll find, and, as values steady after the stampede of the past few years, the sticker price of £40,000 is about right.

Hustling a 996 Turbo through The Snake at Chobham test track is a thrilling experience, balancing the car on the throttle around this corkscrew rollercoaster section.

ANTONY FRASER

JACKY ICKX INTERVIEW

With his distinctive black helmet with its white surround, endurance specialist and F1 driver, off-road racer and trials champion Jacky Ickx is the consummate all-rounder. In his seventies, he's movie-star fit, bronzed with a Monaco perma-tan and speaks fluent English with a strong Gallic flavour. This is the man who, aged twenty-four, rewrote the rules at Le Mans for good when, in 1969, he strolled insouciantly across the track in the traditional driver sprint start, eased – rather than jumped – into his GT40 and carefully buckled up. Ickx won the race, the first of his six Le Mans victories and one of just two not achieved in a Porsche, and, until Le Mans Classic was introduced, there was never another traditional Le Mans sprint start.

A potted history of his career includes winning the 50cc Zundapp trials championship as a teenager; three-wheeling the Lotus Cortina to win the Belgian touring car championship in 1965; his break into single seaters with Ken Tyrrell when he was third fastest around the Nordschleife in the F2 Matra in practice for the 1967 German GP; the five years with Ferrari that brought eight GP victories; how he licked Lauda in the wet Race of Champions in 1974 in a Lotus museum piece; the fiery Ensign crash at Watkins Glen in 1976; six Le Mans wins (1969 in a GT40 with Jackie Oliver, 1975 in a Mirage with Derek Bell, 1976 in a Porsche 936 with Gijs van Lennep, 1977 in a 936 with Hurley Heywood and Jürgen Barth, 1981 in a 936 with Derek Bell, and 1982 in a 956 with Derek Bell); winning the Can-Am championship in 1978 in a Lola; and lastly the Paris–Dakar win in a Mercedes in 1983.

Today, Jacky is a brand ambassador for Porsche-Audi, and a regular visitor to Goodwood and Rennsport Reunion. It's our fourth meeting – two Goodwood Festivals and one Monaco Historic, though in the mid-1970s, when I was doing JPS Team Lotus PR and in regular contact, he treated me to a few exuberant laps round Brands Hatch in journo Pete Lyons' Corvette Sting Ray. I chatted with him ahead of the 2017 Historic Motorsport International Show at London's ExCel where he was a guest speaker.

Johnny Tipler: You're probably more readily associated with the Rothmans-liveried 956 and 962 with which you won the WSC in 1982 and 1983, but actually it was the 936 that you drove over the longest period – from 1976 to 1981 – and scored three Le Mans wins with, as opposed to one with the 956. Which one's your favourite?

Eloquent gesture: Jacky Ickx re-enacts a racing moment during his interview with Johnny Tipler at the Goodwood Festival of Speed. ANTONY FRASER

Jacky Ickx: It was a privilege to do those ten years with Porsche, because I've been part of a number of interesting projects, and the 956 was probably the most incredible Group C car that's ever been built, because it also lasted roughly ten years with very little development. And there is the incredible four-wheel-drive Paris–Dakar project where I was deeply involved, because the 953 and 959 were built to do 230km/h (143mph) in the desert. I only did 210km/h (130mph) because I wasn't brave enough, but my team mate did 230km/h, and that's fast, but more incredible than this was the fact that this is a sophisticated 911 that was able to compete with the people who build four-wheel-drive off-road machines, and yes, we did it.

JT: You still hold the record for the closest-ever unstaged finish at Le Mans, back in 1969, when you beat Hans Herrmann's 908 coupé by 100m in your JW-Gulf GT40. Did you always believe Porsche was going to be the best bet as far as results were concerned?

JI: I'm absolutely convinced; that's why I made a short list of potential winners, where the winning car is in your hands, and it's your job then to stay on the road and go as fast as possible.

JT: You were known as 'the rain master' in the early 1970s – witness your amazing passing move in the Lotus 72 on Niki Lauda's Ferrari around the outside at Brands Hatch's Paddock Bend as rivers flowed across the track. You undoubtedly had very special skills in the wet.

JI: I had some abilities, and I think my style fits those conditions fairly well. I learned some of that in motorcycle trials where I was competing in a sport that most of the time you do in winter, in mud, ice and rivers, and also races like the Suzuki Grand Prix 50. When you only have two wheels you cannot be wrong – with a car you can put a wheel on the grass and hold it there – but it suits my style probably, and I used that experience later on in the Paris–Dakar. I was doing some jumps with the car and I was still lifting the steering wheel, the same way as you do with a trials motorcycle – you lift the front wheel, and I was trying to do that in the car! It doesn't work in practice, but it does help psychologically.

JT: You have painted a vivid contrast between the relative fragility of F1 and the rigours of endurance racing in the 1970s.

JI: Motor racing is a job you have to do without any fears or without having to pay attention to anything. When you are not motivated in motor racing it doesn't work; when you are waiting for the next mechanical failure, you cannot go fast because you are anticipating the worst. You have to have a clear mind. Formula 1 and the World Sportscar Championship are two different worlds and probably two different mentalities. Sure, it is a privilege to run with a make like Porsche because you can be confident, and the reality is, in ten years with Porsche with a lot of endurance racing mileage I never had a single mechanical failure, not one.

JT: Surely that's as much as anything a reflection on your dexterity with the equipment?

JI: No, I think it has nothing to do with dexterity, it has to do with calculation, it has to do with quality engineering to produce the best possible materials, the best possible design, the best possible resistance on certain points. I don't think I even had a puncture in an endurance race; it sees strange how lucky you can be sometimes. But with Porsche I can't remember having stopped for a puncture in ten years and I am not joking.

JT: Your race career lasted three decades, from your motorcycle trialling to the Paris–Dakar. That's impressive in itself.

JI: Yes, I started in 1961 and I finished in 1992. My last real race as a professional was 1992 in the Paris–Dakar, and I'm probably the one who made the largest number of racing miles in their career because I did so many things at the same time. It adds up to a hell of a distance if you count touring cars, endurance racing, World Championship for Makes, GTs, Group C, Formula 1 and Formula 2, and Paris–Dakar. Usually drivers are

specializing in one thing, but in the past there wasn't this exclusivity; we could race anything because there were not the compulsory sponsor activities. And that also meant I've been able to build up a number of good results because I was very often with the right team in the right place at the right time. You can't control that, it's just a fact, things are happening.

JT: Your Formula 1 career began to decline because of budget cuts at JPS Team Lotus in 1975. But you do have those parallel ladders in your career, F1 and WSC, so as you started to descend one, your ascent of the other took off in a big way with Porsche.

JI: Yes, but you don't know at the time that it's going to last for ten years. Still, having no F1 contract in 1975, and as I had already been doing long-distance racing for a long time and with Porsche offering me the most incredible cars (the 935 and 936) with a guarantee of winning, it was a no-brainer.

JT: So, what about the 935? The bulk of your racing in 1977 was in the 935 with Jochen Mass, for example, and you scored four wins and several second places.

JI: The 935 was maybe the most powerful car in those days with 750bhp – let's call it a monster – with which we won almost every race in the 1977 World Championship for Makes, the DRM and IMSA. Then came the 'Moby Dick' (935/78), honestly an incredible car, a spaceframe silhouette of a 911.

JT: Yes, you won the 1978 Silverstone 6-Hours with Jochen Mass in that car.

One of Jacky Ickx's stints in Formula 1 was driving for John Player Team Lotus when Johnny Tipler was JPS motorsport press officer, so they do go back a little way. JONATHAN GILL

(continued overleaf)

JACKY ICKX INTERVIEW *(continued from previous page)*

JI: Yes, I think we were only 4 seconds slower than the F1 lap record at the previous year's Grand Prix, and Moby Dick was also fastest car on the Mulsanne Straight that year with 367km/h (228mph)! It was a real surprise at first, but after ten to fifteen laps you get used to it – it's very powerful and very fast, and nobody saw a car like that before. But I never drove it at Le Mans, I drove the 936. You know at Le Mans on the Mulsanne Straight, before the chicanes, you go 380km/h (236mph) and frankly, it's easy. You could smoke a cigarette at the same time, and as you pass the restaurant in the middle of Hunaudières you could see the people eating at the table in front of the restaurant in the 1970s – it was not easy to see it if it was salmon or beef, but you could see more or less! You say how do you manage to stay six hours at the wheel or whatever, but it's very restful, the Le Mans straight, I don't say you can sleep, but almost.

JT: Your first Porsche win was at Mugello in a 935 in 1976 and your last Porsche win was in 1985 at Selangor in Malaysia driving a 962. But what was your favourite race of all in a Porsche?

JI: The Le Mans 1977 in the twin-turbo 936. You always try your best whatever you do, whatever your world, and sometimes it's even better than all of the other days, and if we're referring to a race that we shouldn't have won, frankly, this was it. We had two cars; I was in one car with Pescarolo and we had an engine failure early on; this happens sometimes, and I was reserve driver on the other one, so at 8 o'clock in the evening I went in with Hurley and Jürgen as third driver, and we were forty-first and twelve laps behind the Renault at the time, and we were convinced that, for us, the race was over. Honestly, you don't bet a single dime on winning a race like that, but when you see the lap chart after every hour and you've moved up three places, and then rather than being forty-first, suddenly you are tenth, you start to believe it's possible, and that gives you wings sometimes. That did happen to all of us – the drivers, the engineers, the mechanics, they did an unbelievable job – and even though the engine went onto five cylinders, at the end we won. The moral of that is, never give up until the flag!

JT: The Group C twin-turbo 956 from 1982 was Porsche's first aluminium monocoque and it had ground effect bodywork, which made it pretty special. Were you involved in the development of that?

JI: We were all driving the prototypes. Weissach is the engineering centre of Porsche, and I'm sure you are aware that they do a lot of studies for other brands, even aeroplanes. I think the group of engineers today numbers maybe 3,000 or 4,000 people and you never know what they do, it's very secret. But in those days Weissach was the very first development centre. There is a small racecourse in the middle of the office buildings, and we were testing all the cars there, so it was very special. The Rothmans 956 was made there, and starting the 1982 season we knew that it was the best possible toy on the Group C grid. We always did a lot of testing, mostly at Paul Ricard, before we went to Le Mans, and it's fast there, but we had no simulators in those days, few computers, and testing was fairly hands on, trying out different spring settings on the cars, different aerodynamic styling, different camber, different torsion bars, different settings for the engine. It was all handmade, not by computers, that's why it was fairly easy for the amateur, and it was an incredible result; at the conclusion of that season I think we had four wins, and by the end of 1986, the Rothmans 956s and 962s had amassed twenty-five wins (not to mention numerous podiums).

JT: What makes a successful endurance driver? A combination of driving talent, race craft and mechanical sympathy?

JI: What makes the success of a car, frankly, is not the driver, it's the group of people who stick together and design and build an incredible race car, and replace the parts at the right moment. Then you as the driver receive a winning car, and then you have to be lucky, and that's how it was for me. I was not too bad, OK, but without the right tool you're nobody. There are no possibilities of winning any kind of race if the background isn't perfect and the team's not motivated and passionate about what they do. And as far as that's concerned it's clear that I had the perfect surroundings, including the perfect partners in long-distance racing. If you take for example drivers like Derek (Bell) or Hans (Stuck), or Mario Andretti, Brian Redman, Gijs van Lennep or Jackie Oliver, at the time they were the perfect team mates, and we shared that together. Maybe mathematically I am the one who won the largest number of long-distance races but if I reached that point it is because I was surrounded by a lot of other talented drivers who share that equally.

JT: Surely race fans at the time wouldn't have been surprised to find you winning; it might not have been so wonderful in F1 in the mid-1970s, but you'd won an awful lot of endurance races with Ecurie Francorchamps, JW Automotive and Ferrari, and in 1976 here you are winning with Porsche in the 935 and 936: you won two races at Dijon on the same weekend in two very different cars.

Jacky Ickx drives the 3.2-litre 845bhp Porsche 935/78 'Moby Dick' at Nuremburg's Norisring street circuit in 1978. The 'Silhouette' Group 5 category ran from 1976 to 1982 and included the 935, BMW's 320 Turbo, 3.0 CSL and M1, the Zakspeed Ford Capri and others. Moby Dick's cylinder heads were welded to the cylinders, and the heads were water-cooled. PORSCHE PHOTO ARCHIVE

JI: Everyone was able to drive every kind of car in those days. Jimmy, Jackie, Jochen, Denny – we were doing all sort of things, saloon cars, GTs, endurance, single-seaters. It was what we did, not because we were more talented than drivers today – drivers today are outstanding and do incredible jobs – but the difference

The 936 Spyder that took Jacky Ickx, Jürgen Barth and Hurley Haywood to victory at Le Mans in 1977, parked here in the pit lane at Hockenheim. During the race, Ickx was drafted in to the Barth/Haywood car after his own retired, and they moved from forty-first on the Saturday night to take the lead, though Barth had to nurse the car home on five cylinders at the end. PORSCHE PHOTO ARCHIVE

The Le Mans 24-Hours was won in 1982 by Jacky Ickx and Derek Bell in a works 956. The same partnership also won at La Sarthe in 1975 in a Gulf Mirage, and again in 1981 in a 936. PORSCHE PHOTO ARCHIVE

between them and us is that in those days there were few sponsors, and those we had made no demands on our time, so we had the freedom to choose to race whatever and wherever we wanted. In that era when I started in motor racing, it was on another planet, where you had to win big to survive. At the end of the 1970s we had huge wings, huge downforce, no assistance for the steering, no power assistance for the brakes, and to us it seemed normal. It's just a matter of era. Today you can't do that anymore: you will become the greatest in F1 or the greatest in long-distance WSC or the greatest in rallying, but you will never have the possibility to do what we all did in the past – to drive all sorts of cars at any time.

JT: Did you have any a special fitness regime in those days?

JI: No, nothing; we were amateurs.

JT: What about for Paris–Dakar? That must have involved a very special type of fitness.

JI: We were fit because we raced forty weekends a year, non-stop. I think one year maybe I did forty-eight weekends of racing if I include everything: motorcycles, saloon cars, Formula 3, Formula 2, everything at the same time. When you take my first twenty years of motor racing, until I went to Paris–Dakar in 1981, that was one type of racing and I call it monorail. I was successful, it was nice, beautiful, filled with glory, but monorail. Then when I started with Paris–Dakar my vision of the world and the people changed completely. That is the most important part of my life, the era when I went to Africa to compete in off-road racing. If you ask me which part of my life I prefer, it's this one. I discovered the world was much wider than I saw it before and then, really, I became somebody different. Like having a vision.

(continued overleaf)

JACKY ICKX INTERVIEW *(continued from previous page)*

JT: You were at the official Porsche centre at Becton last night as guest of Porsche Club GB, so you are now a Porsche brand ambassador. That's appropriate, isn't it, because of all your successes with Porsche?

JI: I am a brand ambassador for the Volkswagen group, and that means all members of the group, depending on the occasion. Today it's Porsche, and it was an opportunity because I was here already for the Classic Motor Show. I have a lot of positive feelings for that type of event, where you find owners, experts and drivers, and it's partly the reason why classic racing is so successful.

JT: And if somebody offered you a drive in a Porsche 911 in, let's say, this year's Spa 6-Hours, would you be tempted?

JI: Do you know how old I am?!! Also, when you are seventy-two, the chance of being competitive with someone who is twenty or twenty-five is pretty slim.

JT: So, going up the Goodwood Hill is fine, and that's as far as it goes?

JI: Sure, because I don't try to speed but Lord March has reunited those who have a passion for motor racing. Although it's a business, everyone feels like a guest of Goodwood and everyone's gone back home with a huge smile, so he has demonstrated that you can be professional and also be human at the same time.

And that's Jacky Ickx too: perfect gentleman, worldly and astute, yet carrying that aura of greatness that only high achievers possess. As he says of himself, 'There are two drivers inside: there's the nice, polite one, and there's the wolf.' It's a privilege to have met one and seen the other in action.

ABOVE: **It's 1977, and Jacky Ickx drives Porsche 935 'Baby' in the Nuremburg 200 miles at the Norisring. Baby was a scaled-down version of Moby Dick, powered by a 2.1-litre turbo engine. The Silhouette formula allowed manufacturers competing in Group 5 to develop race cars that resembled production cars, and could indeed be smaller than the original they purported to represent, but were in reality full-on competition cars.** PORSCHE PHOTO ARCHIVE

LEFT: **On a visit to London's Historic Racing Car Show in 2017, Jacky Ickx guested at Porsche's Beckham OPC, and here he shares a moment with Johnny Tipler alongside his Paris–Dakar 959.** HENRY HOPE-FROST

Highland Games

Forget the scenery; once you've embarked on the dramatic Pass of the Cattle to the Applecross peninsula, if you put a wheel wrong, the abattoir calls. Taking the bull by the horns, I used a 996 Turbo as my partner for a Highland fling. The Pass of the Cattle – Bealach na Ba – in Wester Ross in the highlands of northwest Scotland is one of the most foreboding and remote places in the UK. Comprised of impossibly tight hairpin bends and sheer drops, you cannot afford to divert your attention from the road to check the view for one second: the slightest misjudgement would have you over the edge in a trice.

Capable of punching out 420bhp, the Porsche 996 Turbo is a big-time A-road car, so you could contend that it would surely be off its game in the constricted mountain passes of Applecross. But it is remarkably docile when its power is unbidden, and at least its four-wheel-drive attributes can ease the pain in the direst of circumstances. The drive started off at the Muir of Ord, 16km (10 miles) north of Inverness, in undulating pastoral

countryside, where photographer Peter Robain, Spicer the terrier and I stayed at the sixteenth-century Ord House Hotel.

As I prepared for the run I took stock of the interior. Everything about the controls was refined, still recognizably 911, with switchgear more coherently located than in the days of air-cooled. The electrically operated seats were more comfortable than the 996 C4S I'd driven recently, although I found they didn't cuddle as fondly as the sports seats in my old 3.2 Carrera. Boot space is restricted, as it is on all 4WD 911s, compliant with the front drivetrain assembly.

Once underway, the 996 Turbo came into its own immediately. Power delivery was instant, even alarming. Clutch take-up was light, although it needed a few thousand revs to get it off the line. Between shifts the right foot had to be completely removed from the accelerator before depressing the clutch pedal otherwise the revs soared – a mark of the eagerness of the gearshift as much as anything. It was as well-oiled and slick as any, and the six ratios were perfectly spaced. The twin turbos came in around 3,000rpm, surging car and occupants forward with great pulses of energy. On a clear stretch of motorway at night its 305km/h (190mph) maximum seemed entirely plausible. Overtaking moves that would ordinarily give pause for thought were perfectly possible, especially valuable when making time on congested A-roads. Not that there are many of those in the north of Scotland, admittedly, and those that are not rammed with tourists are bedevilled by speed censors, in both human and robot form.

We took the twisty A832 out of Muir of Ord and joined the A835 north of Marybank. The fast road was flanked by stone-walled woods and bright yellow gorse and broom, with thrilling ups and downs bookmarked by action-packed corners. The going got quicker still once we turned left on the A832 at Garve. The 996 Turbo tackled the empty roads with a sense of urgency, the power-assisted steering civilized and well-weighted, providing a surprisingly tight turning circle when necessary. Incongruously, a vast illuminated roadside sign reminded

RIGHT: **The road sign leaves the motorist under no illusion that this is going to be a tricky drive! The 996 Turbo driver contemplates the prospect of what lies ahead.**
PETER ROBAIN

BELOW: **Scotland's awesome Wester Ross coastal scenery provides a stunning backdrop for the 996 Turbo as well as some great driving roads.** PETER ROBAIN

travellers in several languages to drive on the left, though the roads of our Applecross destination required no such bidding as they were all single-track.

Scrub-covered hills, dotted white with sheep, formed the backdrop, with conifer plantations, deciduous woods and the occasional small loch to one side or the other. Flanked by a single-track railway line, the road colour changed from blue-black to faded grey asphalt, some without markings or cat's eyes, presenting a succession of sweeping 100km/h (62mph) top-gear bends and long straights. As the Strath Bran valley broadened out, poles delineated the road on either side to show its course when buried in snow. Highland weather changes quickly, and now rain showers passed, turning the scenery bleak and inhospitable. At the single-pump filling-station at Achnasheen we opted for the left fork along Glen Carron and the A890, signposted Kyle of Lochalsh and the Isle

of Skye. It was still a very quick two-lane road, though sheep on the roadside were a cautionary factor, especially with the 996 Turbo's rev-counter reading 4,000rpm in sixth gear. The 'wow' factor kicked in just short of Loch Carron when, after cresting a brow, we were met by a hilly vista encompassing the long waterway with its wooded islands heading southwest towards the sea, the road stretching a mile or two ahead.

Now purple-pink rhododendrons abounded, creating an arcade-like canopy over the road. Scots pines, larch and silver birch lined the bendy grey-granite surface. Tackling the succession of bends, my technique was slow in, fast out, in true 911 style, given that I'd be going appreciably faster in the 996 Turbo. It steered with total accuracy, tracking faithfully through corners, demonstrating effortless turn-in to tighter turns, facilitated by unshakable grip from the low-profile rubber and four-wheel-drive traction. Negotiating fast turns, the whole car bucked and heaved, jiffling like a classic 930 and, to a degree, it could be given its head without any arm-wrestling of the wheel. In slower corners and hairpins I could wind it effortlessly round.

We stuck with the A896, and the route turned west at Lochcarron on the brown-signed Wester Ross Coastal Trail. Abruptly, it became single track with passing places, and the quality of the surface petered out. Tall roadside fencing indicated deer, with buzzards, kites, crows and gulls as aerial escorts, entering bleak, heather-clad moorland and bare rock interspersed with sheep. Giving us our first taste of being in the clouds, the single-track road climbed swiftly up and then down into a craggy ravine. With Loch Kishorn to the left, we found the unassuming signpost to Applecross. An ancient blue tow truck before the prominent road-sign exhorted caravans, learners and inexperienced motorists to refrain from taking the turn.

The start of the climb was a gentle gradient and we rushed up zealously. The first of many hairpin bends came up, and as we wound our way ever higher, the islands down in the loch shrank smaller. My attention was entirely focused on the road rather than the view, since apart from a yard of tussocky rock at the edge of the road, there was nothing to restrain a wayward vehicle. Further on, a few short stretches had been fitted with Armco barrier. The passing places were roughly 100m apart to left and right, but if an approaching vehicle was unsighted behind a hairpin higher up, it meant backing down to the previous lay-by. I had to perform this service twice for gaggles of German-registered Harley-Davidsons. Pulling in to a passing place on the left – the side with the perpendicular plunge – demanded extreme caution so the nearside wheels did not go over the brink. The consequences didn't bear thinking about.

We were shrouded in cloud as the road entered the defile between the vertical dark grey cliffs. The uncompromising rock face of Meall Gorm (710m/2,328ft) was stratified with narrow green ledges and tracks just for mountain sheep, interspersed with cascading streams. Drainage channels beside the road revealed drying cross-sectioned peat, while the soggy moss covering the surface revealed a world of bog plants and lichens, little orange blooms and cotton flowers. As we climbed higher, it became apparent that the screes tumbling down the mountainsides were composed of huge boulders, any one of which would flatten a car roof. Painted white lines instead of Armco defined the side of the road and, now, it was impossible to discern what lay to either side, sheer drop or wilderness. More unfeasibly constricted first-gear hairpins followed. Our progress was conducted at less than 40km/h (25mph), with headlights and windscreen wipers permanently on. With visibility down to about 20m (65ft) in the swirling mists, we reached the summit of the pass. The cattle had been and gone. The trig point suggested we were 24km (15 miles) from Portree on the Isle of Skye and, in the opposite direction, 92km (57 miles) as the crow flies from Inverness.

With Loch Kishorn to the left, a prominent road-sign exhorts caravans, learners and inexperienced motorists to think twice taking the turn to Applecross via Pass of the Cattle. The author decides to accept the challenge.

PETER ROBAIN

RIGHT: **White-rendered Applecross House lies amongst woods on the approach to the village and its broad sandy bay, with pub and row of whitewashed cottages forming the heart of the village.**
PETER ROBAIN

BELOW: **Having arrived at Applecross village, the 996 Turbo circumnavigates the peninsula, taking the winding 23km (14-mile) single-track coast road to Shieldaig.** PETER ROBAIN

Off to the right would be Beinn Bhàn, at 896m (2,938ft) the highest peak on the peninsula. If only you could see it.

Despite the fact that high-speed cornering didn't enter the equation, this has to be one of the most daunting and demanding drives anywhere in the British Isles. On the way down, the clouds cleared, revealing the splendour of the Applecross landscape; small patches of moorland bathed in sunlight shone bright green. Across the Inner Sound lay the Hebridean islands of Raasay and Scalpay with Skye beyond, its mighty Cuillin Hills gloomily discernible through the clouds. The terrain mellowed, the hillsides less precipitous now, and the road was visible ahead as it wound down through bracken and heather towards our destination. Rambling, white-rendered Applecross House lay below amongst woods as we approached the village and its broad sandy bay. Strung out along the coast road that doubles as the quayside, Applecross village consisted of the pub and a row of whitewashed cottages.

We did a circuit of the peninsula, taking the winding, undulating 23km (14-mile) single-track coast road from Applecross to Shieldaig. Around every turn was some fresh spectacle to delight the eye: tiny inland lochs or tarns, ruined cottages along the shoreline, huge rectangular boulders among bracken, gorse and heather, views of breathtakingly beautiful bays and a complex of sea lochs intersected by land forms, all the while bathed in sunshine. On the leeward side, the peninsula was sheltered by deciduous woodland, mainly silver birch and mountain ash, contorted Scots pines and evergreen oaks. One or two cottage industries clung on in the remoteness; here a stained-glass workshop, there a wool and weaving mill; oh, and a shell-fish bar, while platforms out in Loch Torridon indicated the important local salmon fishery. Half a mile across the water, Shieldaig's white terraced cottages looked enchanting.

We took the A896 to Achnasheen, via Glen Torridon to Kinlochewe. There were plenty of lovely corners to indulge the compliant 996 Turbo on the ups and downs and blind brows. Occasionally we rattled over cattle grids and open gates that could close the road in the depths of winter. The road wiggled up the valley, and the Porsche wasn't fazed by any of the irregularities and undulations or camber changes. If we did meet something coming the other way, it could stop in very short order.

Between Kinlochewe and Achnasheen, back on the A832, Glen Docherty was less harsh, with gorse, bracken and heather usurping the bare rock. A new two-lane highway was being constructed, with contractors hard at work in the early evening. It's got to be done in the summer, of course. The section that had been completed was terrific – smooth, with fast curves, lined with new stone walls and barriers along the side of Loch a'Chroisg; it felt a relief to be on a two-lane road again. At

ALLAN MCNISH INTERVIEW

This is an opportune moment to reproduce the interview I had with genial Scotsman Allan McNish in 2014, who has won the Le Mans 24-Hours twice, for Porsche in 1998 and Audi in 2008.

Johnny Tipler: Which is the better configuration of car to be in when racing in the rain: Coupé or Spyder?

Allan McNish: Well, they each have good points; the open-top car has better vision, but you get wet. Technically, aero and mechanical grip should be the same wet and dry. So ideally, you want to be in the fastest one.

JT: Would you describe what it's like in the middle of the night at Le Mans?

AM: Le Mans at night? It's a wee bit like driving on a country road on your own when you've just come off the M25 in the rush hour! You have got to be committed, and if you've got good eyesight then it is better than you anticipate because you're on your own. You've got your own very narrow tunnel of light so therefore it is easier to focus and concentrate.

JT: Since 1980 each car has been crewed by at least three drivers, generally doing three-hour stints each and having physio and sleeping in the motorhome during downtime. Getting the cockpit right for three different drivers must be tricky?

AM: The ergonomics have to be adapted for everybody. The cockpit has to be comfortable for all three drivers, because if the others aren't happy with the set-up they'll not perform properly, and ultimately that will slow you down.

JT: Race strategy is all, and races can be won and lost in the pits. It was a close-run thing in 1998.

AM: I thought we were in trouble when the water pipe split because we were leading by a lap at the time, and that put us in the pits for thirty minutes or so, and we were only eight hours from the finish. We had led from midnight and we were looking really, really strong, but I thought at that moment that Le Mans had passed me

Allan McNish chats over coffee with Johnny Tipler in the Goodwood Festival of Speed's Drivers' Club garden. ANTONY FRASER

by. Still, the mechanics did a really good job and got us out in tandem with the Toyota and we were able to keep them under enough pressure that they finally fell apart.

JT: Le Mans prototypes aren't as fragile as they were fifty years ago. Tell me about the Porsche GT1 from 1998.

AM: They were real racing cars and they were intended to be pushed. You didn't have to conserve them as much as I'd anticipated would be the case in endurance racing. You still had to be a little bit careful with gearboxes and clutches, but they were certainly cars that you could push.

JT: It must be an amazing feeling of elation when 4pm Sunday afternoon comes around, presumably?

AM: Not quite. You don't get the elation, you get an extraordinary sense of relief that it's all held together, because you are so focused and under such pressure. In 1998 it was fifty years almost to the day – the Monday was Porsche's fiftieth anniversary – and it was the hundredth anniversary of Michelin too. The board expected a victory; they didn't expect an entertaining race, they wanted a result, and there was nothing else to it. So, from that point of view there were definitely big questions to be answered and thankfully we answered them.

I was speaking to Allan at the 2014 Goodwood Festival of Speed, an event that never fails to provide opportunities to interview people like him in the sanctuary of the Drivers' Club.

Winners of the 1998 Le Mans 24-Hours were Allan McNish, Stephane Ortelli and Laurent Aiello in 911 GT1-98 #003, powered by the 3164cc twin-turbo flat-six, averaging 199.324km/h (123.854mph). The GT1 is passing the Roock Racing 993 GT2 driven by André Ahrlé, Rob Schirle and David Warnock, which finished twenty-second, 104 laps behind the winner. PORSCHE PHOTO ARCHIVE

Achnasheen we'd completed the circuit, and it was a simple matter of covering the same A832 back to the Muir of Ord.

Knowing the road better this time, our progress was swifter and more assured. In that respect, the 996 Turbo was exemplary, inspiring confidence; hardly surprising given its four-wheel drive and Porsche Stability Management systems, but it meant that I could perform more or less any manoeuvre I felt like. The sat-nav was helpful in urban situations, and where I chose to deviate from the designated path, ignoring exhortations to turn around, it very soon adapted itself with a new plan of action. It handled superbly, provided all the acceleration, braking and high-speed cruising ability one could wish for, and was comfortable to sit in for the duration of the 12-hour run between Norfolk and Inverness.

Handsome and purposeful, the 996 Turbo looks like it means business. One of the views I liked best was its rear flanks when seen in the rear-view mirrors – much more muscular than classic models. At 1,829mm (72in) wide, the Turbo body is 58mm (2.3in) broader than the regular 996 C2 coupé. If it were mine I'd probably fit an aftermarket exhaust to give it a little bit more presence to override a slightly muted personality. At trip's end, we had notched up 2,494km (1,550 miles), averaging 82km/h (51mph) and 11.7ltr/100km (24.1mpg), undoubtedly on some of the most arduous roads in the country and through breathtaking scenery.

THE 996 GT2

Compared to in-your-face street racers like the 996 GT3 RS, the 996 GT2 looks positively subdued; not much more extrovert than a 996 Turbo. But looks are deceiving. Porsche have a long tradition of building special models, cars aimed at the weekend racer or the serious track-day enthusiast. Think Carrera RS, or even the later Carrera 3.2 Clubsport. Or, to really sort the men from the boys, models like the GT3 in all its various forms.

At its launch in 2001, Porsche hinted the GT2 was a perfect track-day car, a real enthusiasts' machine, setting the standards by which all other such cars would be judged. On paper, it certainly looked as if that would be the case. Two huge turbos, and over 460bhp delivered via rear-wheel drive only, adjustable suspension and a new race-bred braking system showed the GT2 was not for the faint-hearted. It was not cheap, either, costing just a shade under £115,000, but its technical specification promised that it would be worth every penny of its high asking price.

Simply put, the 996 GT2 was a 996 Turbo, but with two fewer driven wheels, and a bunch of goodies heisted from the GT3 parts bin. The 996 GT2 used an upgraded version of the engine from the 996 Turbo, which means it's a 3.6-litre water-cooled flat-six based on the 911 GT1 motor.

The M96/70 unit displaced precisely 3600cc, thanks to a bore and stroke of 100mm × 76.4mm. Each bank of cylinders featured two overhead camshafts, with 4 valves per cylinder. The GT2 differed from the mainstream Turbo in using a pair of KKK K24 turbochargers, which, aided by a reprogrammed Bosch Motronic ME7.8 injection/management system, helped boost power to 462bhp at 5,700rpm. This rose to 483bhp with the introduction of the Mk 2 version, thanks to new KKK K24 turbos and revised Motronics. The throttle operation was purely mechanical, rather than fly-by-wire, in operation. There were also two pick-ups in the dry-sump reservoir to ensure oil supply under extreme cornering and acceleration. These were small points, maybe, but indicative of the GT2's serious nature – as if the 319km/h (198mph) top speed wasn't enough to convince you. The GT2 was equipped with a six-speed manual transmission similar to that used on the original 993-based GT2. Ratio changes were made

FVD Brombacher's 996 GT2, powered by the twin-turbo version of the 3.6-litre flat-six, rises from 462bhp to 483bhp against the GT3's 360bhp, and though rear-wheel drive only, it is closely related to the 996 Turbo in terms of road-going set-up.
ANTONY FRASER

ABOVE: **The 996 GT2 is fitted with a 3.6-litre water-cooled flat-six, an upgraded version of the 996 Turbo's M96/70 engine, and based on the 911 GT1 motor. The turbochargers and intercoolers are located at the outer right and left of the engine.** ANTONY FRASER

RIGHT: **Close-up of the silencer, tailpipes and turbo installation on the FVD 996 GT2 flat-six.** ANTONY FRASER

via a cable linkage, and the gears kept cool by the use of oil spray nozzles inside the box, and a water-to-air heat exchanger similar to that used on the older Cup race cars.

In line with the normally aspirated GT3 launched some two years earlier, the GT2 features Rose-jointed suspension, making it easily adjustable in the workshop. The days of Porsche's beloved torsion bars had long gone, with the GT2 and its siblings riding on coils all round. Those on the GT2 were of a higher rating than the units fitted to the GT3. It eschewed any driver aids, such as traction control, PSM or anything else that could dampen the buttock-clenching fun on offer. Options were few, with nothing as wimpy as a semi-auto Tiptronic gearbox on the spec sheet – this was a beast that could only be tamed by manually stirring the internals of the six-speed transmission. The GT2's progress was retarded by PCCB (Porsche Ceramic Composite Brakes), which were great when new and hot, ineffective when cold – and expensive when worn out.

The GT2 was based on the wide-hipped bodyshell of the contemporary Turbo but with various aerodynamic aids thrown in for good measure. At the front end, the nose is unique to the GT2, with a rubber-lipped spoiler that sits rather too low to the road to be practical, especially if you live in a speed bump-infested area like London, or if you regularly take your car to the track – you'll hear it scraping at the bottom of Paddock Hill at Brands Hatch, without a doubt.

Air is ducted in through the central 'grille' to the front-mounted radiators and out via a slot across the top of the nose. Not only does this aid cooling, but it also serves to reduce front-end lift at speed. Ducts in the flanks send cool air into the engine bay, too. The rear bumper valance is unique to the GT2, as is the fixed rear spoiler. That has ducts to aid cooling as well.

The GT2 was available in Clubsport and Comfort trim. The names rather speak for themselves, although the word 'comfort' might raise a few eyebrows. Clubsport versions were equipped with fire-retardant Recaro buckets, half-cage with a bolt-in front section supplied for dealer fitment, and no rear seats. A fire-extinguisher was standard, while a battery cutout switch and a set of harnesses were supplied, but not fitted, for track use. The Comfort version used the same front seats and still had no rear seat, but the electrically operated leather seats from the Turbo were an option. Electric windows and central locking were standard, but air-con and a CD player were only available at extra cost.

The 996 GT2 turned out not to be the anticipated hard-core cage-fighter. While the preceding 993 GT2 was a competition car, Porsche elected to concentrate on using the GT3 for motorsport. So, although the GT2 uses a twin-turbo version of the GT3's 3.6-litre flat-six, rising from 462bhp to 483bhp against the GT3's 360bhp, it is more closely related to the 996 Turbo in terms of road-going set-up. Giveaways to the GT2's identity are the distinctive bisected air intakes in the front panel and the air ducts feeding its turbo intercoolers in the leading edges of the rear wheel arches. The rear wing is different too,

LEFT: **The 996 GT2 features rose-jointed suspension, coil springs and dampers, with Porsche Ceramic Composite Brakes, in this instance allied with Brembo calipers.** ANTONY FRASER

ABOVE: **Slow burn: the ceramic brake of a 2001 996 GT2 glows red hot on the test rig.** PORSCHE PHOTO ARCHIVE

LEFT: **Air is ducted in through the 996 GT2's central grille to the front-mounted radiators and out via a slot across the top of the nose, helping to reduce front-end lift at speed.** ANTONY FRASER

996 GT2 (2000–2005)

Layout and chassis

Two-plus-two coupé, unit-construction steel body/chassis

Engine

Type	M96/70 'Mezger' dry sump, horizontally opposed, rear-mounted 6-cylinder
Block material	Aluminium
Head material	Aluminium
Cylinders	6
Cooling	Water-cooled
Bore and stroke	100 × 76.4
Capacity	3600cc
Valves	4 valves per cylinder
Compression ratio	11.7:1
Fuel system	Multi-point injection, two KKK K24 turbochargers
Max. power (DIN)	462bhp at 5,700rpm
Max. torque	457lb ft at 3,500rpm
Fuel capacity	64ltr (19.5gal)

Transmission

Gearbox	Getrag G96/00 rear drive, 6-speed
Clutch	Hydraulic single dry plate
Ratios	1st 3.82
	2nd 2.20
	3rd 1.52
	4th 1.22
	5th 1.02
	6th 0.84
	Reverse 3.44
Final drive	3.89

Suspension and Steering

Front	Independent suspension with MacPherson struts, aluminium links, longitudinal and transverse links, coil springs, gas dampers, anti-roll bar
Rear	Independent suspension with MacPherson struts, aluminium links, lateral and transverse links, coil springs, gas dampers, anti-roll bar
Steering	Rack and pinion
Tyres	225/40 × R18 front, 295/30 × R18 rear
Wheels	Aluminium alloy
Rim width	7.5 J front, 10 J rear

Brakes

Type	Front and rear vented discs with six-piston calipers; optional M450 ceramic discs
Size	380mm × 24mm front, 350mm × 20mm rear

Dimensions

Track	1,455mm (57.3in) front, 1,500mm (59in) rear
Wheelbase	2,350mm (92.5in)
Overall length	4,430mm (174.4in)
Overall width	1,765mm (69.5in)
Overall height	1,305mm (51.3in)
Unladen weight	1,540kg (3,395lb)

Performance

Top speed	319km/h (198mph)
0–60mph	4.2sec

cantilevered from the engine lid with down-swept fins on either end. But despite a 10mm (0.4in) lower ride height than the 996 Turbo, which explains why the tyres touch the inner wheel arches on full lock, the GT2's drag coefficient is slightly higher – 0.34cd against the Turbo's 0.33 – due to the larger expanse of the fixed rear wing.

Germany and North Yorkshire: Two Test Drives

I've driven a couple of 996 GT2s: one on a visit to Willy Brombacher's FVD parts concern at Umkirch, Freiburg, southwest Germany, which I took into the Black Forest and Baden vineyards for our photoshoot, and the other at Specialist Cars

LEFT: **Like its contemporary 996 models, the GT2 cabin is functional yet sophisticated, with half roll cage, full harness and fire extinguisher the exceptions to normality.** ANTONY FRASER

BOTTOM LEFT: **There's never a great deal to see under the engine lid of a modern Porsche, though the FVD 9916 GT2 does at least offer a blue inlet tube as well as its fluid fillers.** ANTONY FRASER

BOTTOM RIGHT: **FVD Brombacher's 996 GT2 is equipped with Bilstein coil-over dampers.** ANTONY FRASER

of Malton, which we ran up on the North York Moors near Rosedale. The wonderful thing about Germany is, as I've said before, the fact that they still have plentiful and lengthy sections of unrestricted autobahn, and it's here that we can really assess the high-speed potential of a car like the GT2.

It's time to nestle into the all-embracing Recaro seat and embrace the controls. Fire up the GT2's flat-six and it plunges into a colossal booming cacophony. The noise of the lightweight flywheel in concert with the gearbox is also quite noticeable. There's a slight tremolo to the throttle at low revs because of the special cams, hinting at the tremendous power available when it comes on song. To begin with, the roads are damp after a shower, and Willy urges caution on account of the Sport Cup tyres, imperious on a warm, dry track but like slicks in the wet. 'It goes absolutely crazy when you have damp roads, and if you accelerate at all hard you would just lose it.' No problem, it's

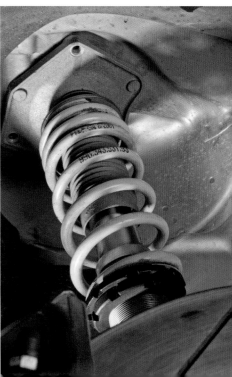

FVD boss Willy Brombacher enthuses about his new range of pistons. ANTONY FRASER

Rear three-quarter view of the FVD 996 GT2 against a bucolic backdrop of Baden-Württemberg vineyards, illustrating the car's permanent rear spoiler and wing structure. ANTONY FRASER

perfectly happy to burble along at a low-velocity 1,500rpm, a docile kitten easing through dignified downtown Freiburg on our way up through the forest to our photoshoot.

New Bilstein PSS10 coil-over dampers are fitted, and the handling is peerless, irrespective of Willy's new enthusiasm for Ohlins shocks and Eibach springs. 'The customer demands Bilsteins, so that's what we've fitted, because he wants to have it a little bit stiffer, and you can actually feel that on the road.' Turn-in is very sharp and assured on the incessant twists and turns and second-gear hairpins of the Schauinsland hillclimb, and in a lot of corners I'm giving the wheel a little bit of an old-school jink to assist the grip. We pause at the halfway house chalet-style restaurant and wooden timing booth before motoring over the top and westward towards the balmy vineyard terraces. Circulating repeatedly round our loop through the back-road vines for Antony's benefit, I sense the wonderfully compliant chassis, the vast grip in the turns and the bottomless resource of power: an awesome machine.

Now comes our autobahn alacrity. Floor the throttle, see what happens. It's like being in a catapult, firing you forward relentlessly in every gear, no matter how tight the belts: your body's tight but your head nods helplessly. It feels like being on a plane taking off without leaving the ground. The backfire is splendid on the overrun, popping and banging like a good 'un. The landscape flashes by, edges of the autobahn a grey-green

blur. Bridges zoom into view and zap overhead as we whizz beneath them. I look as far into the distance as possible, gauging gaps between vehicles to see who's likely to pull into the overtaking lane on this unrestricted section of blacktop. Luckily, they check their mirrors in Germany. A glimpse at the speedo says 300km/h (186mph) as we streak from one *Kreuz* (intersection) to another.

We've been in fifth gear all the time on the unrestricted autobahn. Normally you wouldn't need to do that because the engine is so elastic, so even in sixth gear you know you have power to accelerate – that's how torquey it is. And, happily, it stops pretty thoroughly as well. It's just that you can be maxed out on an unrestricted section and all of a sudden there's a 130km/h sign, likely as not followed by a 120, and without exception everyone anchors up dramatically and falls into line, no matter if they're in the overtaking lane. That's what governs maximum speed in Germany: rigid adherence to the limits. 'Now you understand why we need the big brakes!' All too soon it's over, but it's a taster of just how mental this GT2 can be when 480bhp is unleashed.

And so to North Yorkshire. Talk about moorland magic: there's no shortage of great driving roads around Malton to put the beast to the test, and we target the moors above Pickering and over to Whitby, taking in Rosedale, Blakey Ridge and Goathland: I'll be there in a *Heartbeat*. We have a great

RIGHT: **The FVD 996 GT2 fits like a glove, and the writer finds that turn-in is sharp and assured on the serpentine vineyard lanes, while tweaking the wheel mid-corner to assist the grip.** ANTONY FRASER

BELOW: **Motoring on the moor in the rear-wheel drive 996 GT2, there's so much power instantly available, switching between third and fourth gears, and into fifth on a long straight, and though it's a firm ride, it is a bit softer than a 996 GT3.** ANTONY FRASER

cross-section of asphalt to power down, including cattle-gridded moorland single-track and two-lane A- and B-roads, interspersed with myriad bends, convoluted cambers, roller-coaster dips and troughs: all in all, an exhilarating prospect in this super car.

The GT2 leaps athletically into action. It's heftier than a 996 C2 in terms of the bulk of car I'm throwing down the road, though it has way more than enough power to do that. There's a madness about the delivery – floor it, and it gets cracking without hanging around, and though at first I think I detect a slight lag, that notion is soon dispensed with. Lift off abruptly and the violent forward dash is punctuated by a sideways twitch. The gear lever action is light and feels reasonably slick, and because it's rear drive it's not constrained by the front axle drivetrain.

I'm meandering along the A64 towards Whitby, 1,800rpm cruising at 80km/h (50mph) in sixth, and there's enough torque

Getting to grips with a 996 GT2 on the North York Moors, where there's an exhilarating cross-section of A- and B-roads, with myriad bends, cambers, dips and troughs through which to exercise the car. ANTONY FRASER

to encourage it to get a move on if an opportunity arises – but I have to drop two cogs to inspire it, and at 3,000rpm in fourth it starts to go. Flooring it across the B-road all hell breaks loose and it reveals itself as the crazy monster that I knew it would be. So much power on tap! But oh, the thrill of it, switching from third to fourth, maybe fifth on a long straight, with the power instantly there. It's a firmish ride, softer than the GT3, and the ratios are closer than the GT3 – all but second are the same as the Turbo's. I love the way the front wheels are following all the undulations on the moorland road, feeling their way along. The delicacy of control going round some very tight corners on the wooded hill roads near Stape is wonderful. Going more remote with gorse in full bloom and cattle and tractor mud happily dried on the roads, I can just see Whitby from the top of the moor. It's interesting having the boost gauge in the bottom segment of the rev counter: I see 0.8 bar, accelerating in second gear at 5,000rpm, though I'm mainly concentrating on watching the road ahead.

At the time, the 996 GT2 was the most powerful production 911 ever built. Porsche was never a company to rest on its laurels, however: for model year 2004, the GT2 Mk2 was released, with a massive 483bhp on tap, thanks to revised turbos and a remap of the Bosch Motronic system. Some minor cosmetic alterations also helped contribute to a not insignificant price hike. In fact, by the time the 996 GT2 ceased production in 2005, it would set you back a cool £126,600. The 996 GT2 will always remain a pretty exclusive beast. Worldwide, there were just 247 sold in 2001, 716 in 2002, 233 in 2003 and a measly eighteen in 2004. Of these, 963 were so-called Mk1s, the remaining 324 the later Mk2. A total of 129 cars came to the UK, of which sixteen were the upgraded Mk2 version.

Driving the 996 GT2 on the approach road to Castle Howard, the author observes a certain madness about the power delivery when both applying throttle and lifting off, the car twitching in response.

ANTONY FRASER

Close to Nirvana? A 996 GT2 in bright sunshine on a deserted moorland road: there's a delicacy of control passing through tight corners, and the front wheels follow all the undulations.

ANTONY FRASER

RUF AUTOMOBILE: PFAFFENHAUSEN'S FINEST

They're fast, they're extreme – and every time you look at a Ruf there's that smile-inducing extravagance. But why buy a Ruf when a regular 996 GT3, GT2 or Turbo would surely provide enough excitement? The flipside to that question is, why settle for a regular Porsche when you could have a Ruf? That's the carrot – a Ruf product (rhymes with roof, not rough) is so much more exclusive. Wait five minutes to cross London's Brompton Road and it's like every other car's a 997 or 991. You dig Porsches but fancy going one step beyond? A Ruf could be your answer. Not only is the car more striking and potentially faster than the Stuttgart product upon which it's based, but ownership confers membership of an elite club. In effect you join the Family Ruf, and that's very enticing. You don't

have to be there long for the magnetic personalities of Mr and Mrs Ruf to draw you in. Why would you not want to go on the annual Ruf tour to Valencia or Hockenheim, a long weekend partying with other owners and the charming company staff, with a track day thrown in? Ruf has also hosted driving courses at a small circuit in Austria, with Hans-Peter Lieb (father of works Porsche racer Marc) in charge, and in 2018 we attended a two-day session at Hockenheim, where I drove the SCR 4.2.

Munich is an hour or so's drive from the home of Ruf Automobiles, providers of the fastest incarnations of our favourite German sports car. It's located beside a roundabout at Pfaffenhausen in the heart of undulating Bavarian farming country. The adjacent garage and Aral filling station would hardly rate a second glance if it wasn't for the familiar – yet subtly different – sports cars on the cobbled forecourt outside the small semicircular showroom.

Pop-riveted competition-style wheel-arch extensions typify the Ruf RGT, along with the Carrera Cup-style front panel, rear wing and Ruf split-rim wheels. RUF AUTOMOBILE

An intriguing matt silver RGT Coupé and blood orange RK Speedster vie for attention within, and in the compound behind are the rear-engined RGT, Rt 12 and R Kompressor, and the mid-engined RK Coupé and Speedster, 3400K and 3800S. Behind the showroom and offices is the service department, a fully equipped workshop where I count nine cars up on lifts, including the Ruf-built GT3-RSR that came seventh in the 2009 Nürburgring 24-Hours. To the right of that is the engine shop, where Ruf's highly specialized flat-six engines are assembled.

In the manufacturing area behind the service workshop are two coupés, a brand-new Ruf Rt 12 being finished off and a customer's 996 GT3 receiving the Ruf treatment, which, apart from engine work, includes full interior refit and incorporation of the built-in roll-cage. While much of the elaborate trim, seats and upholstery is created locally, some is done in house and the installation takes place within the building. A pair of engine dynos in soundproof chambers, one for air-cooled and one for water-cooled cars, complete the main building.

Over the road, on the opposite side of the roundabout, is a larger block containing the foundry where all Ruf's metalwork is fabricated, including silencers and exhaust systems, and replacement panels for the classic restorations that form a major part of the business. The central space here is packed with 1970s Porsches, including three 2.7 RSs, an RSR, and three of Alois's own indulgences: a Mercedes-Benz 350SE Coupé, an E-type Jaguar and a 959. Apart from a handsome black R Kompressor Coupé with black wheels, Alois's daily driver is a discreet Mercedes-Benz E500 that's nudging 400,000km (250,000 miles). Two 356 Cabriolets are up on lifts and a third's under restoration, along with a 901 – only the thirty-fifth 911 ever made. They're both likely to be here for a year yet. A curiosity in the workshop is an ancient 1927 Tatra. In the fibreglass workshop, a trio of Ruf front panels is being created by the GRP technicians, while a bodyshell in vibrant blue for an as yet undesignated Ruf model goes through the paint shop.

OPPOSITE PAGE:
The Ruf RtR and RGT are typical of Alois Ruf's indefatigable perception and creativity. The twin-turbo Rt 12's forced-induction system is descended from the original Yellowbird CTR, producing between 550 and 650bhp depending on engine capacity, while the RGT is inspired by the lightweight 1973 Carrera RS and develops 445bhp from its normally aspirated 3.8-litre flat-six. ANTONY FRASER

THIS PAGE:
The Ruf Rt 12 was introduced at the 2004 Essen Motor Show, built on the new 997 platform, and powered by a 3.6-litre twin-turbo flat-six based on the previous 996 Turbo unit. RUF AUTOMOBILE

ABOVE: **The Ruf Rt 12 engine bay reveals slightly more of the 3.8-litre twin-turbo's mechanicals than its 997 Turbo stablemate's.** ANTONY FRASER

RIGHT: **Celebrating eighty years since his father founded the firm, Alois Ruf's fertile mind is constantly pondering new technological concepts to maintain the 911's longevity. Now we have the DTM race car chassis core and carbon body panels.** ANTONY FRASER

The Ruf Story

Alois Ruf is very much the lynchpin. Charming and hospitable, with a deep, soft voice and crisp diction, winning smile and perfect English, his raffish appearance belies a focused authority and a dedication to his business and its history. He warmly greets a succession of clients, potential customers who defer to him as minor royalty, and he spends a few minutes with each of them before handing over to his son Marcel or PR man Marc-Andre Pfeifer.

We sit around the glass table in Alois Ruf's office that's mounted on a 1966 flat-six engine. 'It was the first to use Weber carburettors, but it had the full sand-cast engine case,' he observes as we peer between our knees. The dissected car theme continues in the overhead lights, which started life as 911 cylinder barrels. His desk displays a similar filing system to my own, although his wife Estonia's is neat enough. Alois caught the Porsche bug early.

> It started at age fourteen, when I heard my first 911. It was a rainy day in April 1964, so it was still a prototype 901. And that experience ignited everything

that happened subsequently. It was the music of the early 911 exhaust, which goes through your bones – and that caught my attention. I'm not sure if they ever wanted that sound – it probably just turned out that way. Anyway, this big spray of water followed the car as it flew by, so I could hardly see it, but I saw the contours and the Stuttgart licence plate, and I said to my dad: 'That is the new Porsche!' It gave me goosebumps, and from that moment I was a 911 man. And I still am.

He knows that younger enthusiasts like the older Porsche models, so he and his engineers seek to incorporate certain classic virtues into the modern line-up. 'That quick throttle response of the early 2.0-litre engine, the bite and the sound, this was what made those earlier 911s so fascinating, and we are trying to bring back all of that into our existing cars, because it's all about emotions.'

The Ruf story started with an accident – literally. In 1963, Alois Ruf's father was driving his tour bus on an autumnal Sunday evening and was overtaken by a 356. Its driver promptly lost control and rolled into a ditch.

My dad stopped, looked after the driver – he was OK apart from glass cuts – and then he said: 'Don't worry about the car, I have a workshop and we will pick it up and we will talk after you are over the shock.' A few days go by and the gentleman calls my dad and says he doesn't want this car any more because of this bad experience. He doesn't want to have it repaired, but my dad can buy it if he likes. My dad fixed the car, drove it, and became a Porsche enthusiast himself. A year later we were in Munich and a man begged him to sell the car on the spot for cash – it was a rare Karmann hard-top – and we took his 356 Reutter coupé in part exchange. My dad said: 'I have never sold a car like that before! I love the car, I have

fun with it, and made money on top of it.' So, that car triggered everything that you see today.

The Ruf family has occupied the site for nearly seventy years.

My parents bought the land in 1939. There was a villa on the site that was very fancy for this area. My dad thought it was an ideal place to start an auto business because it is right at the entrance to Pfaffenhausen. So, they converted it and I grew up with the river running right where we are sitting just now. I used to swim and take boat rides. In the late 1970s the river was diverted, and I bought more land so I could extend. We still had the same operation, but the whole shape of the

Unveiled at the 2012 Geneva Show, the Ruf Rt 35 celebrates the company's thirty-five years in business. It's based on the 991 and powered by Ruf's 3.8-litre flat-six, delivering 630bhp. ANTONY FRASER

Rear three-quarter view of the Ruf Rt 35, revealing intercooler vents and ducktail spoiler. All-wheel-drive transmission was via six-speed sequential shift or seven-speed PDK.

ANTONY FRASER

As well as totally state-of-the-art turbocharged modern Porsches, Ruf Automobile also services and restores classic models such as this 356A 1600 Convertible outside the Pfaffenhausen showroom – with conveniently sited Aral fuel station (selling 103-octane!) next door.
JOHNNY TIPLER

buildings changed. But the original building where my dad started is still there, where the petrol station is. It's totally remodelled, but still the same floor plan. I was born in the house and my mother still lives here today.

Twenty years ago, they bought the piece of land across the street and built the factory there where the restoration and fabrication work takes place.

In 1965 we had the first 911, and from then on, we made a name specializing in Porsches, be it collision repair, maintenance, service, restoration – and we are still doing that. We are still charging €76 per hour, which is the same price as the Volkswagen dealer charges you. It's a bargain – we have expertise from the earliest to the latest, and all the equipment. That is still our core business and people with an old 911 don't need to be scared away.

The Yellowbird that raised Ruf from provincial Bavarian specialist onto the international arena was hatched in the early 1980s, when Porsche's marketing people believed the 911 was finished and the front-engined cars, including the 928 and 944, were the way forward. The rear-engined model line dovetailed into the Turbo and SC. 'People were frustrated when they couldn't get what they used to have, and we offered the 911 SCR, the Ruf version of the SC, which was a 3.2-litre with big-bore pistons and cylinders with 217 very strong horsepower, which made the car feel like a 1973 Carrera RS.' Its reception in the press and among enthusiasts convinced Ruf

that there was a need for such a car, so he turned his attention to the 911 Turbo.

We developed our own five-speed gearbox, based on requests from customers, and we set up a bodyshop, so in ten years we could build another new car. Because, whatever Porsche believed at the time, we knew there would be a group that would stick with the 911. In 1987, for the Yellowbird we brought the maximum technology

Alois Ruf is often his own test driver, here behind the wheel giving his Ruf 3.4-litre '2.8 RSR lookalike' a thorough workout – as in hitting the red line in every gear! ANTONY FRASER

available to the good old classic 911. We designed that twin-turbo engine, and the only engine management system that was available and affordable for us was the Bosch Sports Motronic. The results were brilliant and, as you know, Paul Frere ran it at 340km/h (211mph) on VW's test track and it beat all the supercars. And, of course, Stefan Roser turned the Yellowbird into a legend, ragging it round the Ring in a 23km (14-mile) powerslide – and that's before you consider its starring role in Gran Turismo.

Of course, from today's perspective you would find some flaws in the drivability. It is not as subtle as the car of today, but the computer in the engine management system was not as intelligent. We built twenty-nine cars, and we probably modified twenty for customers who didn't want to buy a new CTR.

Ten years after the Yellowbird, the 993-based CTR-2 emerged, following the same philosophy but displaying more aesthetic differences, including a different rear spoiler. 'The CTR-2 is in demand as a collectors' car, which I am glad to see, and now we have the CTR-3, which was at Goodwood in the Supercar section.'

Although Ruf is now an official Porsche centre, the association was always going to be prickly.

We didn't have a professional relationship; a love and hate relationship, I would call it. It also depends on how the factory is doing. That influences the relationship. They used to think what we were doing was unnecessary, because they thought what they offered was sufficient. Mercedes-Benz thought that about AMG for many years, then they bought it. Ruf has been in business for too long and has its own reputation; they cannot wipe us away because, for the traditionalist, we are very much like Porsche used to be in its early days, and that's what they are looking for when they come to see us. Porsche once stated that they see us as competitors. But we have to buy their product first in order to compete with them. So, we are their competitors in one way, but at the same time we are enhancing their product. Every car that we sell, Porsche make money out of, because it's a sold Porsche!

Output is around thirty-five brand-new cars a year, with fifty major conversions. Ruf buys everything it needs from Porsche, from complete cars to bodyshells and drivetrains.

They never make it difficult for us – they tolerate us, let's put it that way. We have a very long-term agreement that Ruf can build cars based on Porsche parts, and Ruf has to put its own chassis number on the car. In the end that makes it a much more valuable car because there are not so many around. If somebody has a car which needs upgrading, we will do it, but our speciality is that we are a licensed car manufacturer.

That status was achieved in 1982, and Ruf has been recognized in the USA in its own right since 1987. 'We are self-certifiers, and we are bringing in cars under this provision, just like the big boys. They don't make exceptions, except that as a small-volume manufacturer we don't have to crash test.' A recent expansion is the facility it has built in Bahrain, at the invitation of the royal family there, making Ruf the first European manufacturer to build cars in the island kingdom.

The whole Ruf scenario is seductive; its exquisite products and clubby aura enchant without fail. Better put mine on the slate, please.

Steep Pitch: the Ruf RGT, Rt 12 and R Kompressor

The Ruf RGT was inspired by the lightweight 1973 Carrera RS, according to Alois. More discernibly, it's based on the 997 GT3 and underlines its visual impact with screw-fixed wheel arch spats front and rear, and Ruf five-channel front intake panel and splitter. Inside the cabin there's an integral roll-cage, clad in Alcantara to match the interior decor and deeply cosseting sports seats. The RGT achieves 445bhp at 7,600rpm from its normally aspirated 3.8-litre flat-six. Maximum torque is 420Nm (310lb ft) at 5,100rpm, and top speed is 317km/h (197mph), with 0–100km/h in 4.2sec. By comparison, the 997 GT3 makes 415bhp and 405Nm (299lb ft) from 3.6 litres, hitting 311km/h (193mph) and 0–60mph in 4.0sec.

Next comes the twin-turbo Rt 12, its forced-induction system descended from the original Yellowbird CTR. Two levels of performance are available, depending on whether you opt for the 3.6- or 3.8-litre engine. The lesser capacity gives 560bhp at 6,900rpm and 790Nm (583lb ft) torque between 3,500 and 4,000rpm, and the larger engine produces 650bhp at 7,000rpm and 870Nm (642lb ft) at 3,500–4,000rpm. It's available as coupé or cabriolet and, as well as the Ruf styling and aerodynamic evolutions to the body, which include air scoops in the rear wheel arches and ducting in the neatly integrated rear valance, the Rt

The 997-based Ruf RGT takes some of its styling cues from precedents such as the 911 Carrera RSR and 993 GT2, with Ruf five-channel front intake panel and splitter. ANTONY FRASER

BELOW: **Inside the cabin of the Ruf RGT there are deeply cosseting sports seats and carbon trim as well as an integral roll-cage, clad in Alcantara to match the interior décor, so to all intents and purposes it's invisible, though it's reassuring to know it's there.** ANTONY FRASER

12 offers sports suspension with hydraulic lifting facility. This raises the front axle – and hence the front splitter – 50mm to clear obstructions such as speed bumps or ferry ramps. Customers can opt for the six-speed manual transmission or five-speed RufTronic paddle shift. Top speed can be 344km/h or 349km/h (214mph or 217mph), depending on selected engine size, with 0–100km/h times of 3.6sec and 3.4sec. Fuel consumption, if it matters, is 21.1ltr/100km and 21ltr/100km (13.4 and 13.5mpg). Porsche claimed the Porsche 997 Turbo produces 480bhp, does 311km/h (193mph) and accelerates from 0 to 100km/h in 3.7sec.

Ruf offers the R Kompressor as an alternative in the forced-induction stakes. It's the supercharged version of the Rt 12 model and can also be ordered in open or closed bodywork. The supercharger is driven by a V-belt, and has an aluminium intake manifold with two water-cooled intercoolers. It works

ABOVE LEFT: **The 2004 Ruf Rt 12 features large-diameter cross-drilled brakes, and accelerates from 0 to 60mph in 2.8sec, with a top speed of 352 km/h (219mph).**
RUF AUTOMOBIL

ABOVE RIGHT: **Another Ruf model with its origins in the 997 Turbo is the Ruf R Kompressor. Fitted with 3.6-litre flat-six, it develops 435bhp, and with 3.8 litres it makes 460bhp.** RUF AUTOMOBILE

RIGHT: **While Ruf Automobile specializes in turbocharging, the firm has also produced supercharged cars such as this Ruf RK Coupé Kompressor, based on the Cayman 987 S.**
RUF AUTOMOBILE

As well as sporting a supercharger, the Ruf RK Coupé Kompressor differs in detail from the Cayman 987 S on which it's based in that the air scoops ahead of the rear wheel arches are located at sill level, and the frontal air intake system has also been revised. The fuel filler is located in the front lid, too.
RUF AUTOMOBILE

out slightly more economical than the twin-turbo Rt 12 at 19.9ltr/100km (14.2mpg), with maximum velocity of 303km/h (188mph) and 0–100km/h time of 4.3sec for the 3.6-litre motor and a shade better with the 3.8-litre.

Celebrating Ruf's twenty-five years as a TüV (Technical Inspection Association)-approved manufacturer, the RK Coupé (Ruf Kompressor) is a customized take on the mid-engined Cayman bodyshell, endowed with a 440bhp supercharged version of the 3.8-litre flat-six, topping 306km/h (190mph) and achieving 0–100km/h in 4.3sec. On this and a 981 Boxster-derived Speedster version that displays more than a hint of retro, even down to those flashes in the rear wing tops *à la* 550 Spyder race car, collaborators on the RK's sublime minimalist styling were Studio Torino, whose name appears discreetly on the rear flanks. If you prefer to adhere more closely to Zuffenhausen's normal mid-engined products without getting into significant bodywork evolutions, the Ruf 3400K, 3800K and normally aspirated 3800S are mechanically enhanced versions of the 981 Boxster and Cayman. And should you wish to simply endow your own Porsche with Ruf technology, the Kompressor kit is available for 996 and 997 Carrera models.

Beam me Aboard: 3400K and 3800K

The supercharged 3400K Roadster and its 3800K sibling are based on the 981 Boxster – Boxsters with attitude, and a 400bhp punch to back it up. There's the really deep vroom of an exhaust note on tickover, and the sound effects department swings into action with an enthralling guttural roar that crescendos into the spine-tingling zone. Each shift, short or long, delivers sustained

power, sending the Roadster leaping up the highway. Here, in the land of unlimited speed, we are content to revel in treble figures without seeking out maximum velocity. It's an extremely competent and convincing machine. Twenty years on from the CTR Yellowbird, it's suave and sophisticated. By contrast, the Yellowbird pensioner now feels relatively crude, with everything from controls and cabin environment to handling and power delivery savouring of racing car – it has more in common with a 1974 3.0 RSR than it does with its modern Ruf siblings.

Ruf logos appear on the 3400K's rev-counter, steering wheel boss, door panels and aluminium pedals, as well as the door plates, gear knob, floor mats, wheel centres, brake calipers and, of course, on the bonnet. The Rt 12 nose gives it that great big smiling face in the front. The only Ruf ID on the back is the number plate, while a couple of large exhaust pipes reveal it's no ordinary Boxster. Its *raison d'être*? Alois explains:

We wanted to show that, for a budget of €95,000 including VAT you can buy a Ruf car. I don't want to call it entry level – that is a phrase that I don't like; let's say that it is an authentic Ruf, because most people think that they would start at €250,000. And you can give the Turbo drivers a hard time with this car.

True, the supercharger delivers with stunning effect and no lag. The steering feels perfectly balanced as I direct it through Pfaffenhausen's undulating B-road bends. It does everything the Boxster S does, but magnified to the extent that I feel invincible, yet at no time out of control. We shall discover how a turbocharged Boxster feels in Chapter 5 on the 718 models.

ABOVE: **Based on the 987 Boxster S, the Ruf 3400 K is endowed with a supercharger, elevating its performance to 997 Turbo levels.** RUF AUTOMOBILE

LEFT: **Driving the Ruf 3800 S through Pfaffenhausen's undulating B-road bends, the steering feels perfectly balanced, while the supercharger delivers with stunning effect and no lag. Why a German car in right-hand drive? It's bound for Singapore.**
ANTONY FRASER

The Ruf 3800 S is powered by the 400bhp flat-six from the 991 Carrera S, with modified exhaust and electronics. This panning shot shows off the exaggerated air intake slats on either side of the rear wheel arches.
ANTONY FRASER

The 997 Turbo was unveiled at the 2006 Geneva Salon and was in production from 2006 to 2014. This is a Ruf Rt 12 S from 2009, based on the narrow 997 Carrera 2 bodyshell and powered by Ruf's interpretation of the 997 Turbo's 3.6- or 3.8-litre flat-six engine.

ANTONY FRASER

CHAPTER THREE

THE 997 TURBO

ABOVE: **The upper section of the split rear spoiler elevates at 120km/h (75mph) and retracts at 60km/h (37mph).**
ANTONY FRASER

BELOW: **Ghosted cutaway illustration of the Gen2 997 Turbo, revealing the innards of the cabin, powertrain and four-wheel driveline, suspension and steering gear.** PORSCHE PHOTO ARCHIVE

Following on from the 996 Turbo, the 997 Turbo was unveiled at the 2006 Geneva Salon, and was in production from 2006 for the 2007 model year to 2014, when it was superseded by the 991. Stylistically, it differs from the preceding 996 in having conventional ovoid headlights instead of the 'fried egg' look, and features LED indicator strips in the new front panel's air intakes, while fog lamps relocate to the outer ends of the panel. The trademark air vents in the leading and trailing edges of the rear flanks are also different, while the retractable rear wing functions on similar lines to the 996 version.

The powerplant is the 3.6-litre 'Mezger' flat-six that employs the casings of the GT1 racing car, developing 480bhp though its twin Borg-Warner VTG turbos that deploy Variable Vane Technology to reduce lag under boost. If more woosh were needed, the Sport Chrono option overrides boost control to provide more torque over a short 10sec period and a narrow rev range. The second generation also ushered in revised 'torque vectoring', meaning the differential dispenses varying amounts of power to the driven wheels according to road and weather

ABOVE: **The internal components of the 997 Turbo engine are discernible within this cutaway rendering of the flat-six power unit, with turbochargers and intercoolers below on each side.** PORSCHE PHOTO ARCHIVE

RIGHT: **A nocturnal cockpit shot of the 997 Turbo Cabriolet against a backdrop of the mighty Falkirk Wheel on the Forth and Clyde Canal.** ANTONY FRASER

conditions. Even the 997 Turbo Cabriolet can perform at this level, in spite of its frivolous canopy, as snapper Fraser and I found when travelling to Bavaria once: we could hold an almost normal 'pop quiz' at 274km/h (170mph) on the autobahn. The inexorable surge under boost to 319km/h (198mph) is sublime. It rushes from 0 to 100km/h in 3.7sec too.

In some ways the 997 Turbo isn't so very different from its siblings. There's always been a homogeneity about Porsche cockpits, and the 997 Turbo is no exception, being agreeably familiar with a dash that's recognizably akin to the Boxster's, and compared with classic models, it seems like the gauges and controls have been rationalized and simplified for the twenty-first century. The 997 Turbo has a more modern steering wheel with the shifter paddles on the two upper arms of the wheel, and electric seat adjustment makes it very easy to find a nice travelling position. In sports damper setting the ride is too harsh for country roads, though the sports exhaust is fun to play with in a context where you can hear it.

FIRST-GENERATION 997 TURBO

The 997 Turbo was built on the wider-hipped C4S bodyshell, with some 20 per cent comprised of aluminium, including the doors and engine lid, leading to a weight saving over the outgoing 996 Turbo. It was underpinned by high-strength and super-high-strength grades of steel in crucial areas, and backed by a ten-year anti-corrosion guarantee. There were subtle visual distinctions too. The rear wings were 22mm (0.85in) wider and the valances were revised, the rear incorporating new exhaust outlets and a horizontal bar at the front containing the now obligatory LEDs, as well as reducing lift by redirecting airflow. The 997 Turbo also featured a new front bumper and air dam pierced by three substantial air intakes, and a split rear spoiler whose upper section elevated at 120km/h (75mph) and retracted at 60km/h (37mph). The front end was also endowed with bi-xenon headlights, along with LED daytime running lights housed in the outer air intakes.

ABOVE LEFT: **The 997 Turbo Cabriolet roof takes 12 seconds to retract and erect, and it can also be operated at speeds of up to 50km/h (30mph). Bizarrely, the author gives it a go in the Scottish Borders – in the depths of winter.** ANTONY FRASER

ABOVE RIGHT: **So, in the depths of winter when it's cold and snowy, the only option is to drive the 997 Turbo Cabriolet with the top down. Obviously, the heater is very effective!** ANTONY FRASER

RIGHT: **The 997 Turbo has a more modern steering wheel with the shifter paddles on the two upper arms of the wheel, while electric seat adjustment makes it very easy to find a nice travelling position.** ANTONY FRASER

The Cabriolet model was introduced in 2007, costing £106,000, an increase of £8,300 over the Coupé, though performance and dynamics were virtually the same. The Turbo Cabriolet was just 70kg (154lb) heavier than the closed car 90kg (198lb) in Tiptronic format, but still lighter than the 996 version – while the aerodynamics remained the same with the canopy erect, at cd0.31. The soft-top itself could be raised or lowered electrically in twenty seconds too.

The 997 Turbo flat-six was, essentially, the same as the 996 Turbo motor with the addition of two Variable Turbine Geometry (VTG) blowers. These electronically controlled blow-ers enabled a power delivery amounting to 620Nm (457lb ft) of torque over a broad rev range, from 1,950 to 5,000rpm. Consisting of a light alloy crankcase and Nikasil-coated cylinder bores, it incorporated lightweight aluminium pistons and forged con rods, with two chain-driven camshafts per bank, employing VarioCam Plus variable valve timing. It also featured dual-valve springs and hydraulic tappets, while the dry-sump lubrication system was actuated by nine pumps. The Bosch ME 7.8.1 engine management system included cylinder knock-control to prevent damaging pre-ignition, while the Sport Chrono Package provided ten seconds-worth of overboost and additional torque.

Power output was 480bhp, enabling the 997 Turbo to reach 100km/h in 3.9sec in Tiptronic mode, and 0.3sec quicker in manual trim, topping out at 311km/h (193mph). Transmission was via a six-speed manual gearbox or five-speed Tiptronic S automatic, with steering wheel-mounted shift buttons, and shift patterns that adapted to driving style, road conditions and available grip. The manual was fitted with a dual-mass flywheel, while both transmissions drove through a four-wheel-drive system. The viscous coupling of the 996 Turbo was replaced by a faster-acting, electronically controlled clutch, supported by Porsche Traction Management (PTM), Automatic Brake Differential (ABD), and Porsche Stability Management (PSM).

997 TURBO GENERATION I (2006–2009)

Layout and chassis
Two-plus-two coupé and cabriolet, unit-construction steel body/chassis

Engine

Type	M96/72 'Mezger' dry sump, horizontally opposed, rear-mounted 6-cylinder
Block material	Aluminium
Head material	Aluminium
Cylinders	6
Cooling	Water-cooled
Bore and stroke	100 × 76.4
Capacity	3600cc
Valves	4 valves per cylinder
Compression ratio	9.4:1
Fuel system	Multi-point injection; two Borg-Warner VTG turbochargers
Max. power (DIN)	480bhp at 6,000rpm
Max. torque	295lb ft at 4,600rpm
Fuel capacity	67ltr (14.7gal)

Transmission

Gearbox	Getrag G97/00 rear drive, 6-speed; all-wheel drive
Clutch	Hydraulic multi-plate
Ratios	1st 3.91
	2nd 2.32
	3rd 1.61
	4th 1.28
	5th 1.08
	6th 0.88
	Reverse 3.44
Final drive	3.89

Suspension and Steering

Front	Independent suspension with MacPherson struts, aluminium links, longitudinal and transverse links, coil springs, gas dampers, anti-roll bar
Rear	Independent suspension with MacPherson struts, aluminium links, lateral and transverse links, coil springs, gas dampers, anti-roll bar
Steering	Rack and pinion
Tyres	235/35R × ZR19 front, 295/30ZR × ZR19 rear
Wheels	19in aluminium alloy
Rim width	8.5 J front, 11.5 J rear

Brakes

Type	Front and rear vented discs with six-piston calipers front and four-piston calipers rear; optional M450 ceramic discs
Size	330mm × 24mm front, 330mm × 20mm rear

Dimensions

Track	1,465mm (57.7in) front, 1,500mm (59in) rear
Wheelbase	2,350mm (92.5in)
Overall length	4,450mm (175.1in)
Overall width	1,852mm (72.9in)
Overall height	1,300mm (51.2in)
Unladen weight	1,660kg (3,659lb)

Performance

Top speed	310km/h (193mph)
0–60mph	4.7sec

The 997 family suspension consisted of MacPherson struts at the front, incorporating ducts feeding cooling air to the brakes, and the multi-link LSA (light, stable, agile) layout at the rear. Most components were in aluminium, and Porsche Active Stability Management (PASM) was standard, with selectable Normal or Sport modes. Analysing inputs from a host of sensors that monitored lateral and longitudinal loads, throttle, brake and steering inputs, the system continuously adjusted the dampers at all four corners. It was considerably more complex than the 996, but it did seal the 997's reputation as a dynamic but secure-handling 911, no matter what the road conditions were like, or how adept the driver. The steering consisted of a variable-ratio, hydraulically assisted rack, while the brakes were 330mm vented and cross-drilled discs, actuated by six-piston monobloc alloy calipers at the front and four-piston calipers at the rear, allied to the latest Bosch ABS 8.0 anti-lock system.

SECOND-GENERATION 997 TURBO

In 2009, the 997 Turbo received a makeover, including cosmetic improvements and new LED tail lights. Engine capacity rose to 3.8 litres, taking power up to 500bhp and 650Nm (479lb ft) of torque, slicing half a second from the 0–100km/h dash, and lifting top speed to 312km/h (194mph). Porsche also claimed reductions in fuel consumption and CO_2 emissions. The new engine introduced a radical reform. There had been no 997 Turbo 'S' version until the arrival of this revised model. The Mezger engine, which had powered the 911 Turbo for thirty-four years, was replaced by a totally new direct-injection unit. While traditional injection mixes the fuel and air in the manifold before it's sucked into the combustion chambers, direct injection, which is derived from diesel engine technology, squirts the fuel directly into the cylinders at very high pressure,

The 997 Turbo Cabriolet is equipped with Porsche Active Stability Management (PASM) as standard, continuously adjusting the dampers to ensure secure handling and traction, no matter what the road conditions, as here in the Scottish Borders.

ANTONY FRASER

A special edition 997 Turbo parked in the Porsche Museum underground carpark, bearing the legend 'Edition 918 Spyder' with lime green detailing. Like other short-run commemorative models – the Boxster 987 RS60, for instance - in this case, 918 units celebrating the 918 Hybrid were completed in 2012.

JOHNNY TIPLER

ABOVE LEFT: **The 997 Turbo incorporates a new front bumper and air dam, pierced by three substantial air intakes, with split rear spoiler whose upper section elevates at 75mph and retracts (when decelerating) at 37mph. It has updated fog lamps, and employs two Borg-Warner VTG turbos. It is equipped with bi-xenon headlights and LED daytime running lights placed in the outer air intakes.** PORSCHE PHOTO ARCHIVE

ABOVE RIGHT: **The 997 Turbo was created using the wider-hipped 997 C4S bodyshell, with 22mm wider rear wings. Doors and engine lid were aluminium, and it was underpinned by high-strength grades of steel in crucial areas, and backed by a ten-year anti-corrosion guarantee. This is a Gen1 model from 2006, evidenced by the fuller sweep of the rear-light clusters.** JOHNNY TIPLER

eliminating loss and providing better control of the mixture, with attendant benefits to power and economy.

One of the refinements of the previous 996 Turbo was the Tiptronic gearbox, an important option on such a sophisticated GT car; by 2000, Porsche was confident that the Tiptronic would cope with the Turbo's torque, and it proved a particularly successful combination. Technology moved on, and the automatic 997 Turbo was fitted with the PDK gearbox, offering the

same levels of refinement as the Tiptronic, and quicker launch than the six-speed manual. The 997 Turbo S was the first 911 to be offered without a manual option. Porsche claimed that the majority of sales would be of the PDK variety, so it was not worth upgrading the six-speed manual gearbox to handle the 700Nm (516lb ft) torque produced by the S variant.

So it was that a seven-speed PDK transmission replaced the Tiptronic unit, ushering in paddle shifters and launch control,

The Gen2 997 Turbo was launched in 2009, and could be specified with manual transmission enabling 0–100km/h in 3.7 sec, or PDK transmission, taking 3.4 sec. Gen2 Turbos are powered by 3.8-litre flat-sixes. Most notably, their LED rear-lights have a sharper profile, they have larger rear exhaust tailpipes, and they run on redesigned 19-inch wheels, On the road, the biggest difference between Gen1 and Gen2 is ride quality, probably attributable to PDDC (Porsche Dynamic Chassis Control) and ceramic brakes.
PORSCHE PHOTO ARCHIVE

There are few sights more purposeful – aside from a race car – than a Gen1 997 Turbo on a determined blast on an empty moorland B-road.
ANTONY FRASER

Inside the carnival cockpit of the 997 GT2 RS, the driver quickly discovers there's no PDK option, just a robust, short-throw manual shifter. The fixed buckets are identical to those in the GT3 RSs, while the dash is plain 997. Acoustically, there's far less induction noise than apparent in normally aspirated 997s.
ANTONY FRASER

and a steering wheel display when incorporating the Sport Chrono Package. After launching the Gen2 997 Turbo in September 2009, Porsche finally unveiled the 997 Turbo S at the 2010 Geneva Show. As with the 993 and 996 Turbo S models, it offered more power and torque than the base Turbo, with 526bhp instead of 500bhp, and 700Nm (516lb ft) rather than 650Nm (479lb ft) torque.

In addition to PSM and PASM (Porsche Active Suspension Management), which lowers the suspension by 20mm (0.75in) and firms up the damping, the Turbo S also employed Porsche Torque Vectoring, as well as the mysteriously named Sport Chrono. Of all the options, the Sport Chrono is one of the most useful: the accompanying Sport button remaps the engine to give a more aggressive response. In the case of the PDK-equipped Turbo S, Sport Chrono holds the lower ratios longer and controls the turbo's overboost facility. It also controls the adjustable engine mounts: in a new development, Porsche's

Dynamic Engine Mounts are fluid-filled rather than the regular solid bushes. As such, they remain pliable when refinement is required, but they harden when commanded by the Sport Chrono to enhance stability during cornering. Porsche Torque Vectoring works by applying braking to the inside rear wheel (an intervention mandated by the PSM), and the effect of torque vectoring is to rotate the car into corners, which is particularly reassuring on wet surfaces and, according to Porsche development engineers, makes the 997 handle more like a mid-engined design. With the Sport Chrono button on, and backed up by the standard mechanical limited-slip differential, which allows earlier application of throttle, the Turbo S can be made to corner at quite incredible speeds, allied with Porsche's standard-fit ceramic PCCB brakes and six-piston aluminium calipers at the front and four at the back.

Putting all this into practice, I'll recount a few tales from behind the wheel of assorted 997 Turbos.

The 997 GT2 RS was priced at £164,107, and with 611bhp and 700Nm (516lb ft) of torque, it was the fastest 911 ever. The driver here at Porsche GB's Silverstone test track is erstwhile journalist and racer Tony Dron.
ANTONY FRASER

Aerodynamically, the 997 GT2 RS is similar to the GT2, with a new splitter and rear diffuser plus additional Gurney on the rear wing, creating almost as much downforce as the GT3 RS. The front wings are new one-piece items, instead of the GT3 RS's extensions, and use of carbon and plastic rear and side windows shaves 70kg (154lb) off the previous GT2. ANTONY FRASER

NORTHERN EXPOSURE

Classic rallying? This event was closer to home than the Monte Carlo Historique, which, as I've said, I love to cover on an annual basis. The Roger Albert Clark Rally is the classic rendition of the former RAC Rally, named for the doyen of 1970s rallying, attracting diehard fans to the northern wastes to relive the epics of yesteryear. Would the classic Porsche 911s trouble the multitudinous Escorts? In 2011, Antony Fraser and I braved the blizzards to find out.

Driving or navigating on a rally is one thing; spectating is another. If the boredom of the wait doesn't get you, exposure to the chill night air surely will. It's only early December, yet as I loiter by the impenetrable conifers, pining for a log fire, I don't care if I never see another Christmas tree. To be fair, the camaraderie among marshals attending the corners is energizing, like being with your pals in the trenches: it's muddy and cold and precarious. On several stages we while away interludes between cars with banter about competing crews, and when cars visit the scenery it's all hands on deck as they push them back on track.

All rally fans are petrolheads and well up with the latest as well as historical info. The Roger Albert, as they call this event, was founded in 2004 and is named after Roger Clark, with his conveniently coincidental initials, the first Brit to win the WRC event back in 1972. For two-wheel-drive cars only, the RAC is the spiritual successor to the national event dating from 1932, which, after several variations, including the Network Q and Lombard RAC Rally, became the Wales Rally GB in 2003. Gravel tracks through Forestry Commission plantations were introduced in 1961, stamping the character of the event ever since, with 'stately home' spectator stages from 1971.

Antony and I have been let loose in a Porsche 997 Turbo by Porsche GB's press office. First docking station for the red rocketship in our complex itinerary of special stages is Duncombe Park on the outskirts of Helmsley, 40km (25 miles) north of York. We sign on in the scrutineering marquee and scour the paddock for Porsches, while two big tractors harnessed together like plough horses struggle to extract service vans from the quagmire. There are three 911s in the main event – out of forty-six entries – and a single 964 in the RAC Open, one of five smaller piggyback rallies. A quartet of Saab

96s, an Ascona, a Sunbeam Lotus, a Fulvia HF and a Stratos provide diversions from the ubiquitous Escort Mk2 1800s, while drivers to watch include 1996 British Rally Champion Gwyndaf Evans and co-driver John Millington (Escort), Phil Collins and Nicky Grist (Ascona), and previous winners Stefaan Stouf and Joris Erard (Escort). Dark horse is Guy Smith, 2003 Le Mans winner and 2011 ALMS Champ, driving a 2.0-litre Mk1 Escort with Patrick Walsh.

The favourite contender amongst our Porsche 911 contingent to challenge the Escorts on the leader board is ebullient Tim Mason: '*Motoring News* predicts we'll get a podium finish but that depends on whether I crash or not!' Tim's had a few offs on this event in the past:

> *We rolled it a couple of years ago on the last morning – we were fourth at the time with two stages to go. It was a full 360-degree job. I knew we were going off and I just shut my eyes. We landed in the ditch where there were tree stumps, rocks and boulders and we managed to find a gap!*

Tim gives us the lowdown on the car: 'It's a 3.0-litre RS on carburettors rather than fuel injection, on a Motorsport gear-box, built by Strasse, with Bilstein suspension. The bodyshell was done by PrepFab.' Tim and Graham Wild won the Malton Rally outright a couple of weeks ahead of the RAC. They're boasting new sponsors too: 'Hot Turtle are a greetings card company – they financed the whole event for us – and Pirelli's worked with us on the last couple of events.' So far, so good. But the car is in its sixth season and Tim predicts this will be its last outing. A new car is in build for next season, 'a fresh 3.0-litre,' he says.

> The bodyshell is done and the assembly process will have a lot of Porsche Strasse influence in it. The car that we've got now has been such a work in progress that we'll probably put the best bits into the new car. Obviously, there's a lot of life left in the old car, but to keep running at the front end you've got to be on top of things like the gearbox, engine, bodyshell; it's continual maintenance really.

An interesting prognosis, as things turned out.

The white 911 with its ducktail looks like an RS, but driver Peter McDowell reveals it's a 1982 SC with a 3.0-litre Supertec engine.

> A guy in the States builds them. I've been running it for five years without any problem. They are 260bhp, torquey, bulletproof engines, and you can't argue with that unless you've got the budget to go to Francis Tuthill – when we were talking about this car it would have cost about £100 grand, but if you want to win the Safari you've got to take one of his cars.

Peter and navigator Matt Utting have done most of the 2011 historic rally championship. 'When they cancelled the Isle of Man we were looking for something to do in the winter. I thought the RAC might be too long for us because we are getting on in years!' Nick Moss of Early 911 takes care of them at service halts.

Nothing is quite what it seems: the Martini-striped 2.7 RS lookalike turns out to be an SC, according to its Belgium-based driver Lionel Hansen. 'It's running a 3.0-litre engine from an SC and a 915 gearbox,' he reveals; 'it's a completely new car, set up for this season's gravel and snow rallies.' He's aiming high: after the RAC he plans to do the 2012 Historic Monte Carlo, Neige-et-Glas and Boucles-de-Spa, all of which demand thermals. This former Renault Sport and Peugeot Sport engineer cut his teeth on modern rally cars and began building classic 911 competition cars five years ago. 'This is my first gravel car,' he says. 'Previously I've built ten 911 racing cars, including two for Kronos Racing on the East African Safari Rally, and a 911 SC RS and an RSR for circuit racing.' While Tim Mason and Peter McDowell have service crews fettling their cars at the designated service halts, Lionel and do-driver Johan Jalet are self-sufficient: 'It's a funny game without a service truck. We can only check the oil and change the tyres like they did twenty-five years ago.'

Running in the Open class, the 964 is crewed by David Rawlings and Philip Weston: 'We bought it as a write-off six years ago and it's taken us that long to get to this stage,' David says. 'Even the suspension's quite standard, though anything rough and we struggle. It's still got its G50 gearbox but it has a 3.2 engine. They won't let us in with a 3.6, 3.5 is the maximum.'

There's a general northwesterly progression to the Roger Albert. Out in Dalby Forest Woodyard on Friday evening, there's that heightened sense of anticipation waiting for the cars to come by in the dark. You hear the distant sound of the engine, then way off you spot the headlights coming spookily through the fir trees. Then the marshal's whistle blows, alerting the 200 or so spectators flanking the stage, and a battery of lights cleaves the darkness. The engines are silenced so you don't really hear them ripping through the forest: it's more of a visual thing – the eerie glow as they emerge through the trees. Then there's a warbling blare of noise as the transmission fights the bumps, and they're gone. I shuffle through the hummocks and tussocks after a fresh viewpoint. Minutes later the cars flash by again over to my right on the return leg of the stage. A couple of spinners, and two more almost come off on the corner, livening things up as we jump behind the straw bale wall. It's a debacle for Tim Mason, whose 911's transmission fails and then it blows a head-gasket. Cue our torch-lit exit. We thaw out with a curry in Pickering and take sanctuary at the Mallyan Spout hotel, Goathland, the picturesque setting for TV's *Heartbeat*.

On Saturday morning it's the Langdale and Gale Rigg woodland stages up on the North York Moors. We position ourselves on a corner where there happens to be a tyre-swallowing pothole, out of which anything on a tight line travelling at a decent speed gets its front wheels airborne. Then the retinue returns to Duncombe Park for service and a short, sharp concrete stage on farm roads overlooking the Georgian pile and the ruins of Helmsley Castle. By teatime we're in the service paddock beside Croft Autodrome for the night-time circuit races. Cars are flagged away every 60 seconds, but the nature of the 'stage' means there are often two or three on track at once, and with

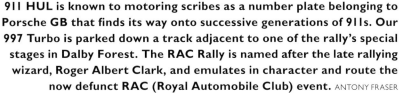

911 HUL is known to motoring scribes as a number plate belonging to Porsche GB that finds its way onto successive generations of 911s. Our 997 Turbo is parked down a track adjacent to one of the rally's special stages in Dalby Forest. The RAC Rally is named after the late rallying wizard, Roger Albert Clark, and emulates in character and route the now defunct RAC (Royal Automobile Club) event. ANTONY FRASER

Road signage in Kershope Forest takes on a different aspect when it comes to protecting local wildlife. ANTONY FRASER

the final bend split in two there's a Race of Champions flavour about the run to the finish, though the innermost car carries on for another lap. Those Escorts look amazingly fast, and their speed is emphasized as headlights draw away from slower cars. Aerodrome circuits are notoriously desolate, and in that respect, Croft is just a little bit closer to Siberia than other wind-chilled icehouses like Snetterton.

Dumfriesshire in the western Scottish Borders is the designated territory for Sunday's action. Hard-bitten (frost-bitten?) fans trudge out into desolate Twiglees forest on Eskdalemuir in the teeth of a blizzard, with visibility down to 50m. One by one the cars appear, and for a few fleeting seconds it's nirvana. The course car (a V8 Discovery) sweeps the stage, there's the distant sound of a race engine at peak revs, and you strain your ears to detect whether it's a flat-six or not.

Ah, an in-line four: that'll be an Escort. Your ears soon become attuned: the whirring 841CC 3-cylinder two-stroke Saab 96s are unique, a reminder of Erik Carlsson's RAC Rally wins in 1960, 1961 and 1962, while the rasping V4 Fulvia is sharper than the in-line fours. Our principal quarry is the 911s, whose 3.0- and 3.2-litre flat-sixes vary slightly in pitch and tone, but the loudest car of all, the Dino-engined Lancia Stratos, has the most

enduring soundtrack, barking for half a mile down the tracks as Steve Perez jabs the throttle. There's a novelty item too: a Mk1 Escort that plays 'Teddy Bears' Picnic' like an ice cream van.

We hover on the mossy bank between track and trees, vainly trying to exclude the horizontal snow from camera internals. Disaster is narrowly averted when, laden with a long lens in each hand, Antony tumbles into the ditch and I haul him out before inundation can take place. The boot's on the other foot when, five minutes later, I have to escape from a sideways Escort into a bog. Wet feet? I hardly notice the difference! The other snapper hazard is flying gravel: you have to know at what point to turn away from the car, its driver's arms flailing from lock to lock as it hurtles by, peppering you with stones. It's not all glamour, this photo-journalism lark!

Next stop is Heathhall near Dumfries, a mud bath of forest tracks with a full-on water-splash as its centrepiece. Only the long-lens wimps stand on the bank: we get as close to the trough as possible and receive a thorough drenching. The drivers take the tsunami-style sheep-dip full throttle and, as a consequence, grapple their recalcitrant vehicles through the 190-degree right that follows, opposite locking around the lake. And now the blue 964 succumbs to a misfire.

That night the weather worsens. Several inches of snow have fallen, and our Hadrian's Wall billet is in a whiteout. What of our personal transport in these treacherous conditions? Pulling doughnuts in a Porsche 997 Turbo in a Cumbrian car park playground, buried deep in virgin snow, is just too tempting to resist. Hard left with the wheel, a tug on the handbrake, a boot-full of throttle, and round she goes. On these Border roads, where the temperature is around zero, the 997 Turbo is a model of tenacity, taking every bit of snow, ice and slush in its stride, unperturbed. It's on the case the whole time, and I can feel the PSM electronic traction control modulating where the drive needs to be going, giving minuscule hints as to where it's sending the power. We're on country lanes and 64km/h (40mph) is as fast as it's safe to go, but this is one confidence-inspiring car. Try as we may, it's well-nigh impossible to break the back end away, even with traction control wilfully switched off. It's hard to think of another 320km/h (200mph) sports car that could do this.

The rally's last shot is its most deadly. The Newcastleton stage in the perishing depths of Kershope Forest catches out most, and even Gwyndaf drops to second fastest. Everyone's pace falls in the slushy mire. It's not merely a question of tyre choice – though Lionel, the quickest of the remaining 911s, is excused a gyration as they haven't managed to change tyres at all. Peter McDowell is in a similar predicament: 'We thought our goose was cooked because we didn't have any snow tyres; we should've put them on at service. But, anyway, we didn't go off.'

So much time is lost recovering spinners from the snowdrifts that the second Kershope stage is cancelled to give them time to make the Carlisle city centre finish in daylight. First up with the bubbly is Bob Bean in the Lotus Cortina, winning Historic

Category 1, while Gwyndaf is outright RAC winner, an achievement he celebrates by showering the snappers yet again – this time with champers. 'It's four hard days and three hard nights,' he says. 'You can never relax.' There have been sixteen retirements due to crashes and mechanical issues. As for the 911s, Lionel Hansen finishes eleventh and Peter McDowell comes in fourteenth. 'The car went well,' says Peter, 'and we only had to change the rear brake pads. It's a Porsche, and you expect them to be reliable!'

I've heard it said that competition technology surrounding Ford's classic models has evolved to a greater extent than Porsche's in the forty years since these cars were built: there's more latent potential, perhaps, and since an old Ford is a fraction of the price of an air-cooled 911, the Escort is now omnipresent in historic rallying – though Tim Mason and assorted Tuthill users would doubtless disagree. Most likely, Roger Albert Clark would abstain from such a debate, believing that driver technique is the key. Heading home in a blizzard in our peerless 997 Turbo, I am in awe of Porsche's technical evolution.

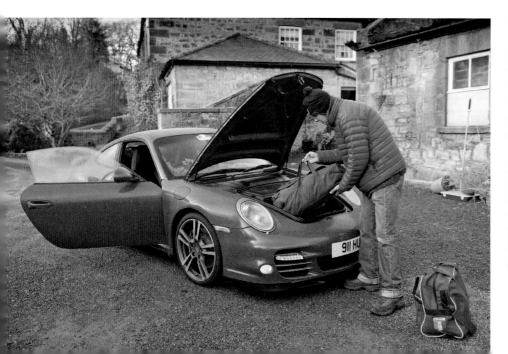

TOP: **On a border road close to Hadrian's Wall, the temperature is around zero, but the 997 Turbo takes the snow, ice and slush in its stride, thanks to its PSM (Porsche Stability Management) electronic traction control modulating where the drive needs to be going.** ANTONY FRASER

LEFT: **It's early December, and we are following the RAC Rally, hence the outdoor gear. Like all water-cooled 911s, the 997 Turbo's front boot provides decent carrying capacity for baggage as well as the snapper's photographic kit.** ANTONY FRASER

WALTER RÖHRL INTERVIEW

Before it's launched, every new Porsche model gets the thumbs-up from two-times former World Rally Champion and racing driver extraordinaire Walter Röhrl. Taking time out with a rare 718/8 sports racer at Austria's Ennstal Classic rally in 2012, the German ace expanded on some of his career highlights.

Johnny Tipler: We saw you travelling sideways in a 911 every lap of the Nordschleife classic marathon at the Old Timer Grand Prix meeting recently, but what turned you on to Porsches in the beginning?

Walter Röhrl: Oh, I have to go right back. When I was ten years old, my older brother was twenty, and he owned a Porsche. It was a 356 SC Super 90. And, of course, on weekends, my parents said, 'You must take your little brother with you.' And so I was in the back of the 356. At this time my brother told me, 'Listen, when you are eighteen years old and you pass your test, wait until you can buy a good car. And the only good car is a Porsche. Forget all the rest.' So, even aged ten, I was Porsche minded. And at twenty I bought a 356 C, and it was my first car. From that time onwards, I've always owned a Porsche, even during all those years when I was driving for Fiat, Lancia, Opel or Audi.

Among the refinements that Porsche's chief test driver Walter Röhrl has been responsible for is servo-assisted steering, which he instigated in 1993; thenceforth all Porsches have been fitted with servo steering.

JOHNNY TIPLER

JT: Your career took off in 1970 with an ex-East African Safari 911S belonging to Jürgen Barth: what was that like to drive?

WR: That was not an easy car to drive. I was using the throttle to steer the car. There's a lot of understeer, so you just have to lift off in the corner and if it's in the right position it turns in, and then you have to be on the throttle.

JT: During the 1970s you drove for Ford, Fiat, Lancia, Opel and Audi, so when did you next compete in a Porsche?

WR: I had a contract with Mercedes for 1981, but before the year started they closed their sports department. All of a sudden, I had a contract but no car. Then Porsche said, 'Now we are able to help you: you have the money from Mercedes, you can have the car from us!' So, I drove a 924 GTP prototype with Jürgen Barth at Le Mans and finished seventh. I won the 1,000km at Silverstone with Reinhold Jöst's 935, and also did the Nürburgring 1,000km with that car. I did the German Rally Championship in a Porsche 924 GTS and won six rounds, and at the end of the year I did the San Remo round of the World Rally Championship with a 911SC.

JT: When did you first start actually working for Porsche?

WR: In 1992 I finished my work with Audi, and the next day Porsche were phoning and said, 'Listen, is it true that you stopped with Audi?'

'Yeah, yeah,' I said.

'Well, tomorrow you can start working for us as an official test driver for Porsche,' they said, and that's the reason I have been nearly twenty years with Porsche, and of course over this time I've had fantastic work.

Walter Röhrl slings a 911 sideways during the Nürburgring Old Timer Grand Prix meeting in 2012, a feat he performed on these Nordschleife bends on every lap. On this occasion he was only beaten by Jochen Mass driving a Ford GT40, which had the legs on the straight.

JOHNNY TIPLER

(continued overleaf)

WALTER RÖHRL INTERVIEW (continued)

JT: Four years ago, you drove me up a country lane near your home in Bavaria in your GT3 RS: do you still have that car? And the 997 Turbo?

WR: Yes!

JT: And your private car is that lovely black 964 RS that you had detailed in orange to match the GT3 RS?

WR: The 964 RS is the only private car that I own; I bought it in September 2006. Before that I had a 3.2 Carrera, but I was always looking for a special car, maybe a 1989 Speedster. That's quite nice: the 3.2-litre engine is the best that Porsche ever made, in my opinion. The 964 RS is good value too, compared with the 1973 2.7 RS, which is so expensive that nobody can afford it, and even the 993 RS is quite expensive. At first people didn't like the 964 RS, because it was like a standard car with no special spoiler. In the beginning the price was OK, but as time went by that also rose. In 2006, I rang all the Porsche centres in Bavaria and said, 'Look, if you hear something about a 964 RS, tell me.' Then, amazingly, 80km (50 miles) from my home town they found this car. It had never been on a racetrack, just twiddling around.

JT: When do you use it?

WR: I only use it for fun, about three times a year with my wife. I'm completely crazy about cars, and if it's raining, or there are too many flies around, I don't bring it out. Most people don't mind driving on gravel occasionally, but with the 964 I go round every stony patch. Originally, I thought about how I could improve it, but apart from new Bilsteins it's absolutely standard; I have not touched the roll bars – they are in the middle position and it's OK like this. I have a second set of tyres too – narrower Pirelli Corsas. If I wanted to corner faster, tenths of seconds quicker, then maybe I would change the roll bars.

JT: Which other Porsche models have you owned?

WR: I've had a 356 Speedster, a 3.0 Carrera, a 3.0-litre Turbo, a 964 C4, and in 1987 a 959; I was doing prototype testing for Porsche although I was still contracted to Audi, and Professor Bott had one of the 959 prototypes rebuilt for me so I could buy it cheaply. I sold it in 2000 because it needed a lot of maintenance and I wasn't using it more than once a year.

JT: What kind of event would you take the GT3 RS on?

WR: I drive it to Nürburgring for my testing job.

JT: What was the most demanding Porsche you developed?

WR: I spent four years (2004–2008) on the development of the Carrera GT. Normally I come to the Nordschleife every three months to test the prototypes, and if I think there's no

At the 1981 Le Mans 24-Hours: Jürgen Barth and Walter Röhrl drove their 924 GTP to seventh overall, and third in class. They covered 4,404.59km (2,736.88 miles) at an average speed of 185.52km/h (114.03mph). PORSCHE PHOTO ARCHIVE

Walter Röhrl was World Rally Champion in 1980 and 1982, and here he tells Johnny Tipler about some of the Porsches he owns, past and present. JOHNNY TIPLER

more room for development (in a road-car context), I make a final test, and I say, 'OK, you can start with the production of this model now.' But with the Carrera GT I did all the test driving from the first day until the last. Of course, it was very interesting. The problem was that the Carrera GT is basically a race car, and we had to make it into something that normal people could use. But you should not kill it completely; it should still give the impression that it is a race car. It's very difficult to find the right compromise between the race car and the everyday car. But I think finally it's OK, because if somebody pushes it, there is traction control. I was always more involved with the development of very sporty cars like the GT2 Turbo and GT3 RS. With the normal Boxster and Cayman, in two years I came just four times and drove the car until I could say, 'it's OK'.

JT: How dangerous is it, being a test driver?

WR: Well, for example, I was in Nürburgring to make the final tests on the current GT2, and on the final test it's always very important to have a good (lap) time to tell the engineers. Then they know exactly if it is faster or not. It's called 'industry week' and it's always on the new Ring, with firms like BMW, Conti and Pirelli. All the test drivers are buddies, everybody knows each other, and these guys are so fast that you don't have problems. I did my fast lap at 7min 29sec, even with the tyres done, and I passed eleven cars. Because you're going so fast they don't see you coming, and that's dangerous. You go 310km/h (193mph) and you've got to look out… and there was this lady in an Audi A3, and she was not watching, and I passed her at 310km/h, and she was all over the place. After that test drive I told Porsche, 'It's finished with these fast cars on here: either you have a closed road

As Porsche's chief test driver, Walter Röhrl is responsible for fine-tuning the prototype of every car the firm makes. This is mainly done by driving them on the Nürburgring Nordschleife, and when he thinks there's no more room for development he declares them to be ready to go into production.

JOHNNY TIPLER

or I don't do it; it's too dangerous now.' But, even so, I'm still testing cars on the Nordschleife. (Directly after Ennstal, Walter went to the Ring to spend a week driving Porsche prototypes.)

JT: How far will a car have travelled in the development process before you get involved?

WR: The first time I see the car, I would say 85 per cent of the basic setting up is done. Because they know which springs to use, and the weight of the car, it's just the small things that need fine-tuning. Then maybe I say, 'You could use harder springs, you can use stiffer roll bars; we can change something on the shock absorbers, we should try to get better response from the engine, the brakes have too much bias to the front, the car is rolling too much'… things like that. With standard cars like the GT3 it is always the small changes that make the difference, like harder springs. If you are really hard on the brakes you sometimes have the feeling that the car is not exactly following the steering – you notice it is pulling to one side, because obviously something geometric is moving. Then they change things like this, very slightly. Normal people never reach this level of driving. But there is one very important thing Porsche are doing: we are really trying to make the car drive up to the limit, 100 per cent. It's a fine line: if I go 8min 0.02sec at Nürburgring, the car is probably perfect. But if I go 7min 59sec, suddenly the same car is beyond the limit. That's a big advantage for Porsche: that we are able to find the limit and make it drive up to that point.

The face that launched a thousand Porsches: Walter Röhrl puts a 997 Turbo through its paces. Since this is a finished article, he has obviously signed it off already.

PORSCHE PHOTO ARCHIVE

(continued overleaf)

WALTER RÖHRL INTERVIEW *(continued from previous page)*

JT: What's the most significant innovation you've made?

WR: In 1993, I said we need servo steering: there was no servo until then. We tried it at the Nürburgring with a 3.8 litre RS, with and without servo. Immediately I was 1.5sec quicker on the new circuit with servo steering because it was so much easier to control. So, from the 993 onwards all Porsches had servo steering. The four-wheel-drive system changed too from the 964 Carrera 4 to the 993. I was in the winter-time Arctic testing cycle, and although I was a bit faster with the old system, our regular test drivers were much faster with the new one. So even though we had less good traction we had much better handling. That was the biggest thing I brought in.

JT: In 1990 Porsche made a Tiptronic 964 racer for the Carrera Cup and you drove it at the Nürburgring. Did the four-speed semi-automatic shift work in a racing context?

WR: Weissach built fifty Carrera Cup 964s for the original series, and fitted one car with the brand new Tiptronic semi-auto

Walter Röhrl cornering the Porsche 718/8 RS Spyder provided by the factory museum through the streets of Gröbming during the Ennstal Classic Rally in 2012. Back in the day, this 2.0-litre flat-eight-powered 718/8 scored class wins in the 1962 Targa Florio (Nino Vaccarella/Jo Bonnier) and Nürburgring 1,000km (Graham Hill/Hans Herrmann), going on to win the 1963 and 1964 European Hill Climb Championship in the hands of Edgar Barth (father of Jürgen). JOHNNY TIPLER

transmission. I drove it in round 7 on the combined Nürburgring F1 circuit and the Nordschleife, starting from sixth on the grid. I thought at the time, 'This is good, it is easy, I cannot over-rev the engine: this is the future of road cars, given the intensification of traffic; it's the future of gearbox technology.' But in fact, it was very hard for me in the race because I had only three useable gears, as the first one is too short. I could manage to compensate on a circuit like the Nordschleife, but I was 7 seconds slower than the best Carrera Cup lap time. During practice I was alone so I could carry the speed into corners, but in the race the other cars slowed me down, so after the corners I had no momentum, because with one gear less the jump in engine revs was too big.

JT: You obviously love racing and rallying classic Porsches, like the 718/8 you were running at the Ennstal Classic.

WR: Yes, I won the first Ennstal Classic twenty years ago in my Austin-Healey 3000 Mk II with my wife co-driving, and then six years later in a 356 Carrera 2 with Peter Falk (Porsche's race director for thirty-four years) as my co-driver. It's become a lot more professional and attracts many more people now. And I won the Targa Tasmania last year with Christian Geistdörfer in a 911 SC. I prefer to drive rallies on fastest times: I don't much like regularities. Back when I was champion we drove everything as fast as we could, flat out.

JT: You scored fourteen WRC victories as well as two World crowns: what's your favourite rally car?

WR: I drove the 1981 San Remo Rally with a works 911SC, entered by Alméras with my regular co-driver Christian Geistdörfer. Even today I'm sad I didn't win, as I was uncatchable; even on gravel the car was fantastic – 1 minute ahead of the Audis. But again, I retired on the last stage with a broken half-shaft. That was my dream car. It was always more interesting to be driving a car which was not the big favourite. That way the driver can make the car. That was the motivation for me. The Ascona was a good car, but if I have to pick my favourite rally car I would say my 911SC from San Remo. My preference for light cars is well known. That is the reason the 911 is so fantastic and, if it's raining, the 911 is so easy to handle.

I've interviewed Walter several times, including one time when we visited his home and he memorably rushed me up his local hill roads in his black-and-orange GT3 RS. There was a white 991 Turbo in the garage: pity we didn't ask him to get that out under the circumstances.

THE RUF CTR-3

In 2011, Alois Ruf wowed us with an exclusive first drive in his masterpiece, the 633bhp CTR-3. We'd seen the prototype run up the hill at Goodwood, drooled over its magnificent curves, and now the production car was a reality. The mid-engined Ruf CTR-3 coupé is nothing less than a supercar, delivering on several different levels. Performance-wise it lacks nothing, it's stylistically unique, and its mid-engined chassis provides a motoring experience par excellence.

Alois Ruf's third iteration of the CTR (Carrera Turbo Ruf) is a steroidally fast mid-engined coupé. As you've already read, the original CTR was the famed 343km/h (213mph) Yellowbird 911 that outran allcomers in a 1987 showdown, superseded in 1996 by the 993-shaped twin-turbo CTR-2. 'Now,' Alois declared, 'we are going more into the depths of Ruf engineering, showcasing what we are capable of doing. The CTR-3 has features like ceramic brakes and centre-lock wheel system, which the connoisseur will appreciate.'

Aesthetically, it's a succession of treats. From the gladiatorial stance, fostered by its low ride height and helmet-like engine cover, to the swelling wheel arches, the CTR-3 is an architectural tour de force. Drive it and the view through a relatively narrow windscreen is of the twin ellipses either side at the front

ABOVE: **The mid-engined Ruf CTR-3 supercar coupé is powered by a water-cooled, KKK-turbocharged 3.8-litre flat-six, based on 997 Turbo casings, with different crankshaft, titanium con rods, barrels, piston sleeves, camshafts and cylinder heads all to Ruf's own design.** ANTONY FRASER

RIGHT: **From the gladiatorial stance fostered by its helmet-like engine cover and Mohawk air intake to the swelling wheel arches, the CTR-3 is an aesthetic tour de force.** ANTONY FRASER

and, in the mirrors, those beautiful spheres over the back wheels. The front wings' greater radii make them slightly more swollen than the standard 997's, while they are perfect orbs over the rear arches.

'Conceptually, it's a modern, more usable GT1,' Ruf asserts; 'a road-worthy race car.' Indeed, comparisons with Porsche's GT1 and the Carrera GT are inevitable, but Alois Ruf is a master and his approach is more subtle than simply to copy obvious precedents. There are plenty of original design cues in the CTR-3, but Ruf also refers way back to the profile of the pre-war, mid-engined Auto Union GP car for a styling influence, and more specifically to the mid-engined Porsche 550 Le Mans coupé of 1953. Like the 1930s GP car, the Ruf has a cab-forward profile. 'I love the shapes of these cars,' says Alois. 'They are a German breed with the DNA from German racing history, and I think this car should reflect that.'

The CTR-3 is not a novel idea; Alois had in mind to do something similar in the mid-1980s, but when Porsche announced the 959 supercar his project was mothballed.

> I still have hidden away somewhere the beginnings of that mock-up. Instead, we did the CTR Yellowbird, which had its own charm, like the removal of the gutters, inch-wider fender flares at the back and a slicker front end. When the second CTR came along we were already showing different aesthetics, and now, with the third generation, we gave the car our own silhouette – and that was my dream, to evolve. So now you could call the car 30 per cent Porsche and 70 per cent Ruf.

That's the nub of it: previous Ruf models were overtly 911, wolves in sheep's clothing. The CTR-3 proclaims its ferocity.

Although the clay buck and original running prototype had a distinctive nose and special light clusters, Ruf took a pragmatic view and used the underpinnings of the 997 front end so he wouldn't have to crash a car to obtain TüV type approval. Alois muses:

> You still see that it is Porsche-derived because of its front and the shape of the doors, but the wings, the silhouette, the roof, the windscreen, all of this is our own. I think we have something unique. You cannot really compare it with anything else out there. You only have to put a Carrera GT next to our car to see the difference. Ruf is a car manufacturer and we want to show what we are capable of doing, externally as well as under the bodywork. That was the idea, to

> bring something to the market where emotions make you want this masterpiece. It's about performance and emotion and the exotic. That is very important, because there are too many wind-tunnel cars nowadays, and they don't stir the emotions any more.

Ruf's brainchild was drawn by stylists Ben Soderberg (twenty-six) and his father Richard. The latter was for thirty years a designer in the Porsche drawing office, so the CTR-3 has an exalted pedigree, too, its form supervised by the man who designed Zuffenhausen icons like the 908/3, 959 and 968. The design was complete by the end of 2005, and the clay model was painted silver on Christmas Day 2006, having been refined in a wind tunnel at Stuttgart. From this buck they assembled the prototype over a six-month period. Much of the R&D and styling was carried out in the laboratory at Ruf's Pfaffenhausen base. A local firm built the carbon chassis, while Ruf technicians assembled suspension and running gear. The prototype CTR-3 that we saw at Goodwood in summer 2008 is also in the workshop. 'We are going to use that car for a couple more tests, then we're going to upgrade it as a production car.'

Ruf employs 'Sideways Stefan' as development driver – that's Stefan Roser, famed for outrageous tyre abuse in the iconic Yellowbird Nürburgring video, which is another neat tie-in with Ruf's past.

> When Sideways Stefan is satisfied, we know it has to be good for everybody, because he is very difficult to please. We were recently celebrating thirty years' friendship, because we actually met through the very first Ruf 911 in 1977. But I also drive the car during development because I want to know what is going on before I sign it off.

As you would expect, the CTR-3 bodywork employs the lightest state-of-the-art materials. Crouching Sphinx-like, with bulbous hindquarters, it sits 120mm (4.7in) lower than a 997, and is a little longer overall. That strange matt paint job enhances the animal enigma – you want to stroke it and feel the surface resist your touch. We tour the body, gently tapping the panels to assess their fabric. The rear wheel arches and the whole of the back envelope are carbon, as are the spoiler and rear wing. The engine lid is carbon and the cabin roof is also carbon. The doors are aluminium and the front bonnet lid is aluminium, but the front wings and the entire front panel are carbon.

The detailing is superb, typical of a Ruf product. Check out the way the oil radiators are directly accessed by the ducting behind the doors, the carbon-fibre door-mirror housings that each contain a side indicator light, and those archetypal Ruf front grilles in the valance segmented by monumentally thick pillars. The sidelight pods contain a small bulb for daylight running and LEDs for the indicators. Alois is proud of the 'dynamic hinge' sited in the rooftop NACA air duct where the roof panel meets the engine lid, allowing combustion air to pass through without impeding the opening mechanism.

I call it the air dynamic hinge because the hinge is in the middle of the airflow. The importance of the air scoop – what we call the Mohawk – is that it picks up and compresses air like a ram-air system and goes straight to the air filter. It's a typical race car feature, but it is also a good styling element.

Those ducts in the engine lid dissipate hot air from the rear brakes, while ovoid exhaust pipes protrude where the bodywork rises over the top of the central licence plate niche, with a diffuser beneath – this is a flat-bottom car, and a certain amount of downforce is thus generated. Above that is an outlet grille, with the rear spoiler and retractable wing on top. The spoiler is a big Gurney flap, housing a central reversing light, with Boxster-derived rear lights on either side. The rear wing elevates when the car reaches 15km/h (9mph) and retracts at 60km/h (37mph) when decelerating, although it can be overridden at the press of a button and, as a further sophistication, the rear-view camera pops back into its niche when you turn off the ignition.

Under the svelte bodywork it's an intriguing cocktail of engineering excellence. The CTR-3 is a chassis of two halves, exactly like the GT1 race car. At 2,624mm (103.3in), the wheelbase is 274mm (10.8in) longer than a 911 and 208mm (8.2in) longer than a Cayman, and it manages to be 127mm (5in) wider than a 911. Aside from Ruf's modifications, it's basically a 997 from the front of the car as far back as the engine bulkhead, then there's a tubular steel subframe that extends

Ruf Automobile hosts track days and tours for clients, owners and associates, one of which was held at Hockenheim Circuit near Mannheim in 2018, where this CTR-3 was in evidence.

JOHNNY TIPLER

within the cockpit to serve as Ruf's trademark integral roll-cage. The engine and gearbox are cradled in the tube frame and mounted directly behind the cockpit. Huge, heavy-duty bracing bars spring from the centre of the machined aluminium cross-member at the rear of the spaceframe and span the upper engine bay for extra torsional rigidity.

The inboard pushrod rear suspension is another engineer's delight, taken straight from racing car practice, beautifully made and well considered. Along with its horizontal shock absorbers, which help reduce unsprung weight, the rear suspension also includes lower wishbones. The front suspension is classic 997, with special dampers and incorporating the hydraulic lifting system that raises the bodywork by 76mm (3in) so it can clear sleeping policemen and ferry-boarding ramps. Whereas it rises gradually, it just drops in one go once the obstruction is cleared.

The liquid-cooled 3.8-litre flat-six is based on the 997 Turbo unit, but all the innards have been completely reworked, to the extent that all that's left of the donor 997 engine is the casings. Alois explains:

> *We use a different crankshaft and titanium con rods, and the barrels, piston sleeves and cylinder heads are a different design. We are also using different camshafts and the air intake system is enlarged: the turbochargers are KKK, though not the VTG (Variable Turbo Geometry) version found in the 997 Turbo. We are using the simple turbo because that is still applicable, and it gives excellent results, with maximum performance and the way the power builds up. We are now*

Like the 911 GT1 race car, the CTR-3 is a chassis of two halves, a 997 from the front as far back as the engine bulkhead, whence a tubular steel subframe cradles the engine and gearbox, while bracing bars spring from the aluminium cross-member at the rear of the spaceframe providing additional torsional rigidity.
JOHNNY TIPLER

> *at 675 horsepower. We don't need the advantages of the VTG for our engine because we already have the perfect ensemble, the optimum match between the size of the turbocharger and engine displacement,*

The CTR-3's inboard pushrod rear suspension is taken straight from racing car practice, along with its horizontal shock absorbers, and the rear suspension also includes lower wishbones. All the rear axle components are located on the machined aluminium subframe that forms the tailpiece of the tubular spaceframe assembly.
ANTONY FRASER

*which means power develops nicely from the low end
with no turbo lag. That's what we are known for.*

For the record, the CTR-3 is said to do 375km/h (233mph)
and make 0–60mph in 3.2sec.

The Ruf-specified six-speed gearbox is a completely new
design, manufactured by German transmission specialist Hor,
which produces gearboxes for the Porsche LMP2 RS Spyder.
'This gearbox is very strong, with big gears, designed for 1100Nm
(811lb ft) of torque – about the strongest you will find in a passenger car and similar to a Bugatti.' In practice, the torque figure
it does handle is 891Nm (657lb ft) at 4,000rpm. 'The gearbox
is transverse, rather than longitudinal, which means we can have
a fully effective uninterrupted diffuser. To make the gearbox
transverse you need a 90-degree drive system off the crank,
which is something else for the connoisseur to appreciate.'

All the rear axle components are taken off the machined
aluminium subframe, which forms the tailpiece of the tubular
spaceframe assembly. To fine-tune the suspension, Ruf called
on Toronto-based MTC Multimatic, which also has a factory
in the UK at Thetford, Norfolk.

*They do a lot of engineering work for the race car
industry and they carried out engineering and dynamic studies with us, specifically new shock absorber
technology and the suspension lifting device that lifts
the front so you can get over the speed bumps. Those
new dampers come strictly from racing, and they have
a certain intelligence: they learn what kind of road you
are on and they adapt mechanically using electronics,
and this is used by many Formula 1 teams now.*

The gargantuan 400mm (16in) cross-drilled carbon-ceramic
brake discs and six-pot calipers are made by Brembo. 'Some
car's wheels aren't even that diameter!' Tyres are Michelin
Pilot Sport, 255/35ZR-19s on the front and 335/30ZR-20s
on the back.

Like all Ruf products, the cabin interior is superbly finished,
clad in a sumptuous blend of suede and its hardwearing Alcantara lookalike. The headlining is thickly quilted Alcantara and
the glovebox door, shift-lever gaiter and centre console are
also swathed thus, while the top of the dashboard is leather-
clad. There are Alcantara door pockets, suede banding on the
Ruf steering wheel, and the carpets rival the headlining for
palatial quilting. The carbon-fibre 935-replica seats with their
distinctive lollipop-shape headrests are upholstered in quilted leather with quilted Alcantara squabs and backrests. Personally, I could do with a bit more support under my thighs,
maybe resolved by tilting the squab a tad more. The dials are
Ruf-badged and the layout is familiar Porsche fare, as is the
switchgear, although a revised instrument cluster unique to
the CTR-3 is in the offing and will eventually replace the one
you see here. The pedals, in drilled aluminium and embossed
with the Ruf logo, provide a finishing touch.

Split Personality

Time to get motoring. The gently undulating farmland round
Pfaffenhausen provides a melange of fast two-lane A-roads,
winding country lanes and a leg of autobahn where the car can
really stretch its legs. The only hazards are the unfathomably
large tractors they use a lot hereabouts. Getting acquainted with

**The Ruf CTR-3 is the closest thing
to a 911 GT1 race car: acceleration
is astronomical in each gear above
4,000rpm, and it dispenses huge
surges of relentless power in
every ratio.** ANTONY FRASER

this Bavarian blockbuster is a steep learning curve. To start with, you're confronted by the man-size sequential gearshift lever. Fortunately, it tells you on the dash what gear you're actually in: back towards you for first, all the way up to sixth, and away from you back down to neutral. Press the knob on the top of the shift and then forward a notch and you're in reverse. You have to be positive about making the shift, otherwise it doesn't engage. Basically, it amounts to two co-ordinated hand movements: you nudge it out of the ratio you're in, and then into the next one.

I'm driving the closest thing to a GT1 race car, and there's no rear screen and, although I still have door mirrors, there's a camera on the engine cover that projects the image onto a TV screen on the dashboard where the sat-nav would be. Effectively, I'm looking at a panorama of the road behind me beyond the rear wing, which is always in shot to tell you where the rear of the car is. You'd get accustomed to this in time, no doubt, but I found myself using the side mirrors more. A further refinement is that warning information is flagged up in the periphery of the rear-view screen.

Once you're away from a standstill and out on the open road, it feels liberated, exulting in the freedom to lash away at the tarmac. It's not too partial to being driven in a low gear and prefers to be running over 3,000rpm. The faster you're going, the better it likes it, though once or twice it was a trifle edgy when a change of tack was mooted during fast cornering. Best let it feel its way through the corner, and once you've set up the line it tracks perfectly. The massive ceramic brakes are superhuman, a giant hand hauling the car inexorably to a virtual standstill when faced, as I was, with the prospect of

oncoming slowcoaches overtaking the ubiquitous mega-tractor. Acceleration is similarly astronomical, like a rocket sled in each gear above 4,000rpm. It dispenses huge surges of relentless power in every ratio and, though I dared not take my eyes off the road, we must have been doing 300km/h (186mph) through some of the long, smooth curves.

It's just an immense car. It makes no secret of its competition stature: you may be cosseted in the cabin, but there's a raw edge to the CTR-3. That's manifest in a pronounced transmission whine like a race car, omnipresent especially at low speeds and when you're accelerating through the gears. Each shift is a physical statement of intent as you work your way up and down the sequential box, juggling your feet with each shift. That demands precision, too, so you must get your foot smartly off the accelerator as you depress the clutch to avoid revs blipping upwards. The temptation is always to drive it very fast, and you could easily get out of shape. It's so powerful you'd be hard pressed to plumb its potential on the road, though on track it would be absolutely awesome. Alois fully intends to institute a Ruf Driving Academy to hone his clients' skills – and maybe even a one-make race series for CTR-3 racers, probably centred on his Dubai base.

There are two facets to the CTR-3's behaviour. There's manic Nordschleife if you want, and there's Grand Corniche. Cruise along at 2,500rpm doing 140km/h (87mph) in fifth gear and it feels very refined, all that latent performance bottled up. I drove it consciously in both modes: as quickly as I thought reasonable with only brief acquaintance of the car, and also as if I was going on a touring holiday with leisurely use of the

The driver's view through the arching curve of the Ruf CTR-3's windscreen: the scenery comes up awfully quickly, though there are two facets to the car's behaviour: manic Nordschleife, and Grand Corniche. ANTONY FRASER

controls – and it's superb at that level as well, with seamless power delivery. It pulls in third from 1,500rpm, and it's extremely well planted to the road, cornering flat through the bends, so you can have a civilized ride in it. If you're relaxed with your sequential shifts and don't try to emulate the rally boys it works very well. If needs must, you could even do the grocery shop, since it has the front luggage space of the regular 997.

Here's the hard part. The CTR-3 will cost you €420,000 without VAT. That's less than half Veyron money, though, and not far off Carrera GT values. The road-going variant of the GT1 is much dearer – DM1.7m in old money, and only twenty-eight street-legal examples were made. 'The CTR-3 is never going to be a big-volume car,' says Alois, although he predicts they'll make between fifteen and twenty units a year out of a total Ruf output of thirty-five cars. 'Each one is built by hand at Pfaffenhausen, so it will always be rare. There's about a year's delivery time.'

The workshops and foundry across the roundabout from Ruf's showroom are full of classic Porsches belonging to Ruf clients in the throes of restoration, and there are another six cars aloft in the garage beside the showroom. Ruf also undertakes conversions on customer cars, which can be as comprehensive as you like: 'You do have an excellent candidate for a Ruf Carrera Turbo – the RCT – based on your own 964,' Alois breezily tells me! I am toast.

At the end of the day, the true test of a car is whether you want one yourself. And I sort of do. But, intriguing as the CTR-3 is, I'm so wedded to the 911 shape that I'd probably take Ruf's Rt 12 – same running gear, equally exotic fabrication, but more familiar lines. Everyone else should sign up for a CTR-3.

THE RUF RT 12 S

Alois Ruf greets us in the hurly-burly of the Supercar paddock at 2008's Goodwood Festival of Speed. He's got the CTR-3 and the electric 997-based Greenster Targa there, and is charged up about his latest hydro-electric power station. But there's something missing: the last word in 911s, the Rt 12 S. 'You must come to Pfaffenhausen and drive it!' he exhorts. A fortnight later we're on the plane to Munich.

The Rt 12 S presents as a ball-breaking uber-Porsche, bent on gobbling up anything short of a Veyron. And in true Ruf tradition, it jolly well can. The difference is that it is just as happy doing the slow-mo pootle. That's the secret of the Rt 12 S: it covers both ends of the performance spectrum, and it's a joy to drive in either mode.

There's a certain mystique about Ruf cars. They go their own way. The 911-shape Rt 12 S shares the same water-cooled flat-six that moves the mid-engined Ruf flagship, the CTR-3, but it comes over as a very different character. All the donor car's standard 997 Turbo internals have been switched for Ruf spec'd items, including crank and titanium con rods. Barrels, sleeves, heads and camshafts are all different, and the twin KKK turbos are a different design to the 997. Only the casings are retained. Ruf's 3.8-litre flat-six is mated to a six-speed close-ratio gearbox with short-throw shift, and produces 685bhp at 7,000rpm and 880Nm (649lb ft) torque at 3,500rpm. Testing at Nardo in southern Italy, it nudged a whopping 361km/h (224.3mph), with 0–60mph coming up in a scant 3.2sec.

The engines are built in the laboratory at the Ruf workshops. There are two dynos, one for engines belonging to classic

THIS PAGE:

The Ruf Rt 12 S is based on a narrow-body 997 bodyshell, produced at Pfaffenhausen with distinctive Ruf front panel, splitter, rear wing and rear wheel arches.

ANTONY FRASER

OPPOSITE PAGE:

LEFT: **The engine bay of the Ruf Rt 12 S, with powerplant topped by cast aluminium intake pipes.** ANTONY FRASER

RIGHT: **Exclusive chassis plate with US Federal bias gives the VIN number of this particular Ruf Rt 12 S, including date of release and recommended tyre pressures.** ANTONY FRASER

Porsches in the throes of restoration, and another for new Ruf development engines. Alois explains:

> We use our own custom pistons, titanium rods and all special parts for the engine because we want to ensure that a car with this power will last just as long as a normal Porsche turbo engine. We achieved that because we've bench-tested it to 300,000km (186,000 miles), no problem. A customer who lives in the next village to Pfaffenhausen and owns a 550bhp 996 R Turbo recently brought it in for a service, and it had done 224,000km (139,000 miles).

When a customer orders a Ruf product, the donor car is bought from the Porsche production line, deconstructed at Ruf's premises and re-created as the relevant Ruf model. There's enough flexibility for the customer to specify certain trim and cosmetic properties. Construction can take several months, depending on the chosen car. Once an engine has been built and tested on the dyno and installed in the car, it doesn't need to be run in because it's already been done on the dyno. After final assembly, each car is taken for a long test drive and for a V-max run on the autobahn.

> Even though all engines are identical, you'll have one car going maybe 358km/h (222mph) and another going 360km/h (224mph). There will always be a very tiny difference, but every car achieves speeds above 358km/h on the V-max drive. That is a benchmark speed. We actually say that the car runs above 350km/h because we can't say the top speed is exactly 361km/h or 362km/h, because there'll be that difference.

The gearbox is also assembled in house, based on the Porsche transmission with a stronger clutch. 'The transmission is also reinforced – you cannot use the completely standard transmission because of the power the engine makes,' Alois says.

There's obviously an ocean of difference between an Rt 12 S and an off-the-shelf 997 Turbo. If you're not yet convinced of why you would want one, the bottom line is, surely, Ruf's exclusivity – and the fact that you're getting a hand-built car, created and tested to the highest possible standards. You literally become one of the family, whisked off to the Alps or wherever on the annual Ruf Rally. However, points of comparison with the stock Zuffenhausen product are not really valid, as the Rt 12 S is configured to behave unlike either the Porsche 997 Turbo or the GT2. The engine produces its power in a distinct way, and puts it down differently, so you can't really compare it like for like. There is a point of reference, and that is Ruf's own flagship CTR-3, which sports the same powertrain, though mounted amidships, which creates a particular feel to the handling behaviour. We know that the CTR-3 is a scorcher, too, though being a dyed-in-the-wool 911 fan, I prefer the known quantity of the Rt 12 S's handling.

The suspension is different from the 997 Turbo. It's to Ruf's own idiosyncratic formula, which is a good compromise between a race set-up and a daily driver. You could quite happily drive to the Nordschleife and have an awesome time, although there's no harshness about the ride quality. Ruf claims it will go from 0 to 300km/h (186mph) in 24.7sec, almost half the time it takes a 997 Turbo. The power is just tremendous; accelerating in third gear, the car pulls pulverizingly hard. Only a GT3 comes close. And this is impressive by any standards. The Rt 12 S is track day capable, but also docile enough for daily use, with shopping capacity in front boot and rear quarters. Could this be the perfect sports car, or is it too good to be true?

The aerodynamic refinements are all defined in Ruf's wind tunnel, and that means that the wraparound front, splitter and cooling ducts, the rear arches with their characteristic cooling cavities, and the wing and door mirrors are nothing like standard Porsche equipment. Ruf claims to have found more downforce front and rear, complementing the suspension and aiding stability at high speeds.

Materials wise, the shell and subtly reprofiled front and rear wings are in galvanized steel, with new cooling ducts carved in the rear wings. The engine cover is carbon-fibre, the doors and front lid are aluminium-skinned – a carbon-fibre roof and doors were tried, but there were problems achieving neat shut-lines – and the front apron and tail end are plastic, which in practice is easier and neater to attach and no heavier than carbon. Ruf maintains that the cooling ducts' revised location on top of the rear wings brings an aerodynamic advantage, so the air goes the shortest way to the intercoolers, which are not in the same position as in the 997 Turbo. There's a small Gurney flap at the trailing edge of the rear wing, which is mounted on hydraulic rams like the CTR-3, rising at 150km/h (93mph) and falling when speed drops to 60km/h (37mph). Rear-view mirrors are from the CTR-3.

The forged alloy wheels are specially made for Ruf by OZ Racing; they measure 8.5 × 19in front and 11 × 19in rear, shod with 235/35 and 325/30 ZR19 Continental V-Max sport tyres. German TüV regulations call for correct tyre size complying with a speed index – and since the Rt 12 S can top 360km/h (224mph), there is only one tyre they can use. Tyre pressure sensors are accessible via the on-board computer. Slowing down is a nuisance in a car like this, but it just has to be done from time to time. It's helpful, then, that the Rt 12 S's brakes are as impressive as its acceleration. Brembo six-piston calipers at the front and four-piston at the back get the job done, acting on 380mm and 350mm ventilated and perforated ceramic composite discs, allied to Bosch ABS 8.0.

Part of the Ruf package is the revised cabin upholstery. You can have more or less what you want in terms of fabric and trim, within basic guidelines: a vegan customer eschewed leather, another specified an unusual carpeting throughout. For the last twenty years, Ruf's bespoke interiors have been fashioned 35km (22 miles) from Pfaffenhausen, and the trim and upholstery are the only thing Ruf doesn't tackle itself. In the Rt 12 S here we are looking at beautifully tailored grey leather, opulently stitched in red. The Porsche sat-nav is retained, as is the switchgear, while the dials bearing the Ruf logo include oil pressure, speedo and rev-counter, plus temperature, fuel gauge and oil pressure. The ensemble is completed by drilled aluminium pedals and a Ruf kick plate on the sills. There's a beautiful clunk to the doors closing, and the seats are sculptured and clad in Alcantara and leather, with Ruf logo carpets in wool, and head-lining and visors in Alcantara. The wheel is nice to touch, bound in leather and Alcantara with a Ruf central logo.

Typical of all Ruf products, the instrumentation and gauges are customized with the maker's logos.
ANTONY FRASER

Front tracking shot of the Ruf Rt 12 S: seamless acceleration rushing from gear to gear, steering pin-sharp and beautifully weighted, turn-in unerring as the front end scrabbles for grip. ANTONY FRASER

The attention to detail is such that in the glove compartment there is another CD player, a Ruf pen and pair of Ray-Bans, along with the handbook and all the documentation. One thing you won't find in a Ruf Rt 12 S, however, is a sunroof. That's because the pressure inside the car at high speed would be so great as to make it pop out – even a sliding roof could be susceptible.

The integrated roll-cage plumps up the A-, B- and C-pillars without detriment to visibility, and lends solidity to the general impression of invincibility. In practice, it also stiffens up the shell no end, bracing every corner for extreme tautness. Not only are occupants much better protected in the event of an accident because the chassis won't flex, the car is also sprightlier in a track-day context. Alois shows us how the cage is wrapped by the pillars and window bars, extending through to the floor and then along to the back of the chassis. 'This cross-bar can save your life,' he points out, 'because if you have an accident you may hit a tree, and this prevents the chassis from bending; it actually helps more than it appears, so if you have an accident you are pretty much safe, no matter what you are doing.'

Transcontinental Express

My test car is chassis 1, finished in time-served Guards Red, which first topped the Porsche paint charts in 1978. I settle into the seat and buckle up; it's so, so snug and womb-like in here. The barrier to the workshop yard lifts and I ease the red rocket onto the street, taking second gear for the run through town. The gears are closely spaced, and Alois has warned me not to use first for anything other than starting off. After a couple of miles across farmland, the hills start. Here there are storks in meadows, buzzards over trees, tractors making hay while the sun shines, and I'm going to follow their example – metaphorically, of course. I take a sharp right and the Rt 12 S seems to understand instinctively what's expected. Its turn-in is unerring, encouraging me to feed in more power. In an instant we rocket

up the hill and I have to pause for breath. This is no more than a country lane and, thanks to the meadows that flank the crest, I can see there's nothing coming along the spine of the hill.

Seamless acceleration starts to come in about 2,500rpm, and builds with the snap of the fingers to monumental proportions. It rushes from gear to gear, and through these tight little turns I feel the front end scrabbling to give me the bite I want. The steering is pin-sharp, beautifully weighted, and it turns in with a flick of the wrist. All the time the car is communicating with you through its steering and suspension and its power delivery. There's a moment's hesitation – infinitesimal as I press the throttle – and then it's going again, accelerating faster than the senses can cope with. I gun it between 3,000 and 4,000rpm in the next three gears, and almost as quickly have to haul it back down again. The carbon-fibre brakes are equally sensational; firm pressure brings things right down commensurately with the speed I've just been going. Whew! This is exhilarating – a wake-up call to the potency of Ruf creations. And yet, it is as sweet as *Kirschtorte* pottering through the sub-Alpine villages.

Unlike Alois's other new toy, the silent, all-electric Greenster Targa, this is still very much a 911, and I want to bask in the flat-six soundtrack. The Rt 12 S exhaust emits a boom rather than a roar, slightly strangulated by the turbochargers as it comes in with each fresh shift. It's unlike the standard flat-six Porsche exhaust note, partly because it's an entirely hand-made system, liberating a small amount of power in the process.

It's about 2bhp extra, but you won't feel it. The goal of a sports exhaust is to enhance the power and the sound. We always say 'form follows function', so the power comes first and then the sound. You can hardly see the difference between a Porsche and a Ruf car, but you can really feel it!

To be fair, I'd need a back-to-back situation to verify that, but the Ruf Rt-12 S is mightily impressive, and it is a sensory feast.

The Rt 12 S is powered by the Ruf-built 641bhp, 3.8-litre twin-turbo flat-six, driving the rear wheels via a six-speed manual transmission.

ANTONY FRASER

RIGHT: **Driving the Ruf Rt 12 S on sweeping Swabian A- and B-roads, it tracks unerringly through the turns with phenomenal traction, and since the field-boundary corners are easily visible, the appropriate gear can be selected well ahead of the turn.** ANTONY FRASER

The author samples the Ruf Rt 12 S as it tracks unerringly through the turns, finding it comes alive between 4,000 and 5,000rpm, running out of space on the open roads around Pfaffenhausen.

ANTONY FRASER

Rural Bavaria is blessed with the best of all roads. Forsaking the lanes that wind up and down the hills, I find myself on fast, sweeping A- and B-roads with great visibility, enabling me to sample the Rt 12 S's versatility to the full. It tracks unerringly through the turns, and I'm looking well ahead, like a motorcyclist, to the bend ahead of the one I'm going through. It really comes alive between just under 4,000 and 5000rpm, but on these open roads I simply run out of space. At least the angular field-boundary corners are easily visible, give or take a maize field, and I can plan a course though them and select a gear long before I arrive at the turn. The traction around a tight bend is phenomenal; I keep my foot down and it grips.

Next, I head for the Munich–Lindau autobahn to finally give the car its head, but my escapade is hindered by a bout or two of the inevitable truck wars. Off I go again, revelling in its mega performance from second through to sixth. It will pull from low down at 1,500rpm, but it's not really happy much below 2,000rpm, over which the slightest dab on the throttle, even in

fourth, will give you an instant response. Then, if you floor the throttle, it erupts with a brutal scream, as if to say: 'Is this what you want? Well you asked for it!' Torque is astounding; I can stay in sixth gear all the time on the autobahn, provided I'm above 2,000rpm. Apply the throttle, another adrenaline rush and we're away. I'm doing 275km/h (170mph) and, with each gearshift, I'm thrown back into my seat – or would be if the belts didn't restrain me. It's a formidable force, yet rock-solid stable at these speeds on the autobahn and eminently controllable. It's awe-inspiring to know that it will carry on with undiminished vigour up to 340–350km/h (211–217mph).

This is a transcontinental express par excellence. You can lap up the miles – and it is also relatively fuel-efficient, because you can run at high speeds without using any turbo boost. You can average 160–180km/h (100–112mph) and not use more than 13 litres per 100 kilometres which, with its 65-litre (14gal) tank, means a potential range of 850km (that's 530 miles, which is an amazing 37mpg). That matches a train or even a plane if the traffic is with you. Travelling at night, you could drive from top to bottom of Germany – 800km (500 miles) – in not a lot more than five hours. You wouldn't be stressed, either, because the car and cabin are built to do that.

Alois Ruf is a visionary. With a stake in three hydro-electric power stations and two electric prototypes based on 997s – the eRuf and the Greenster – he's got more than just a weather eye on the future: he is actually part of it. Over dinner, I hear his next pronouncement with horror. 'The Rt 12 S is the maximum that we can get out of the 911,' he says. My jaw drops. This surely can't be the end of the line? His next statement is reassuring: 'The next logical step with this kind of power output would be not to look for more horsepower but to pursue lightness – to become lighter to enhance the performance.'

The Ruf Greenster is based on a 997 Targa, but powered by a Siemens 270kW electric motor that produces 950Nm (695lb ft) of torque. It's mounted in the same amidships location as the flat-six petrol engine, with a complete recharge achievable at a 400-volt power outlet in less than an hour. The Greenster carries two Gaia batteries in the engine compartment but the majority are housed where the rear seats would normally be. It is parked up next to one of Ruf's small hydroelectric power stations that's hooked up to the local electricity network. The sign says, 'Weir: no entry'. JOHNNY TIPLER

Aha! In the true spirit of Lotus founder Colin Chapman, 'add lightness…'. So all is not lost, then; we're going the RS route.

This is what we have to shoot for, because now the cars have become very comfortable, but at the same time they have also become much heavier. The next step would be to reduce weight, but to look for more efficiency as well. You can look for extra horsepower, but I think that we have to go for another engine system to what we have now with the flat-six, which is pretty much exploited to the maximum. Who would have ever believed that we are finding 700 horsepower in an engine that was designed to give 130, that was not designed by computer animations or calculations, just by rule of thumb, and the experience of the people who engineered it?

So that means we can expect Rufs with carbon panels and lightweight exteriors?

I don't know if it has to be carbon panels. That could be one of the things, and we have to delete some of the comfort items and products that are not really necessary in a sports car. The construction of the body has to be reduced by weight, not by discarding safety features; those have to remain as we are used to those now.

Nothing ever stands still in this Swabian hive of activity. In 2012, the Rt 12 S headed the line-up of Ruf's 997-derived cars, but it was only a matter of time before it was superseded in the performance stakes by something more elaborate – which we shall see in the next chapter. Back then, the Rt 12 S would have set you back €256,000 (£220,000) – plus €10,000 for four-wheel drive.

The true test in evaluating any car is the personal one – how much do I want it? And I do, very much. It's so addictive I don't want to say goodbye. Not that I'll afford one this side of eternity, but I do find myself wondering about residency in Pfaffenhausen. At least there's no shortage of electricity, thanks to Ruf's own power station.

The Ruf Rt 12 S is a transcontinental express par excellence, effortlessly consuming the kilometres, while it is also relatively fuel-efficient with the capacity to run at high speeds without using any turbo boost.

ANTONY FRASER

FREISINGER MOTORSPORT

The front door's locked, so Antony and I saunter around to the side entrance. It's like we've trespassed into Aladdin's cave. The ground-floor car park of Freisinger Motorsport's new premises, in uptown Karlsruhe, is brim-full of exotic Porsches – and there's no one about. Fraser and I stand awestruck for some minutes. Conscious of being watched, we turn around and there's the genie, Manfred Freisinger himself, giving us the beady eye.

He knows full well who we are from the GB-registration 997 Turbo Cabriolet parked in front of his vast new premises, which we've been lent by Porsche GB's press office and driven down in. But he's disdainful. 'Ja, there are some magazines out there now,' he says, matter-of-factly flicking through our proffered copy of *911 & Porsche World*. 'To be honest, we do all the business we want without advertising.'

He's thawed out by lunchtime – and proves more gentle giant than ogre, with an encyclopaedic knowledge of Porsche competition history. He speaks respectable English in deep, measured tones, but it's only when we trade obscure racing drivers' names, races and dates that he starts to relax, and we can tell we've earned a modicum of respect.

He's not exactly cheerful, though a wry sense of humour bubbles under the surface. Team principal, racing car dealer and restorer, parts specialist and sometime race driver, in two decades Freisinger has cornered the market and is not shy of the fact. 'I try to monopolize it, and I spend more time searching for original bits for a particular car than I need for the whole restoration.' He can afford to play the long game. 'I have always got thirty-five restorations running, and swap a bit more time for one car or another. We manage to complete ten cars a year for ourselves, so it makes absolutely no sense to take on a car from a customer and restore it.'

Freisinger's father (also Manfred) set up the business in 1965, buying a damaged, disassembled 356 and tripling his money by selling it in pieces. He repeated the process to the point where he stopped buying individual cars and bought entire workshops, instead. 'My father used to buy businesses all over the world, and the last company we bought was Dauer Racing, in Nürnberg, three months ago.' Right now, the main event is relocating the impressive Freisinger stock of rare Porsche competition spares from one side of Karlsruhe to the other. Moving from the family firm's original site into this three-storey former carpet factory has been a huge undertaking, with over 400 truck trips from the old shop to the new. As well as the Porsche parts, which occupy half the two upper floors – 100m × 25m (330ft

× 82ft) each – the restoration business is also being installed, including the paint shop and its attendant emissions flues.

Factory is not too grand a definition of the operation. It's fronted by a showroom, relatively cramped given the space it prefaces, containing Freisinger's personal favourites:

The red 908 was built in 1969 and raced by the factory in the Daytona 24-Hours (driven by Elford/Redman). It had pole position and retired after 360 laps with broken camshaft drive. It was built as a long-tail coupé; it went back to the factory and was modified to a 'Flounder' body 908/2 Spyder. All the 908/2 Spyders were coupés originally. Then the car was sold to the Japanese driver Kazato, but he killed himself in a Chevron in 1972. The Kazato family kept it until 2001, and I managed to buy it from the US in 2004. We only restored the engine, gearbox and suspension and fuel tanks, and the car is race-ready. The 904 next to it was bought new by Guy Ligier, who later had the Formula 1 team. My father bought it in 1969 and we restored it in 1999. When you look at the old photos of this car it always had an air scoop on the roof, but we cut it off.

125

Next up is a 917 coupé, particularly special because it is effectively brand new. Freisinger explains:

> The frames were built by Baur, and when they ran out of money they had two things hanging on their wall: the last new 917 frame and the last new 959 body. I missed buying the 917 frame, as I could not believe an original frame was lying around and I thought it must be a reproduction. That was a big mistake, and the frame went to Carl Thompson, at Long Beach. He built it up with new parts and I bought it from him. The only thing that was missing was the windshield wiper, but we had those in stock.

Freisinger can't drive the car, as he's too big, though I watched it in action two years ago at Classic Le Mans with Stephane Ortelli driving.

Alongside is another icon, a 917 Can-Am Spyder (917/10 006). Freisinger completed a restoration begun by Vasek Polak's mechanic using brand-new parts. Back in 1972, Polak's driver was Milt Minter, though he was up against George Follmer in Roger Penske's works-backed car and, as Freisinger puts it, 'He was always one step back.' He's sourced a prototype 5.6-litre unit that Porsche developed from the normally aspirated 917/PA unit, which it never ran with in-period.

> *The Can-Am authorities decided in 1972 to forbid them, so the engines were never sold. It has a bore of 92mm and much bigger heads and bigger valves. The exhaust is completely different, with 76mm (3in)-diameter headers, and there are more blades to the cooling fan than normal. It makes approximately 850 horsepower, and you won't find another. I enjoy driving it very much. No turbo lag, of course, and it handles like a go-kart, it really does.*

I saw Freisinger win the historic Orwell Supersports race by a country mile in it at Hockenheim's Jim Clark Revival meeting in 2008.

He's modest to the point of diffidence about his efforts on the track: 'I raced a little bit in club sport in 1988 and now I do a little bit in historics. Historic racing is nice. There's no stress, no politics, in contrast to modern racing, which is dominated so much by politics it's unbelievable. Especially with the constructors.'

At Donington Park's Rennsport Collective meeting I had the opportunity to drive Claudio Roddaro's 917 #008, originally a 1969 long-tail car driven at Le Mans by Richard Attwood and Vic Elford. The car was sold to JW Automotive in 1970 and used for aerodynamic testing, principally at Zeltweg, where it was driven by Mike Hailwood. It has since been restored three times by Freisinger Motorsport. ANTONY FRASER

Manfred Freisinger completed the restoration of 917/10 Spyder #006 that ran in Can-Am in 1972 using brand-new parts and a prototype 5.6-litre flat-twelve engine, an effective specification that enabled him to win here at Hockenheim in April 2008.

JOHNNY TIPLER

Manfred Freisinger storms through the field in his 917/10 Spyder #006 to win the historic Orwell Supersports race at Hockenheim during the 2008 Jim Clark Revival meeting.

JOHNNY TIPLER

Up in the stores, every part is categorized on dedicated shelving. He gives us a sweeping inventory:

Wheel bearings only. Headlights only. Window frames – whatever you need to build a car. Only genuine Porsche; we don't deal in any reproduction stuff. Here we have some engines and gearboxes, some reconditioned. What you see is only 20 per cent of the engines that we have. We could store about 1,000 engines and 2,500 gearboxes. At the very end you will find wheels and suspension parts. So, the whole length of this building carries parts and the whole of the second building is workshops. We never throw anything away, whether it is 914 or 356. There's always going to be a use for it somewhere down the line. Most parts have been sitting with us for thirty years, and at the moment there is a huge run on the old bits.

Freisinger is definitely not a modern Porsche person.

You will never see a Cayenne around here. It is racing only, from 550 Spyder to 917 or Indy Porsche, and we have many prototype parts. We have more or less the entire stock of Vasek Polak and Dauer. We collect the bits little by little from all over the world, and we supply Porsche specialists all over the world, too. You'll find everything you need for injection pumps; all kinds of sway bars from the first prototype to the 962.

He walks us through endless corridors, composed of lofty shelving, stacked full of intriguing mechanical and electrical titbits, commenting at random.

Notice all the titanium screws for the prototypes. You know about the 16-cylinder 917? Here is a new injection pump for it. Compared to the flat-twelve, it is 5cm (2in) longer. This is a turbo from the 12-cylinder 917/30 Can-Am car. Over there are gearbox cases for 924 GTR and GTS, 356 Carrera, 959; all the parts for the 1992 Dauer Le Mans car – you can see the numbers written on it. Items that we sell nearly every day are gear sets for all the cars, from the first 901 gearbox to the 950. All this line is gear sets only, for 917, 930, 956 and 962. A set might cost €1,000 and there are about 3,500 gear sets.

I spot camshafts labelled 908 and 917, but Freisinger has camshafts for all Porsche engines. Here are crankshafts for the 917, 4.5- or 5.0-litre, electrical equipment from looms to spark plugs and headlights, rev-counters, ignition boxes, twin-plug distributors, single-plug distributors. It's mind-boggling. He even has gems like a Formula 2 engine from 1960. 'It was just tested and never sold and never raced. Also from the 1960s I've got an 8-cylinder Bergspyder engine, ex-factory and brand new. Here's one from an RSR Safari. Whatever you need!'

On the floor above are all kinds of bodywork.

Once again, no reproduction parts, all original. Aluminium fenders, and all types of racing wheels for 907, 908, 917, 935 and 956 magnesium, in all sizes. You will also find the finned vents for all the different sizes of wheels. When you do a nice restoration, this is the last part to put on the car so it looks perfect. The engine covers and fin tails are from 917s used in the film Le Mans. We've owned those since 1973. The tails were not good for racing because they were designed to accommodate 15in wheels, and in those days they used to race 17in, so they were just prepared for the film.

Freisinger Motorsport has diligently amassed a vast collection of original NOS and used components relative to historic Porsche racing cars, such as this mechanical injection pump from the one-off, never-raced 917 Spyder #027 from 1971, presented for study by Manfred Freisinger; surely the epitome of connoisseurship! In fact, four such engines were built, under the direction of Hans Mezger, with parts to create possibly ten in total, and the 917 was tested at Weissach by Mark Donohue, who reckoned in turbocharged format it could make 2,000bhp. That never happened, as the turbo flat-twelve was, correctly, deemed to have the right balance of power to weight in the 917/10. ANTONY FRASER

We drive across town to his original workshops, the size of an aircraft hangar in more leafy surroundings. Our eyes fall on what at first sight appears to be a silver 935. It turns out it's a 2.7 RS, transformed into a Turbo lookalike back when that was considered a normal sort of thing to do. 'We will strip it, sandblast it, and rebuild it,' Freisinger says. He appears resigned at such foolhardiness, an attitude that masks the high level of connoisseurship required to perceive the nugget at the heart of such a concoction. I spot a couple of spaceframes. One is a 906; the other has the lines of a 911, but I can't place it. Freisinger explains:

Tucked away in Freisinger
Motorsport's old Daxlanden
workshops on our visit was
the tubular spaceframe chassis
of 935/78 #007 'Moby Dick',
which has subsequently been
restored to its original glory.
ANTONY FRASER

*That's 'Moby Dick'! It's the second works car, chassis
number 935/007, a really raw Porsche prototype. It
was stored in Nevada, but we took it apart so we can
paint the structure. The first works car that did the
24-Hours of Le Mans was 006 (driven by Manfred
Schurti and Rolf Stommelen to eighth overall). This
car was planned for 1979, incorporating ground
effects. After 006 won at Silverstone, nine laps ahead
of everybody else, the FIA forbade this car, so 007
was never ever completed. But we have all the pieces
– we found the original bodywork at Jöst's, and we
found an engine and gearbox from 006, so this car
will be finished for the next Classic Le Mans.*

An exciting prospect.

Freisinger's car park of completed projects and turn-key cars
contains a host of gems, but it's a tad sterile compared with the
restoration workshops, where a succession of Porsches is in
the throes of greater or lesser refurbishment. Another 906 is
being sanded and its panels honed. Here's a 924 GTR, one of
a trio created by Freisinger from brand-new parts.

*The factory stopped production and sold all the bits
to three different parties; we received some bodyshells
and some other people had some other stuff, so we
brought everything together and we will build two more
cars out of new bits. The chassis were stamped those*

*days by the factory – this, for example, is 019; 018 is
still in Stuttgart, but not assembled, and 020 is in North
Carolina and not assembled. Also 001, the first prototype, is standing in the States, only as a bare bodyshell.*

A pea-green 934 race car from Portugal is getting a new engine.
Freisinger is scornful: 'They fitted some Mickey Mouse engine
in it and now it is receiving a proper 934 engine as the owner
wants, with full water cooling for the intercoolers, a proper fuel
cell, oil tank and oil lines. We're installing correct 934 brakes, as
well.'

You go months without seeing a 934 and four come along
at once. This one's Aubergine, and I imagine I saw it at last year's
Old Timer meeting. Freisinger puts me right:

*No, there is a second car racing in Germany in the same
colour. There's a very good history to this car. It was
bought new by the biggest Porsche dealer in the south
of France. He raced it at Le Mans twice and sold it to
Thierry Perrier, who raced it another four times at Le
Mans, always in these colours, and in 1981 it won the
Group 4 class, running a mixture of half alcohol and
standard fuel. I raced it at the Nürburgring Old Timer
this year.*

A 914/6 GT replica on its way to salvation provides another
talking point. 'The car was crashed in the rear right and we put

it back together, and now it's a week before painting.' He indicates another tranche of panelling.

> We have fifty times more than you see here, but we are not really happy to sell because every piece you sell you might need for your next project, and also because today pieces that Porsche are selling are such bad quality and fit that you need days to make them close like genuine ones.

This 914/6 includes all the reinforcements of the GT, plus original oil-cooling system, bonnets, the kit that makes the lights open, original cooling, engine, gearbox and the big fuel cell of the GT.

Next up is a 911S under construction.

> There is currently a demand for clones for racing rather than collecting. We have customers asking for S/Ts up to 1972 with 2.5 engines. They've made a new three-hour race series, ten events, so a lot of people want cars like this to race. I think the clone makes more sense if you want to race it hard – and also I think it could be more competitive, because we build more reinforcements into the chassis than were done in the old days. I've sold three; this one goes to Los Angeles. Most things we work on are sold or close to being sold. We don't advertise, we've never had to; 99 per cent are sold during the building period.

Freisinger is scathing of the current Zuffenhausen regime.

> I don't follow the new cars any more. The cut-off is the 993. I don't think you'll have to restore a 996 as a historic car as there will be none. Take the production for the 993 Turbo, which was approximately 1,300 cars a year; now we have more than 5,000 Turbos a year

The factory entered three 924 Carrera GTs for the 1980 Le Mans 24-Hours; this one, sitting here in Freisinger Motorsport's garage, is the Derek Bell/Al Holbert car, which finished thirteenth overall and sixth in the GTP class. Best-placed of the trio was the Jürgen Barth/Manfred Schurti car, which came sixth overall and third in the GTP class, having hit a rabbit in the night and damaged its radiator. Next best placed was the Andy Rouse/Tony Dron 924 Carrera GT, placing twelfth overall. ANTONY FRASER

for the 997. The first year they changed 5,000 engines – this was a big problem on the Boxsters and the 996s, and this is a huge number. On the new models, not even the engine is Porsche any more. It comes as a complete unit from Kolbenschmidt for all the Carreras. Porsche only build the Turbo engine and the GT3. The engine cases used to be forged by Mahle, in Stuttgart; now they make them in Spain, and they are so much longer in the casting that they crack. Quality is way down.

Back in the garage, he singles out the sparkling jewels. The red 908/2 with the earlier 'Coca Cola' body shape was driven in period by Hans-Dieter Dechent and Reinhold Jöst, then went to the States, where Vasek Polak fitted a 917/10 body. Later it went to Gustav Brunner Racing before being restored.

> Here we have the Alméras Freres' Carrera 3, which did Monte Carlo in 1982, where Jürgen Barth finished ninth overall. Next is a 924 GTR, which has all the last updates, like twin water cooling. The next one is a GTS that was built for the owner of Porsche Munich, with full leather and air conditioning. The next car is a lightweight 2.2 S, and the red car in front is a 934, which spent twenty years in the Matsuda museum in Japan. It went to the Canadian collector Byzek, but French customs asked him to pay VAT on it so, as he was a friend of my father, he sold it to him. I managed to buy it back three months ago, untouched since 1978. I've only seen one in the world like this.

His current obsession is 964 and 993 Cup cars and RSRs.

The first is a 993 RSR that competed at Le Mans in 1998, and in 1999 it won the GT class at Road Atlanta Petit Le Mans. Next is the Supercup Championship-winning GT2 from 1997, driven by Patrick Huisman, and the third car is a 934 run by Kremer for Bob Wollek, Marie-Claude Beaumont and Didier Pironi, who came nineteenth at Le Mans in 1976 – and this was the car that later raced in the Jägermeister colours. Later on, it was sold to Stefan Rattel, and then restored at Weissach.

He indicates a 3.8 RSR that is off to the USA. 'I exchanged that for 906/017, which is the dark-blue car from Daytona 1966 (Herrmann and Linge finished sixth).' There are also cars that Freisinger has run under his own banner, including a 996 RSR.

This was my dream car in 2004. We won the Spa 24-Hours with it and four other FIA races. The next car is our European Le Mans Series 996 GT3 RSR, driven by Stephane Ortelli and Manual Collard, but we lost the championship because my refueller left out 15 litres (3gal) of fuel in the last pit stop at Nürburgring.

The list goes on. These are extraordinary cars, but Freisinger is no sentimentalist. 'Everything is for sale,' he says, 'everything except family.' He doesn't have a particular favourite. 'As long as they are all original, I don't care which one.' There are a few road cars, as well.

Here is the last new 959 bodyshell, last seen hanging on the wall at Baur, which explains why it's lacquered. We had six and I sold two red ones, and we will assemble this one when we have time. The 959 is totally underpriced. People are asking today in the €200,000s, which is crazy for what it is. It ought to be €1m, you know. We had two or three in 1988, but we sold them to Japan for over DM1m. And today they run between €150,000 and €250,000 and you don't sell them, and that's bad. The maintenance is pretty expensive, but when you have a car like this you don't run it every day.

So, what drives him, I ask.

The final product. When it is finished, I am not interested in it any more. The goal is achieving that perfect car, fitted with perfect components. When it is finished and drives off, then for me the fun has gone. It's all about getting there, making it as good as possible, with all the right bits.

Much as he rails against the company today, Manfred Freisinger is merely emulating the brand whose rarefied parts he specializes in. With Porsche the most profitable car maker on the planet, almost everything else appears to belong to him.

Freisinger Motorsport restored 917 #008 three times. The author gets to drive it at Donington Park circuit in 2019. ANTONY FRASER

CHAPTER FOUR

THE 991 TURBO

The 991 Turbo superseded the 997 Turbo in 2013, followed by the 991 Turbo S in 2016. Cabriolet versions were offered simultaneously, in 2013 and 2016. The 'standard' 991 Turbo delivers 513bhp, while the 991 Turbo S develops 552bhp. Standard versus optional equipment constitute the differences between the Turbo and Turbo S. At launch, the Turbo was priced at £118,349, with the Turbo S retailing from £140,852. The S-model's 3.8-litre flat-six is a heavily revised version of the twin-turbo (variable-blade) engine used by the 997 Turbo. It's strengthened internally to cope with increased boost pressure, and prodigiously fast acceleration – 0–100km/h in 3.1sec and 0–200km/h (124mph) in 10.3sec – is augmented by the Sport Chrono package, fitted as standard. This endows it with an overboost function that stumps up with an extra 50bhp for up to 20 seconds in the mid-range. A red light confirming the Sport Plus programme for the engine management is currently engaged glows from the centre console. In terms of illumination, the S's self-levelling and self-dipping LED headlights that shine around corners are optional on the Turbo.

The 991 Turbo's transmission is via the seven-speed PDK gearbox and, like the contemporary GT3, there is no manual gearbox. Steering is electrically power-assisted so turn-in to an apex is intuitively spontaneous. The 991 Turbo is equipped with new Porsche Dynamic Chassis Control, or PDCC, which plays the role of an active anti-roll bar by keeping the car flat through corners and planting the wider new tyres with a broader tread pattern on the road. Electro-hydraulic control for the multiplate coupling of the four-wheel-drive system

OPPOSITE PAGE: **Head-on shot of Gen1 991 Turbo on Salisbury Plain.** ANTONY FRASER

THIS PAGE: **The 991 Turbo seen here was released in 2013, followed by the Gen2 and 991 Turbo S in 2016. Both open and closed versions, Coupé and Cabriolet, went on sale at the same time.** PORSCHE PHOTO ARCHIVE

means that the torque is bounced between the front and rear axles quicker than before, and more of it can be directed to the front end, making the 991 Turbo more agile and capable through the corners. The front axle has the potential to work so hard that it is equipped with water cooling.

Active rear-wheel steering, also used on the 991 G13, is a necessary feature because the 991 wheelbase is 100mm (4in) longer than the 997. It's also 28mm (1in) wider than the 991 Carrera 4 models, two-tone forged 20in alloys filling its haunches. Active rear steering is modulated by a pair of electromechanical actuators instead of normal rear track-rod arms, so that, at speeds below 50km/h (30mph) they steer the rear wheels in the opposite direction to the fronts by up to 2.8 degrees, creating the dynamic effect of a shorter wheelbase and making the Turbo more deftly manoeuvrable. Above 80km/h (50mph) the rears steer the same way as the fronts, generating the effect of an even longer wheelbase, which makes the car even more stable in high-speed changes of direction. In both cases, rear-wheel steering makes the overall steering sharper than with a conventional chassis. Porsche Torque Vectoring Plus (PTV Plus), which is standard on the Turbo S and optional on the Turbo, works through an electronically controlled, fully variable rear differential lock, so that, on slippery surfaces, the system applies light braking pressure to whichever of the rear wheels is struggling to find grip, and during turn-in, it brakes the inside rear wheel slightly, thereby improving turn-in at low to medium speeds. The 991 Turbo is slowed down by PCCB carbon ceramic discs, measuring 410mm in diameter at the front and 390mm at the rear, and these are standard issue on the S.

ACTIVE AERO

The 991 Turbo features an innovative concept known as Active Aerodynamics. Common to both models, these active front and rear aerodynamic devices – identified in typical Porsche parlance by the acronym PAA for Porsche Active Aerodynamics – match an extending three-piece lip spoiler that glides out in multiple stages depending on conditions, with a slotted rear wing that automatically adjusts for height and attack angle. Up to 120km/h (75mph), both front spoiler and rear wing remain in situ, the latter looking quite discreet compared with

ABOVE: **The controls of the 991 Turbo make life easy for the driver, since transmission is via the seven-speed PDK automatic gearbox, and steering is electrically power-assisted so turn-in to an apex is intuitively spontaneous.** ANTONY FRASER

LEFT: **Cabin interior of the 991 Turbo S, resplendent with Alcantara seat cushions and wheel rim, plus PDK shift controls.** ANTONY FRASER

The Gen1 991 Turbo displays perfect turn-in and unwavering handling as it tracks through the Rossfeldstrasse hairpins.
ANTONY FRASER

previous Turbos, while the former allows better ground clearance and ramp approach angles than the 997 Turbo. Above 120km/h (75mph) the system moves into Speed mode, and in this setting the two outer segments of the three-piece lip spoiler extend, pushing air around the sides of the car and reducing lift on the front axle. At the same time, the rear wing rises 25mm (1in) to balance the aerodynamic loading.

Pressing the aero button on the centre console activates the downforce Performance setting, triggering the centre section of the lip spoiler to project forward and thereby divert more air around the sides of the car and create a low-pressure zone behind the spoiler. At the same time, the rear wing elevates itself 75mm (3in) above its basic position and is angled forward by 7 degrees, creating 132kg (291lb) of downforce at 300km/h (186mph) in the process. Let's see how the spec stacks up in practice.

ABOVE: **Back end of the 991 Turbo, showing the slotted rear wing that automatically adjusts for height and attack angle, actuated utomatically at 120km/h (75mph).** ANTONY FRASER

RIGHT: **A Gen2 991 Turbo press car on the North York Moors. It's in good hands, being driven here by Ingrid Fraser who happens to own a 996 GT2. The most obvious visual difference between Gen1 and Gen2 is the front sidelights.**
ANTONY FRASER

WHERE EAGLES DARE: THE ROSSFELD HILLCLIMB

Our steed for this road trip is a 991 Turbo, lent by the Porsche GB press office, and we're visiting the Rossfeld Hillclimb, once a significant venue on the international motorsport calendar, and scene of countless Porsche successes in its 1960s heyday. The course nestles within a glorious, wild, mountainous setting, the peaks soaring resolutely upward, some sheer, some merely vertiginous. In winter I daresay we'd be deep in snow. This is the land of low-pitch roofed chalets, their balconies gaily festooned with flowers, and external walls muralled with religious iconography. Villages feature very tall maypoles, about 15m (50ft) high, and churches with onion-dome steeples.

Antony Fraser and I have motored down to the German–Austrian border, close to Salzburg, having ferried our way into France, belted through Belgium and autobahned south through Germany via Cologne and Stuttgart. While long stretches of autobahn are under reconstruction – making it a tight squeeze with trucks on the contraflows – there are plentiful sections of derestricted motorway where we can give the 991 Turbo its head. To this end, my colleague clocks a majestic 282km/h (175mph) while I manage only a paltry 257km/h (160mph). the Turbo's potential top whack is 318km/h (197mph), so we're not even close, though I can attest to its 0–100km/h time, achieved in a blink-and-you-miss-it 3.1sec. This is such a competent car that there is little drama, just the sensation of extremely high speed that most of us only experience briefly as a plane takes off.

Skirting Munich, we find ourselves passing briefly through Austria, south of Salzburg, due to the vagaries of the frontier boundaries. As in Switzerland, a toll is payable for travelling on Austrian autobahns, but our on-board sat-nav says we'll be heading off into the neighbouring mountains in a few clicks so we desist. We're still on the valley floor when we hit Berchtesgaden, an Alpine resort offering plenty of café opportunities, and we plot a course up to the minuscule-signposted Rossfeldstrasse.

The road becomes a lane, winding narrowly upwards, and we emerge by an incongruously large, modern visitor reception centre where coaches disgorge tourists bent on visiting The Eagle's Nest, an eyrie that served as Adolf Hitler's summer residence seventy-five years ago. So, now we know where he lived, the other question my colleague wishes to address is that of his approximate height. The road system was all pretty new back then, with mountain views to die for – on a sunny day, which isn't the case right now with the mists wafting whitely on the steep slopes.

Hillclimbs are fascinating events: a cross between a single stage of tarmac rally and a short section of a road circuit such as the Targa Florio or Carrera Panamericana, where the obvious objective is to set best-time-of-day by getting to the summit faster than anyone else. Cars are flagged off one at a time and hurtle uphill, snaking through a succession of daunting curves till they pass the chequered flag and time control at the top. Rossfeld-Berchtesgaden is one of the longer ones, at 6km (3.8 miles), rising 505m (1,657ft) in altitude from start to finish at 1,500m (4,920ft) above sea level. By comparison, British

Once a significant venue on the international motorsport calendar, the Rossfeld Hillclimb was the scene of many Porsche successes in its 1960s heyday. The 991 Turbo proved an admirable contender for a quick time, though rain dampened the proceedings later in the day. ANTONY FRASER

BELOW: **Rossfeld Hillclimb is a designated section of the Rossfeldstrasse, 6km (3.8 miles) long, located near Berchtesgaden.**
ANTONY FRASER

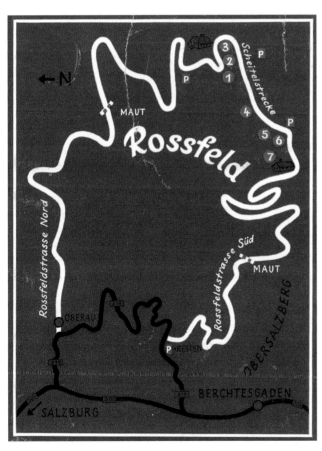

Flagged away from the Rossfeld startline in 1967, Toni Fischhaber won the 2000 GT class in his 2.0 911 S. PORSCHE PHOTO ARCHIVE

hillclimbs tend to be short and sweet, like Shelsley Walsh, 1,000 yards (914m) long with a 100m (330ft) ascent, but on the other hand Pike's Peak in Colorado is a monster 20km (12.4-miles) long, rising 1,440m (4,700ft) on the way.

Rossfeld's heyday was the 1960s, though as we shall see, its origins were in the 1930s, and a clubby revival event is staged annually now. Rossfeld was on the European Hillclimb Championship calendar during the late 1950s and 1960s, along with Mont Ventoux (France), Trento-Bondone (Italy), Ollon-Villars (Switzerland), Gaisberg (Austria) and Freiburg-Schauinsland (Germany), a series contested by top drivers and ambitious manufacturers. We've only got to look at Porsche's works participation with the 910 Bergspyder programme in the late 1960s to see just how seriously they took hillclimbing back then. In fact, Porsche factory cars won the European mountain-climb series twelve times between 1958 and 1969.

The Rossfeldstrasse dates from 1927, when the notion of a scenic Alpine road known as the Deutsche Alpenstrasse took off, running along the entire mountain range between Lake Constance and Lake Königssee, ostensibly to promote tourism in this fantastically picturesque region. Construction of the road began in 1933 at the town of Inzell, with the Rossfeld Höhenringstrasse section planned as a dedicated mountain loop off the eastern end of the Alpine Road, winding between the villages of Unterau and Oberau, with superb views of the Obersalzberg mountains along the way. Although construction started in 1938, the last stretch to Hinterbrand wasn't finished until 1955. In fact, the final section to Königssee was never finished – though that village is but a ten-minute drive along the valley from Berchtesgaden. In the 1950s, the Rossfeldstrasse was classified as a privately owned national road and a toll was introduced to cover building and maintenance costs – rather like accessing the Nürburgring Nordschleife today. The tollbooth also marks the hillclimb startline. The whole Rossfeld-Panoramastrasse winds around the mountains for 16km (10 miles), with a maximum gradient of 13 per cent and an elevation of 1,560m (5,100ft) above sea level, and it's also Germany's highest permanently accessible road.

The first hillclimb events for motorcycles and cars were staged from 1925 to 1928 on the steep, sandy track leading from Berchtesgaden to Obersalzberg. Billed as the Salzburg races, renowned Silver Arrows drivers like Hans Stuck (Snr) and Rudolf Caracciola were early competitors. Fast forward to 1958, and the Rossfeldstrasse race became an international venue for touring cars and GTs, sports cars and smaller single-seaters, when it counted towards the European Hill Climb Championship. By this time Porsche had already been contesting hillclimb

events for a few years, Hans Herrmann winning at Freiburg-Schauinsland in 1953, Huschke von Hanstein at Ollon-Villars in 1956 and Sepp Greger at Gaisberg in 1957. The following year, Greger notched up Porsche's first success here at Rossfeld, and Porsche RSKs also cleaned up in 1958 with wins at Mont Ventoux (Jean Behra), Trento-Bondone (Wolfgang von Trips), Freiburg-Schauinsland (Paul-Ernst Strähle), Gaisberg (von Trips) and Ollon-Villars (Behra, von Hanstein). Porsche's next victory at Rossfeld came in 1961, scored by Heini Walter in an RS61.

In 1963 the floodgates opened, and Greger took the 1600 class with a 356 Carrera, while Edgar Barth (Jürgen's father) won the 2.0-litre category using a Porsche-powered Elva chassis (like a low-slung Lotus 23). Team mate Herbie Müller drove the regular mountain championship car, a 718/8, while Barth also took the Rossfeld GT class in a 2000 GS Carrera. He went on to win the rest of the 1963 Hillclimb Championship rounds at Trento, Sestrière, Schauinsland and Gaisberg to scoop the title. Rossfeld continued to be a successful venue for Porsche, with Barth the overall victor in 1964 in a 904/8, Gerhard Mitter in 1965 in a 904 and 1966 in a 910 coupé, with Rolf Stommelen victorious in 1967 in a 910 coupé, and Mitter again in 1968 in a 910 Bergspyder. And that's the last time Porsche raced at Rossfeld.

The mountain-climb events had been a major stepping stone, an arena in which Porsche quickly secured a dominant role, and a proving ground alongside its increasingly concerted assault on the World Sportscar Championship during the mid- to late 1960s – although after the 1969 Le Mans 24-Hours the works team was withdrawn from racing and the competition reins handed to JW Automotive (Gulf) and Porsche Salzburg (Martini).

By way of a souvenir, I came across a charming video from 1963, 'Alpen Bergpreis am Roßfeld 1963 (Bergrennen/Hillclimb)', watchable on YouTube, which features racing cars such as Edgar Barth's Elva-Porsche and 2000 GS in action, one or two Lotus 23s, plenty of Porsche 356s, Carrera Abarths, BMW 700, DKW, Glas Goggomobil, Ferrari Dino, works Abarth spyders – one driven by a cameo'd Hans Herrmann – and around ten VW Beetles functioning as ambulance/rescue cars. The hillclimb was organized jointly by ADAC (the Automobile Club of Germany) and Berchtesgaden Automobilclub, and there are advertising banners on certain corners where spectators watch from the banking.

The 1973 oil crisis precipitated the end of hillclimbs at Rossfeld, but twenty-five years later, in 1998, Günter and Heidi Hansmann instituted a revival in the same spirit as other modern reprises of vintage events. The Rossfeld Historic hillclimbs up the Rossfeldstrasse lasted until 2010. Then Joachim Althammer

a 1966 Porsche 2000 GS-GT, Walter Röhrl in his 1987 'Pikes Peak' Audi Sport Quattro E2, Jochen Mass aboard a 1928 Mercedes SSK, and Prince Leopold von Bayern in a 1961 BMW 700 RS. In 2014, some seriously well-known cars participated; for example, an ex-Hans Stuck/Ronnie Peterson BMW 3.0 CSL Batmobile, an ex-Niki Lauda BMW M1, 1970s Schnitzer and Alpina 2002s, hordes of Porsche 356s, a 718 RSK 8-cylinder Spyder, a handful of 911s, a Simca-Abarth, Mercedes-Benz 300SLR and Ford GT40: an eclectic mix indeed.

Toll paid, we get ready to tackle the Rossfeld Hillclimb in the 991 Turbo S, with just 50m to the first left-hand hairpin. ANTONY FRASER

set up another revival in 2013, identified as the Internationaler Edelweiss Bergpreis Rossfeldrennen – a grand enough title to persuade Porsche, Mercedes-Benz, Audi and BMW to dispatch cars from their respective museum collections, along with 140 other entrants, enabling fans to witness Hans Herrmann driving

The Rossfeld Hillclimb in a 991 Turbo

Let's do this properly, then. We ease up to the checkpoint barrier and engage the attendant in a spot of banter, hoping he'll waive the toll. No joy there, but no worries. He raises the bar and I move on up. The 991's back end squats, and I gun the scarlet Turbo off the Rossfeld startline, 50 short metres into the first left-hand hairpin, adding more rubber to the swathes of tyre tracks bedecking the asphalt. The 991 sticks like glue, and apexes out onto a quarter-mile straight, snarling through three swift upshifts and back down again through the gearbox as I brake for two more hairpins that rush towards me in quick succession. It's remorseless, and it's also addictive; what goes up must come down, and, having reached the top, I motor back to the start for another crack.

The majority of the course is lined with pine forests interspersed with alpine pastures and cattle, and the overriding impression is of high banks on one side of the road and drop-offs through trees on the other. A final rush through a couple of hairpins takes us past the timekeepers' box, located on a curve right at the summit. There would be fabulous vistas across the valleys if we weren't up in the clouds – and, by late afternoon, in pouring rain. There's an assembly area below the start, and a collecting lay-by after the finish line. A paddock just over the summit consists of a hillside web of single-track roads with individual grassy pull-ins where cars are fettled prior to their runs. The Rossfeldstrasse effectively forms a circle, so, unlike most hillclimbs, where the competing cars have to descend the route they've raced up in batches after each category has performed, at Rossfeld they can carry on going down the other side of the hill and back to the start line collecting area.

It's very easy to see how the slightest distraction would have you off the edge and into the trees. Rossfeld is fast, well surfaced, and consists of a succession of curves, esses and sharper bends interspersed with very few straight bits, and a dozen or so challenging hairpins. In a quick car they come up on you

A mask of grim determination envelops the author's face as he strives to keep the 991 Turbo S on the sodden black bit amid Rossfeld's uncompromising scenery. ANTONY FRASER

very swiftly. Providing my colleague with ample opportunities to snap sharp shots for this feature, I drive around bends that we've earmarked as being somehow special, and that means driving to and fro between safe turnaround points, maybe eight or ten times. Ruminating bovines wearing enormous bells round their necks regard us with indifference from their alpine meadows. There's method in the madness, because it gives me the opportunity to learn some sections of the track quite thoroughly, and as we've driven the whole Rossfeld Strasse in both directions several times scouting for locations we've come to know the whole route reasonably well.

This is one heck of a demanding stretch of road, and no wonder they decided to run a competition up it. Cars are flagged off at 30-second intervals, and from the starting kiosk where they take off, there's that scant 50m before the first hairpin, where tyre marks and indelible tread patterns on the asphalt provide testimony to the aggressive getaways as cars power away from the start. Our Red Rusher is extraordinarily fast by any standards, and I reflect that, with 560bhp on tap at 6,500rpm, I must be going up the hill at least at a similar pace to the 1960s race cars, benefitting from my on-board traction control systems. The turbo cuts in smartly and it's like a rocket blasting off when the car shoots forwards. The slightest throttle pressure has it dropping a couple of gears and the revs soar and off it goes again. I address the hillclimb with a bit more vigour, and I'm surprised to find I've got quite a sweat going on, because it's actually quite demanding.

I surge up to the corners and attack them, finger-tipping the paddles and braking hard while it drops a couple of gears, and I can turn in with total precision, keeping the throttle on round the apex, and power out again, steaming up the hill to the next hairpin, round that and then hurtle upwards with blasts of power between each curve, left-right, left-right, straight-lining the bends wherever possible to get the optimum line up to the next hairpin. There's an urgency, an incessant, repetitive quality to it.

There must be at least a dozen hairpins on the way up as well as numerous interestingly cambered bends. Some are more open, others tight where the road narrows, with stone walls lining the drop-offs in places, and buttressing the banks in others. Sport mode is irresistible, and we have a real cacophony echoing off the walls. I flash over a couple of bridges too, oblivious to the rushing torrent beneath. There are only a few buildings beside the track, though we break at lunchtime to investigate a couple of café-restaurants overlooking the course.

Tributes to fallen comrades grace many racetracks, and Rossfeld has one of its own. Halfway up, I pause by a big boulder close to the edge of the track that bears a workmanlike metal plaque dedicated to Lodovico Scarfiotti, who was killed here on 8 June 1968. It consists of a steering wheel and a painted portrait of him. A works Ferrari star who'd won Le Mans in 1963, 'Lulu' was also two-time European Hillclimb Champion

(1962 and 1965) in a Ferrari Dino, and on that fateful day was handling one of three works 2.0-litre flat-eight 910 Bergspyders (think 910 without roof and with minimal screen, precursor of the 908/2 Flounder). Though the monument is alongside a straight bit, the Porsche actually went off on a nearby right-hander, where 50m-long skid marks led over the edge and into the trees below. Its luckless driver was thrown out and suffered fatal head injuries. One rumour suggests he was distracted by a spectator, another that the throttle stuck open, and it may be coincidental that he crashed just after his team mate Rolf Stommelen had also gone off lower down the hill, wrecking the car but sustaining only a broken arm. Maybe he was fazed by that. Whatever, Gerhard Mitter, driving the third works 910 Spyder, posted fastest time up the hill to win the event and clinch the championship. Perhaps it was odd they didn't pull the team after Scarfiotti's death. But it was a bad year, 1968, with Scarfiotti's friend Jim Clark killed at Hockenheim, as well as Mike Spence at Indianapolis and Jo Schlesser at Rouen. Mitter also died a year later on the Nordschleife, and Stommelen succumbed at Riverside in 1983. It's a tough sport, motor racing; even something as apparently innocuous as hillclimbing.

The heavens have opened – and up here we couldn't be much closer to them and still be on terra firma. My colleague sloshes about, still grasping for the quintessential shot from behind a hairpin parapet with, likely as not, just fresh air behind him and the valley 300m (1,000ft) below. So we call it a day, ease down the hill – which now resembles a fast-flowing river – and point the Red Rusher northwards.

Halfway up Germany we try a different route, hooking off at Karlsruhe for Saarbrucken and then up to Luxembourg. It's such a consummate mile-muncher, this car. Nothing comes close to it, though we are occasionally overtaken ourselves by even more dedicated speed junkies. Without exception they all anchor up obediently when the 130km/h (80mph) signs appear. Most of this is autobahn and, eventually, autoroute, apart from a stretch where they appear to be thinking about duelling it near Kaiserslautern. I almost resent having splashed out for Aral's 102 RON fuel as we can't exploit the high-octane adrenaline lift-off like we could on the unrestricted three-laners. We overnight beside the Meuse river at Namur, Belgium, and by midmorning next day we're at Calais, boarding P&O's SS *Spirit of Britain*. So far, our 991 Turbo has travelled around 2,250km (1,400 miles) on this trip, averaging 10.1ltr/100km (28mpg) in all manner of conditions. We hunker down in the Club Lounge for a spot of R&R. There's a sea haar rolling in, and here we are, even at sea level we're in the mists again. A foghorn booms dolefully. Thanks, but I'll take the clonking Alpine cowbells every time, please.

On the damp Rossfeld Hillclimb, the 991 Turbo S hustles from one hectic hairpin to another, ignoring the fact that the photographer is growing more drenched by the minute.

ANTONY FRASER

RUF TURBO FLORIO

Ruf's 991-based Turbo Florio unites Porsche's 991 Targa model with forced induction – and pays homage to the great Sicilian road race where Porsche cut its teeth. The world's oldest motor race, the Targa Florio was a round of the World Sportscar Championship from 1955 to 1973, and it's a scenario typical of the event's halcyon days when Porsche ruled the roost on the 116km (72-mile) mountain course. With eleven outright victories and numerous podiums and class wins during a seventeen-year period spanning 1956 to 1973, the Zuffenhausen marque celebrated its successes by identifying its top-off 911 variants as the Targa from 1967.

It's also commemorated in one of the latest offerings from the Bavarian tuning and manufacturing wizards Ruf Automobile, which is why we're at Pfaffenhausen – to see what makes Alois Ruf's Targa substantially different to the standard factory 991 version. Well, for starters, it uses the turbocharged Mezger-based engine, twin turbos lifting power output to 700bhp against

The Ruf Turbo Florio revisits Porsche's topless Targa series, which has been a key model in the factory line-up since 1967. Porsche took a break from that convention with the ingenious glass-roofed 993, 996 Mk2 and 997, and then reverted to the distinctive Targa roll-hoop incarnation with the 991 in 2014.

JOHNNY TIPLER

the no-slouch 400bhp of the standard model, and what's more they'll build it in two- and four-wheel-drive format as required. And with overt Ruf styling modifications it is a distinctive variation on the Targa theme.

Taking the Targa name and applying it to the removable roof version of the 911 (the Targa shield doubling as the lid of the car), the topless format has been a key model in the line-up since 1967 with the soft-window version, through to the ingenious glass-roofed 993, 996 Mk2 and 997, and then as the distinctive Targa roll-hoop incarnation with the 991 in 2014. The current car emulates the Boxster's electronic decapotable roof mechanism to lift the ceiling panel over the heads of the occupants and set it down in the well at the rear of the cockpit, leaving roll hoop and rear screen in place, just like the original 911 Targas.

Alois describes the thinking behind his new car:

> The idea of the Turbo Florio was to combine the new technology of the Targa with the drivetrain of the Turbo 991, adding a touch of Ruf, which is the extra performance of the 3.8 engine that delivers 630bhp. And it's also about the stance of the car when you look at the front end, so we have a different appearance and a sportier vehicle. One of our special touches is the signature Ruf air intake, which is very subtle, and that makes it a unique car.

No one is more conscious of the status of his marque in the historical framework, and since Alois grew up with Porsches at his father's garage he's intimately acquainted with their race history.

> The name came from the Targa Florio, because Vincenzo Florio was the founder of that race, and we thought it would be good if his name could also be on a car named after him. We were thinking of his inspiration, and how brave he was to bring the first automobile to Sicily, and so we thought that this open-top car that's essentially designed for good weather driving should have his name. I don't think that's ever happened before. It's a unique car for the individualist who likes to have a Targa-top car combined with turbo power, driving with the double-clutch gearbox, and lovely flat handling.

Though Porsche never raced a works 911 Turbo in the Targa Florio, a couple of privately entered 930s placed fourth and eighth in the swansong 1976 race, legitimizing the Ruf Turbo-Florio connection, if any justification were necessary.

Ruf's Turbo Florio has a more aggressive demeanour than the factory model, including turbo power. Air scoops top the rear wheel arches rather than the flanks. JOHNNY TIPLER

Hunky rear-three-quarter static of the Ruf Turbo Florio, showing the ducktail spoiler that Ruf considers perfectly adequate for generating sufficient downforce at speed.
ANTONY FRASER

Though it's finished in a familiar Porsche Sapphire Blue, the Ruf components on the Targa contrive to differentiate it markedly from the factory model, and I'll highlight those in a moment. Perhaps most strikingly, it's the air intakes in the top sides of the rear wheel arches, tapering off subtly into the rear three-quarter panel to the sides of the rear window, that provide the most surprising visual departure from standard, plunging deep into the recesses of the rear wings and optimized to supply the intercoolers without being affected by the heat dissipating from the engine and the brake discs.

The design and creation have all been all done in-house, together with an external freelance designer, so we're using the original part from the Targa, cutting the shape of the holes and then welding in extra metal that's shaped in detail to make this design. The decreasing size of the duct accelerates the air to provide a better

flow to the intercooler, so we're using the shortest, most direct way to the intercooler here, behind the wheel, instead of ahead of the wheel.

Vast, mesh-clad ducts behind the wheel arches each side of the rear apron help vent hot air from intercoolers and brakes. 'These are basically just the exits for the air that has gone through the intercooler, and this mesh is really a visual thing so that you don't see the insides, but they also protect the intercoolers from stones thrown up by the tyres.'

The ducktail rear spoiler is another obvious addition:

There's no movement in the three vanes on the engine lid because the turbochargers are sucking the air in so you don't need to optimize that by lifting this up, and as regards the aerodynamics we get the maximum downforce we need with the ducktail because the airflow pours over the low angled surface of the rear window. Anyway, we don't need so much downforce at the back because the car would become too light at the front.

The exhaust tailpipes protrude from either side of the carbon-fibre diffuser – a conceit that serves more aesthetic than practical purpose though it is in keeping with the turbo iconography, likewise the carbon-fibre door mirrors. 'The diffuser is not going underneath the complete body, so it doesn't have a huge function because the downforce from the ducktail is already more than enough – we really didn't want to have more downforce with the diffuser.' The wheels are hunky Ruf five-spoke alloys, shod with 325/25 ZR20s on the rear and 255/30 ZR20s on the front. The carbon front lid sports the Ruf logo, as do the door-shut kick plates, while the engine lid displays the subtle Turbo Florio signature. The instruments are inscribed with the Ruf legend, and the logo is embossed in the headrests, which is a nice touch of class.

Then there's the front panel. Really, this is the car's signature, if you discount the Targa roll-hoop; starting with those vast air intakes and corresponding slits beneath the small light clusters, central gaping maw, and the twin semicircular outlet slats in the upper surface of the front panel. The sculpted upward aerodynamic slashes on either corner are echoes of the deep carbon-fibre front splitter traversing the leading edge. It's an exquisite artwork in the chunky, no-messing, Giacometti style.

What about the Ruf power hike, though? I'm with Marcel Groos, Alois's son, and he describes the mechanical DNA of the Florio: 'We started with a 991 Targa chassis and fitted our Rt 35 twin-turbo engine with a double clutch transmission, so we can achieve up to 700bhp. So that's the drivetrain, and then we have designed these air intakes in order to supply enough air to the intercoolers.'

Handling and stopping have also been addressed in respect of the extra horses.

The Turbo Florio brakes are carbon ceramic, with 380mm discs on the front and 380cm discs at the rear. The suspension is a coil-over system that we've developed and set up especially for this car. It also has the hydraulic lift system as a standard feature so you can always push the button and the car lifts up and lowers automatically when you go more than 70km/h (44mph).

Indeed, the button in question is mounted in the centre console just ahead of the armrest; flip a lid to reveal a Ruf logo'd switch, which I press, and the nose rises up, enabling me to negotiate rough ground or sleeping policemen. And when we are travelling at 70km/h (44mph) the nose will drop again. Price comparisons? Ruf products have never been cheap, but they are without exception fabulous and awesome supercars. The 991 Targa S costs £97,000 ex-factory; think twice that and you are in Ruf's ballpark pricelist.

The blistering bluebird awaits us in the compound outside the workshop. I slip into the lush Ruf-upholstered cockpit interior. We need to get the top off for the photoshoot. Opening the Florio's roof is simplicity itself. A pair of switches located in the centre console, one to make it go up and one to retract it, and the whole operation is accomplished in twenty seconds. The roof even unclips itself and, in a mechanical ballet, rises gracefully overhead as the Florio's hoop moves out of the way and the stowage compartment lid lifts up, then eases into the chamber behind the cockpit. Finally, the hoop and greenhouse rear window re-establish themselves. It sounds a tad complicated compared with the good old Targa lid lift-off, and the glazed version of the 993 and 997, but that was then, this is now.

We have a sunny day, so we trundle the Turbo Florio out of Pfaffenhausen and into the mellow, undulating landscape for a blast on the smooth Swabian blacktop. I open it up and immediately I sense that the power is sharper than the 911 Turbo that we journeyed down here in. This is an extremely fast, formidable car. It demonstrates storming acceleration, the power

The Ruf Turbo Florio's Targa top operates automatically, rising upwards and over the top of the cockpit, while the rear greenhouse simultaneously lifts up to accommodate it, resting it in the niche behind the rollover hoop, and, in external appearance, perfectly emulating the original 911 Targa. ANTONY FRASER

With the Targa roof retracted, the occupants of the Ruf Turbo Florio are better connected to nature, being subjected to all the rustic farmyard smells along the road.

ANTONY FRASER

A blast on the smooth Swabian blacktop asserts that the Ruf Turbo Florio's power delivery is sharper than the 991 Turbo in which the author and photographer journeyed to Pfaffenhausen.

ANTONY FRASER

delivery is just awesome, and the way it sprints and stops is incredibly efficient. Handling is flat and neutral, steering and turn-in at curves and corners is accurate; it's everything you would expect from a sophisticated Ruf product.

The other amazing thing about the Turbo Florio – indeed, any Targa – is that, with the roof off you're getting all the rustic farmyard smells as you go along as well. That must have all been part of the heady lap of the Piccolo Madonie countryside – if only the aces had time to appreciate it as they rushed through rural Sicily.

Heat Shield

The Targa saga commenced in 1906, when Sicilian nobleman Vincenzo Florio, inspired by contemporary Gordon Bennett Cup races, consolidated his own vehicular excursions by staging the first Targa Florio around the Grand Circuito delle Madonie, 147km (91 miles) of country lanes in northwestern Sicily, linking seaside Bonfornello, Cerda, Caltavuturo and Campofelice. The last three towns became famous on the Piccolo Madonie circuit used from 1932, on which Porsche came to be so successful in the 1950s and 1960s. The elevation rose from 10m (30ft) above sea level at Bonfornello to 1,010m (3,300ft) in the mountains near Collesano.

Back in 1906, eligibility rules called for production cars, of which at least ten had to have been built. Only ten cars made it to the starting line due to strikes at Marseilles and Genoa

docks, preventing some racing cars being shipped to Sicily. The course wound crazily up mountain roads unchanged since the Romans fought Hannibal over 1,000 years previously, and there were serious changes in climate, plus bandits and wolves to contend with. Even in the 1960s, drivers still needed to be wary of herds of goats, agricultural vehicles, crumbling roads and stray dogs. Each hairpin was flanked by race fans and their cars, unyielding stonewalls, or possibly a sheer drop-off. As Vic Elford told me, 'On practice days you could meet anything:

Watching out for stray animals and other sundry impedimenta, Vic Elford swishes his work's 907 through Sicily's myriad curves, en route to victory in the 1968 Targa Florio.

PORSCHE PHOTO ARCHIVE

The 1968 Targa Florio-winning 270bhp 2.2-litre flat-eight powered Porsche 907 #025 of Vic Elford and Umberto Maglioli out on the hectic Sicilian road course. PORSCHE PHOTO ARCHIVE

The maestro shows how it's done: Vic Elford on full opposite lock in the Cayman 987 course car, lapping the 45-mile (72km) Piccolo Madonie course during the Targa Florio Centenary event of 2006. ANTONY FRASER

cars, mopeds, shepherds with their sheep or goats – they were all there; there were stories that the shepherds were there on purpose, because if you killed one of their sheep you'd have to pay for it, and pay way over the odds!'

The first Targa shield, a plaque in fact, was commissioned from René Lalique, later famous for his cloisonné jewellery, by the sizzling Sicilian automobile adventurist, Signor Florio. It was a bas-relief image in bronze, gold and enamel, featuring an Itala amongst pines and cacti with a seascape background, its two-man crew wrapped and goggled against the dust, bearing the legend Targa Vincenzo Florio 1906. It's on display in the Targa Florio museum at Collesano. First recipient was winner Alessandro Cagno, and his Itala averaged 46.8km/h (29.06mph) for the 445.5km (276.8-mile) race, which took him 9 hours, 32 minutes and 22 seconds. Two other leading contenders were eliminated when a mechanic mistakenly refuelled their petrol tanks with water. There are no such issues here at Pfaffenhausen, though Antony and I are disappointed not to find 103 octane at the Aral gas station alongside Ruf's headquarters to refuel our 991 Turbo press car. No matter – 98 will have to do; if it's good enough for Alois, it's sure enough adequate for us.

AUTOMATIC SELECTION: PDK TRANSMISSION

Some might say that an automatic gearbox was never going to be the first choice of the press-on motorist. To put this contention into context, I assessed four different generations of Porsche's automatic transmission on Dartmoor.

Autos are for aunties? Not necessarily. Back in 1967, Vic Elford and his co-drivers, Hans Herrmann and Jochen Neerpasch, blitzed the Nürburgring's Süd- and Nordschleife for 84 hours (covering 9,096km/5,652 miles) to win the Marathon de la Route with a semi-automatic 911 Sportomatic. And then, moving on a generation, Walter Röhrl helmed a 964 Cup Car in clutchless Tiptronic format in a round of the Carrera Cup in 1990. Today, the Cayman GT4 Clubsport competes in PDK mode in the Michelin Pilot Challenge. A few laps around Porsche GB's test track at Silverstone in such a car testifies that PDK is vastly quicker than manual. And that's the point: automatic doesn't condemn you to the slow lane. Hence this evaluation of automatic Porsches down the ages. Saltash-based Williams Crawford sportingly provided the four

OPPOSITE PAGE:

TOP: **Putting a cross-section of Porsches with automatic transmission to the test, this group posed on Dartmoor consists of a 991 Turbo in the foreground, with 911 Sportomatic, 997 and 964 to the rear.** JOHNNY TIPLER

BOTTOM LEFT: **The latest PDK shift arrangement enables the normal four automatic modes, plus manual control when the lever is moved to the left. Paddles on the steering wheel also allow finger-shifting.** ANTONY FRASER

BOTTOM RIGHT: **A fabulous moorland road for a sprint in the Gen2 991 Turbo, allowing the PDK to do the sensitive shift work.** ANTONY FRASER

The shift stick of the 911 Sportomatic, essentially the same as the manual lever, but with four slots and two pedal controls. The gear knob is labelled L, D, D3 and D4, with L for Low, or, basically, first gear. There is no D2.

JOHNNY TIPLER

The shift lever of an early Tiptronic gearbox, located aboard a 964 Targa. It's a conventional P, R, N, D, 3, 2, 1 automatic, and, with the lever slotted to the right in the gate, offers a sequential shift pattern where an upward push on the lever engages a higher gear, and a downward push a lower one.

JOHNNY TIPLER

The second-generation Tiptronic system was introduced in the water-cooled 986 Boxster and 996 range in 1997–8. With just four slots for Park, Reverse, Neutral and Drive, plus Manual for use in association with steering wheel-mounted shift buttons, this shift was more refined.

JOHNNY TIPLER

iterations for me to try, and with a party of drivers, we hustled them up onto Dartmoor.

We automatically think of automatic as something that gets done for us without having to think too much about making it happen. Porsche's first venture along these lines was the 905 Sportomatic gearbox, introduced in August 1967 and just about hanging on until the 1979 model year. Unsurprisingly, it proved especially popular in the USA and Japan, where a quarter of 911s sold were Sportomatics. In the first place, it was clever terminology, turning the lacklustre 'automatic' word that dismayed the enthusiastic driver into something less drab by prefixing it with a dynamic pronoun.

My experience today suggests that it was something of a misnomer. The red 911T is a four-speed semi-auto, with stick shift and two pedal controls. The hand throttle, the little black lever between the seats, helps with firing up the fifty-year-old flat-six. The Sporto system was developed with Fichtel & Sachs and consists of a hydraulic torque converter and vacuum-operated diaphragm clutch mated to a conventional four-speed 901 gearbox. The gear knob is labelled L, D, D3, and D4, with L for Low, or basically first gear. There is no D2. The torque converter takes over for starting off and stopping, while the automatic clutch handles the in-between shifts. In theory. Merely touching the gear knob is sufficient to activate micro-switches at the base of the lever that control a vacuum servo that actuates the clutch. The torque converter replaces the flywheel, smoothing the transmission's electro-mechanical shifts, and allowing the car to be stationary with the clutch engaged.

Sportomatic was a no-cost option, though not available for the 2.2 S of 1970 on the basis that it just wasn't sporty enough, and two years later, with the 2.4-litre cars, it was only available to special order. Rising torque levels meant that, with the 2.7-litre 911s, the 925/09 Sportomatic was reduced to three speeds. In practice, it can, of necessity, work as a two-speed. My experience with a recalcitrant Sportomatic, by now fifty years old, demonstrates why many owners converted theirs to manual shift.

There was a dearth of auto action in the Porsche model line-up till 1990, when the 964 C2 was available with Tiptronic, a dual-function system developed in consort with ZF and Bosch, offering a conventional P, R, N, D, 3, 2, 1 automatic shift. With the lever slotted to the right in the gate, a shift was sequential, whereby an upward push on the lever engaged a higher gear, and vice versa to obtain a lower gear. Whether this was quite as intuitive as the present-day PDK shift, which works the other way round (back for downshift, forward for upshift), is a moot point. A computer calculated the right ratio for the throttle-induced loading on the transmission, achieved without interrupting the torque flow, which was a major improvement over normal automatics. However, the downside was that an early Tiptronic was a second slower than a manual in the 0–60mph sprint.

The PDK paddle switches are located behind the arms of the steering wheel, and are sensitive to fingertip operation for manual shifting. For normal auto mode, just leave them alone. ANTONY FRASER

Come August 1994, and the advent of the 993 in Tiptronic guise, the system had been improved and sales of cars thus equipped with this no-cost option accounted for 60 per cent of the 993 market. With this model, Tiptronic S allowed the driver to use the stick to shift modes, or use the rocker switches on the steering wheel arms. The system could sense varying road resistance, and downshifted accordingly when braking was detected. The second-generation Tiptronic appeared in the water-cooled cars, the 986 Boxster and 996 range in 1997–98, and that was rather more refined.

PDK transmission first became available in 2005, in seven-speed format, in the 997 and the Gen2 987 Boxster and Cayman. It was not that new, in fact, originating in the Group C 956 WEC racing cars in 1983. PDK stands for Porsche Doppelkupplungsgetriebe (Porsche Double-Clutch Transmission). It incorporates two concentric shafts, one for even gears and the other for odd gears, each driven by its own clutch, so it starts to engage the next gear as soon as the clutch on the previous gear's shaft starts to disengage, enabling a continuous flow of power.

Acoustically, automatics splurged indolently from one ratio to another, though the sound of auto shifts has grown increasingly livelier, till today's sequential PDK change is positively arousing as it blasts through the gearbox, blipping the revs to suit the ratio. Between Sportomatic and PDK we have Tiptronic. The 964 Targa is equipped with the earlier version of Tiptronic, where the lever resembles a manual one, topped with large black button and passing through a simple P, N, R, D, 3, 2, 1 slot, plus the opportunity to knock right from D into M + or –. I opt to pop it across to manual, and going up and down the four-speed gearbox in sequential mode. Once acclimatized to that, I imagine that's how you'd probably always use it, apart from in town and on the motorway. It's deploying the torque very nicely as I tackle the steep hills, and I'm modulating the revs as it eases round the corners. Auto does funny things with the engine note, though, and the flat-six is moaning as it slurs across the ratios, rather than snarling in its usual strident manner.

Next up, the 997, offering the newer and sharper version of Tiptronic – still with just the five ratios, though. This later Tiptronic is more user-friendly, if not necessarily intuitively so, because it's labelled as P, R, N, M and D, providing a slightly less convoluted set of instructions, selected by a sleek, aluminium-topped, palm-shaped lever. The gearbox sorts itself out on the hills, dropping from one ratio to another in a much more co-operative way. It's obvious that, in terms of operation, it's way more refined and less clunky than the earlier Tiptronic, while on the move it responds to throttle inputs much more readily and helpfully than its predecessor.

The 991 Turbo with its PDK transmission is an entirely different kettle of fish, upshifting and downshifting and revving the engine for you in the middle of the shift. It's staggeringly fast in operation, and there's no question that to be able to drive as quickly as this without having to dip the clutch and shift gears manually is way more sophisticated. During braking the downshifts can be really dramatic. I've got Sport mode turned on for enhanced aural effect and sharper handling, whilst watching out for errant sheep and moorland ponies as well, delighting in the wonderful popping and waffling on the overrun. I've barely got to graze the throttle for it to jet forward with subtle alacrity. The Turbo's PDK is in another league, and it is, unsurprisingly, the crowning glory of the assortment.

Back at base, I have a debrief with Adrian Crawford. 'I have sold loads of Tiptronic Porsches,' he declares – and this is relevant because of course it applies to 996 and 997 Turbos fitted with automatic transmission.

Let's discuss Tips rather than PDK, because people are generally very enthusiastic about PDK, whereas you'll have a split opinion about Tiptronic. Around the world, Tiptronic has been the most popular choice. Japan and America bought more Tiptronics than manuals, and a Tip can be a really good solution for a broad market place. People can change their minds too. The typical thing is, customers will say they definitely want a manual, and I say, 'But have you considered a Tip?' and sometimes I'll dig down and ask, 'OK, how are you going to use it?' 'Well, probably 2,000 miles a year, and I'm going to go out with my missus at the weekends.' So I say, 'Do you want a closed car or an open car?' and they say, 'Oh, I think I might have a Targa or a Cabriolet,' and my response is, 'So, you want stress-free, catch-the-breeze enjoyable 911 motoring: try a Tiptronic, because there's very little to actually go wrong with them.' There's a difference in values between Tiptronic and manual, but most people are buying modern cars now with automatic gearboxes of some description, and I suspect that the Tip will become more acceptable.

There's another angle:

ABOVE: **Darting over Dartmoor in the 991 Turbo, Tipler appreciates the slick shifting of the PDK system. Nothing comes close to PDK in traversing the ratios, especially if you let it do the work for you.** ANTONY FRASER

LEFT: **Great Dartmoor panning shot of the 991 Turbo. We borrowed the automatics from Saltash-based Porsche specialists Williams Crawford, and the driver here is Lilly Smith, who works there.** ANTONY FRASER

Times change, and for a lot of people manuals are actually feeling more difficult to use, and that's because the market's getting older, the cars are getting older. Now people just want an experience, they just want to enjoy the car, and they're using it in a different way. Tiptronic people are enjoying it differently: they've got a stress-free driving environment, which they can share, so if necessary their mate or partner can drive them home from the pub from time to time.

And then you have the interaction of the buttons on the steering wheel if required.

You need to know how to use them, and how to get the best out of them. They've got different maps in them, and you can encourage them to change differently. You can influence the more modern Tips through the throttle pedal, so, if you move your foot quickly like you're in a rush to get home – on the throttle, off the throttle rather than brake quickly, it's sensing that and it's changing its map and it's going to go with you. What no automatic can do, whether it's PDK or Tiptronic, is predict what silliness we're going to get up to; it is not predictive.

Tiptronics are cleverer than you might think, though. There are five different 'maps' that influence the way the car runs; so, for example, if you press your throttle pedal twice, really fast, it will go into the sporting map immediately, like old-fashioned kick-down. This way you can immediately spark the car up without actually doing anything other than that very fast double-tap on the accelerator. And it's checking that all the time. That is true of all Tiptronics; it's just that they became more responsive.

In Adrian's opinion:

The PDK is an entirely different thing, and in some ways the Tiptronic does a better job than PDK for that market that's wanting a two-pedal car, because the PDK is overly sensitive, overly reactive. I can more easily trundle along in the gear I choose in the Tiptronic, but where the Tiptronic loses out to the PDK is in the ultimate performance. Where it gains over the PDK is in general ease of use.

Each of these automatic gearboxes is a product of its era, and they became increasingly sophisticated with each successive generation.

The 991 Turbo's PDK transmission upshifts and downshifts with greater alacrity than Tiptronic, revving the engine on your behalf in the middle of the shift. ANTONY FRASER

TECHART 991 TURBO S

The leading German tuning companies are nothing if not prolific, and they need to be to stay abreast of their competition and keep their ideas fresh to maintain customer interest. TechArt's 991 Turbo S earned its stripes one day on the Black Forest's hilly bends – narrowly missing a speeding citation along the way. Speed traps? There's an inherent risk with my job as a Porsche car journalist, maybe more so than regular Porsche ownership: that of getting caught going over the limit. Because we all want to know how quick these cars are, and we have to pick our moments. Stretches of autobahn with no speed limit, for instance, would be just the ticket for the TechArt 911 Turbo S with its 305km/h+ (190mph+) potential. But that doesn't reveal the car's dynamics on a switchback B-road. A dragster is fast in a straight line, but that tells us little about its chassis.

So, when my snapper buddy Antony and I depart TechArt's Leonberg premises, him in the snappermobile, me in the 991 Turbo S, and make off for the winding hill roads in the arable Flacht district – by coincidence, a stone's throw from Weissach – I let him get maybe half-a-mile ahead in the snappermobile so I can get a decent run down the valley. No sooner have I floored it than I spot a blue van half-hidden in a roadside copse two-thirds of the way down the hill. Thank god for these mind-blowingly efficient brakes: the enormous speed already attained is annulled in a few yards. But a couple of blue-clad figures hasten to leap into their van and, horror of horrors, the blue lights begin flashing.

Pumping adrenaline turns to vinegar, and I slink towards them, tail between my legs. You can't hide a sparkling white Porsche, and to halt completely will arouse more attention, though the assumption is that my lusty charge of horsepower has already been clocked. Trying to look completely normal, I tool past at about 30km/h (20mph). They come out after me with their blue lights flashing, and I think, 'This is it, this is the reckoning,' and begin to tot up the likely cost in euros – but no! They overtake me and carry on going! Nee-naw, nee-naw… The paddywagon speeds off down the hill, overtakes Mr Fraser and disappears from sight. I catch my colleague up and we proceed gingerly through the village, and there are the cops, having apprehended a truck. Around the next turn a shattered motorcycle tells a tale.

It is one heck of a car, this Turbo S. I've driven TechArt offerings before, of course, and while it's not a major innovation, this one doesn't disappoint either. The company introduced its latest take on the 911 Turbo at the 2016 Geneva Salon. The spec includes technical, aerodynamic and cosmetic evolutions, most obvious of which is the aerodynamic kit, made from lightweight carbon and polyurethane RIM composite, comprising the front spoiler that smartens up the aerodynamics at the front apron, various ducts, and the rear wing. The front splitter extends fully at the press of a button when going at under 100km/h (62mph), or it'll emerge automatically when the car hits 60mph in any case, retracting automatically at 70km/h (44mph). Matching the front end aero, the rear spoiler improves overall airflow, which TechArt claims 'improves driving dynamics and stability' as well as echoing the curvature of the 991 coupé roofline. Likewise, the 'aero wings' that are integral with the front air inlets, and the vents in the front apron, aid streamlining and contribute to the firm's trademark visual characteristics and aggressive design cues. These include the headlamp bezels, side skirts and diffuser trim, framing the stainless steel, dual-oval tailpipes.

While the silhouette of the Turbo S is pure macho white tornado, the actual appearance of the car is dominated by the TechArt striping, and with all the competition references that evokes it does take you to a different standpoint, visually. White car plus blue stripes equals traditional American racing colours. That makes me mindful of American racing cars, from

As well as performance hikes, another TechArt speciality is lifting the appearance of the standard-issue Porsche model to a new aesthetic level, which can be an attractive proposition for those who wish to proclaim their individuality.
ANTONY FRASER

ABOVE: **The TechArt 991 Turbo has a small diffuser underneath the back panel where the exhausts protrude, while the aerofoil wing is purposeful and workmanlike, rather than swoopy and elegant.** ANTONY FRASER

RIGHT: **TechArt's interior styling for their 991 Turbo includes elements of coloured carbon fibre, and the colour highlighting extends to the detailing in the stitching in the seats and dashboard top.** ANTONY FRASER

Cunningham to GT40, Corvette to Panoz, which is no bad thing, and might also indicate the market that TechArt has its sights set on with this model. In any case, stripes are an image lifter. The artwork makeover is enhanced further by the Turbo S graphics on the sides, while the rear-view mirrors match the blue of the metallic detailing in the car. It's all tastefully done, if you like your Turbo to stand out even more than normal. Personally, I would have carried that blue stripe right over the top of the car, but for some reason it stops on the roof and finishes halfway up the bonnet.

The lowered suspension also accentuates the length of the car, and perhaps that is also to do with the positioning of the Turbo S graphics along the bottom of the door. It seems too curtailed, and maybe it should run right around the entire lower quarters, because, as it is, it runs in front of and behind the front wheel arch, but the rear wheel arch is neglected, while the main detail in that panel is the trademark air intake for the intercooler. Looking at the front of the car, it's obvious there are some areas where the aerodynamics have had an influence on the shape of the front splitter, but generally it's a relatively boxy, rectangular affair, and there's no front-projecting splitter as one might have expected. The side skirts, or sills, have a slight knife-edge projecting along their centre lines. Around the rear there's a little

diffuser underneath the back panel where the exhausts protrude. The aerofoil wing is purposeful and matter of fact, rather than swoopy art nouveau; it's not elegant, it's workmanlike. And yet the whole thing integrates very well into a coherent package.

The luminous TechArt aluminium door-sill guards welcome you aboard the salubrious saloon, while the ergonomically shaped tri-spoked multifunctional sports steering wheel with its designer paddle shifters entices. It's flattish across the bottom to give space between rim and thighs. Your feet ease onto the aluminium pedals and adjacent footrest. There's a coordinated design theme running through the upholstery trim, with decorative threads in contrasting colour stitching the leather panels together. TechArt's interior styling packages also include elements of coloured carbon fibre, while the dashboard instruments are also refined versions, presenting legible dials, bezels and the leather wrapped Sport Chrono clock. The attention to detail is evident in sewing and the carbon fibre on the centre console, the needlework in the leather on the dash and on the chairs, and the matching blue of the panels around the PDK shift lever.

Beneath the front bonnet it's the same layout as a regular 991, providing exactly the same luggage-stowing capability; open the engine lid and, like on all modern Porsches, that too is a manifestation of plastic covers so you won't see much in

LEFT: **The TechArt power kit raises their 991 Turbo's power output from 560bhp to 620bhp, boosting torque by 130Nm to 830Nm (612lb ft), and on full boost to 880Nm (649lb ft), dispensed at the touch of the standard Sport button on the centre console.** ANTONY FRASER

BELOW: **Helming the TechArt 991 Turbo along the leafy lanes flanking the Weissach proving ground, the driver is awed by its acceleration and handling competence.** ANTONY FRASER

the way of a driveline. It's tempting to try and lift the spoiler, but the engine lid is in an even smaller panel that just lifts up to access the fluids, like a Boxster.

Its enormous 21in wheels are slightly dished to set the rim out a little bit more, and they're fitted with Michelin Pilot Sports, 245/35 ZR up front and 305/30 ZR on the back. Plenty of grip there, then, which is reassuring considering the prodigious power on tap. From the stance of the car it's obvious that its suspension is lowered by 30mm (1in), as it's quite squat. The suspension is fundamentally original, but the springs are replaced by TechArt's sport springs, fitted front and rear when the 'Noselift' system is installed. Speed bumps and potholes are easily negotiated by raising the front of the car via another console button that operates the suspension hydraulics. This kicks in without delay at 50km/h (30mph), lifting the nose of the car by 60mm (2in); it lowers itself automatically after around seven seconds.

All the trimming and mechanical enhancements are carried out in house at TechArt's multi-level premises in dedicated craft workshops, which is as amazing as it is laudable. No farming-out of functions here. Hanging hides and multifarious leather-bound wheel-rims speak of hands-on endeavour, while techies toil beneath ramps in the garage. It's quieter in the design studio, where renderings for future design themes are on show. The white riot theme is carried over into the Cayman that I also drove on this occasion, but the quartet of demonstrators on display in the rotunda showroom are, if anything, more hardcore poseurs, bejewelled bling-babes each one: a 991 Cab, Macan, Cayenne, Boxster and the wild, swamp-green 997 GT2.

As we know, the Turbo is stonkingly fast, by any standards. Beavering away in their subterranean workshops in the bowels of the main building, these engineers have made it quicker still. The TechArt power kit raises power output from 560bhp

to 620bhp, boosting torque by 130Nm to 830Nm (612lb ft), and on full boost to 880Nm (649lb ft). It's all dispensed by the touch of a button: the power kit springs into life when the standard Sport button on the centre console is pressed. For maximum aural treats, the Sport exhaust system with 'sound muffler kit' dispenses a beefy baritone boom and blare.

Back to the road test, then. This car is but six days old, and that's a rare thing as far as I'm concerned. Even Porsche GB press cars have usually seen a few thousand miles. Immediately I'm impressed by the car's sheer ability. Like a jet fighter pilot, it endows me with an awesome feeling of confidence by its downright competence. The controls are broadly standard Porsche equipment with PDK shift, but the experience it delivers is perceptibly on another level. I ease on the accelerator and it rushes forward, the immediate sensation being that it's immensely fast. After my close shave with the traffic police, progress is inescapably slow for a few kilometres. You can trickle along with a PDK automatic and it does all the work for you. You know that you're the boss of enormous latent power, sizzling away in anticipation of relaunch.

Soon enough, my confidence is rekindled, and the urge to surge takes control again. At first, it's just seamless, linear acceleration. But when the turbos enter the fray there's a positive lunge, signalled by the exhaust note changing to a deep boom. I've got it in Sport Plus, using the PDK paddle shifts, and there's a lovely burble on the overrun. And just as it's tempting to play tunes going up and down the gears, it is also irresistible to floor it just for the hell of it; as we found, however, there's quite a formidable police presence in the Weissach hinterland, so maximum prudence is required. It's a Porsche fest around these back roads, where every other car is a Porsche of some sort, and I lose count of the Boxsters and 991s that glide by during our static photo session, though the 918 and Carrera GT grab my attention: a big 'wow!' moment. It's a car spotter's paradise, such is the volume of exciting cars at large. They all look curiously at our candy-striped TechArt Turbo, and I construe that it is seen as an interloper, though in town it's a regular head-turner as old and young pay tacit homage. I activate noise-boosting Sport Plus to further pique their interest.

Out in the sticks, the car is extremely lively and poised. Around these helter-skelter corkscrew turns it's a pussycat, driven sensibly, but I know that there's a bottomless pit of porking grunt lurking to catch out the over-zealous right foot. It's a big car, relatively, on these tree-lined lanes. Easing the power on and off to get the nose to dip in and out, the steering is very direct, the turn-in is pin-point acute and the balance of the steering is just right, to the extent that the thick, padded wheel invites some twirling, given a broader set of curves.

Having blasted the byways I calm down a bit, settling back for a more objective review of the white wazzer. I've got the sunroof open now. It's no bigger than a normal one, but you can have three different configurations of aperture by pressing different buttons: with just the back cranked up, wide open, or a combination of the two. I'm looking for trouble in the rear-view mirror and I'm distracted by the spoiler, with its neat blue and grey detailing.

There's one last chance for a burn-up along a few, too-short miles of smooth asphalt, winding up and down through the fringes of the Black Forest. Heart in mouth, I go for it, hoping not to find a tractor around the next bend, though a swift overtake or two is feasible when the dotted white line's in my favour. The Turbo plunges into dips and hurtles skywards to crests, and I'm totally gripped with the concentration and the thrill. There's no apparent limit to the available performance. Job done, I cool it and we slink back to TechArt's Leonberg HQ, relying on the console sat-nav for directions. All in all, the TechArt Turbo S is visually striking, an extremely competent and very exciting car.

Around the corkscrew turns in the Weissach neighbourhood, the TechArt 991 Turbo is lively yet poised, demandinga modicum of care, given the vast reserves of power available. ANTONY FRASER

The TechArt 991 Turbo plunges into dips and hurtles up to crests, winding through the fringes of the Black Forest.

ANTONY FRASER

THE RUF CTR-4

The latest Ruf Yellowbird CTR-4 is the most radical offering yet to fly the Pfaffenhausen nest. Yellow plumage is about all that the latest Yellowbird has in common with its trend-setting ancestor. In production in 2018, it is a true technical tour de force, because although it presents itself as something approaching a 964, ruffle those feathers and you'll find it's anything but. This freshly hatched CTR employs racing car construction technology, miming the same structure as a DTM (Deutsche Touring Meisterschaft) saloon, for which the regs stipulate a common-chassis construction of carbon-fibre monocoque and steel roll-cage, with front, rear and lateral crash elements, which also serve to locate the suspension componentry.

Alois Ruf's vehicular affections proudly embrace the imagery of the classic air-cooled 911s, and to that end the Yellowbird's body shape emulates a 964 rather than a 991. Our run out into the Swabian countryside with both examples, old and new, side by side emphasizes the growth of the modern car's girth and stature. The new car is only 911-esque, because what you're looking at is a carbon-panel-clad chassis. While the cabin interior corresponds exactly with normal 964 proportions, the exterior has swollen, very subtly, and it takes Alois's guided tour to appreciate the niceties.

Three decades separate the two Yellowbird CTRs, one introduced in 1987, the latest in 2017. As Alois tells us:

The original idea was to make a motor car that was not so large, because, remember that in the same year, 1987, we had the 959, which was a very big car, relatively, and we wanted to follow the same principle with the new car, and make it smaller than the current 911. The entire monocoque is carbon, whereas the Ultimate that you saw last year only had a skin of carbon, but here it's the whole monocoque. Most people think it's based on a 964 or a 993, and think it's some kind of a backdate. But it's based on a Ruf, and it's coming from a clean sheet of paper.

In fact, there's a full-blown Le Mans race car underpinning this traditional-looking car:

It could have a modern body, but we wanted it to look as much as possible like our original Yellowbird. This is why the car handles so nicely and feels so great, because it's a modern, state-of-the-art race car underneath. The pushrod suspension includes upper and lower wishbones, and at the rear there are the horizontal cross-mounted shock absorbers with coil-over springs, while in the front they are longitudinally mounted, and that's pure race car engineering.

Nothing is left to chance or done on a whim.

We needed to accommodate these larger wheels and tyres to have an adequate stance for the horsepower, because output is 700bhp and it's a lightweight chassis, so we made it wider, but the eye does not read it as a very wide car. To start with, we put 40mm (1.5in) more in the tail lights, and when you compare that with the old one you'll see the difference, that the tail light and that section of bodywork has broadened out.

Typically for a Ruf, the Yellowbird roof has no rain gutters.

The old one didn't have gutters, and neither does the new one. But what we've done here is to give the doors and the wings more shoulder. When you open the door, you'll see how much thicker it is than normal. The size of the cabin inside hasn't changed; the glass area is still the same; we still have the same side-window glass and the door frame that the old one has, as well as the windshield and the rear window.

However, the glass in the rear-three-quarter windows has changed because it's acrylic and there's a discreet air intake either side for the combustion air. The two large ducts in the

Alois Ruf prefers the imagery of classic air-cooled 911s, which is why the Yellowbird's body shape emulates a 964 rather than a 991, and the CTR-4 is actually a carbon-panel clad chassis.

ANTONY FRASER

tops of the rear wings (fenders) provide cooling air for the intercoolers.

Take a few steps back and you will notice we have a 70mm (2.75in) longer wheelbase, and the eye doesn't notice that, because the overall length of the car hasn't changed. It is still the same length as the other one, but we have less overhang, front and rear. The

headlights have been moved up by 20mm (0.75in), and nobody can tell that. The rear axle has moved by 50mm (2in) towards the back of the car and the front one by 20mm (0.75in) towards the front. We've lengthened the door by 25mm (1in), and although it's longer the pivoting points have not changed because that would make it more difficult getting in and out when you're parking next to another car.

**Yellowbirds old and new: Alois Ruf and Johnny Tipler out
for a drive in the original CTR-1 (right) and the latest CTR-4.**

ANTONY FRASER

The strong resemblance to the original CTR-1 Yellowbird is deliberate, because Alois Ruf loves the traditional 911 look and believes the market agrees with him. ANTONY FRASER

The **CTR-4 Yellowbird may bring to mind the shape of the air-cooled Porsche 964, but it is broader and the wheelbase is actually 70mm (2.75in) longer, with headlights 20mm (0.75in) higher than the classic model in whose idiom it was conceived.** ANTONY FRASER

Was it difficult to accommodate the front edge of the door within the structure because of its extra length? 'All the body parts are different,' says Alois. 'There is nothing structural that you could exchange with a 911. You can carry over the wipers, the windscreen, the side glass and the door frame, and that's all; the rest is completely new.' The LED headlights are specially made for Ruf, and the door mirrors are also to Ruf's special design, while the rear bumper corners are slatted in the interests of heat dispersal. 'We've just put it on Dunlop tyres as part of the testing programme; we had been trying Michelin tyres, and now we're trying the Dunlops to see if there are any significant changes.'

To access the cabin, I first press the button on the door lever and the lever swings out a little way in the fashion of a similar Jaguar item, revealing a discrete Ruf logo. You only have to get into any Ruf and you're sitting in something rather special. In this case, the seat upholstery is black and cream hound's-tooth cloth, and the seatbelt passes through an aperture in the side of the sports seat beside your thigh. The steering wheel is characteristically black padded leather without any of the gizmos that infest modern wheels, so you're looking through the apertures in the wheel arms rather than having switches to operate. Of the gauges, the rev-counter is Ruf logo'd, the digits are in green against a black background, and the whole car has been retrimmed so that the panel gaps in the elements of the interior are all pretty well perfectly aligned.

There's Kevlar cladding to the inside sills and the outer skins of the footwells, and the cabin rear has flat surfaces and a storage bin where the rear seats would otherwise be in a conventional 911. There's a carpeted roof and Alcantara around the A-posts and B-posts, cladding the integral roll-cage. The inside door handle levers are very neatly concealed by the armrest and door-pull, and we have trademark Ruf aluminium pedals and a serious footrest for the left foot. Overall, the interior is deliberately minimalistic because it's a CTR. There's no glove compartment; instead there are what resemble sponge bags in the lower door liners, which provide storage nooks.

I pull the engine lid release knob and the lid lifts of its own accord, revealing a very different engine as far as the visible ancillaries are concerned. The oil filler in particular is handily placed, projecting backwards for easy filling. Alois prevents my colleague from taking any photos of it as the motor is still a work in progress and could eventually look somewhat different, certainly more refined and less race car than it does currently.

It's functional the way it is now, but not photogenic. To give it the feeling of the air-cooled engine we've put the alternator into the centre, and we have relocated the air conditioning compressor to the front with an

electric motor. The power steering pump is also in the front with an electric motor, so we can afford to have a very clean engine here.

Back in the day, we thought the 964's suspension was radical when it shifted from torsion bars to wishbones: the Yellowbird is in a different league, taking a leaf out of its mid-engined CTR-3 sibling's set-up – and then some. Its coil-over spring-damper units, assistor shocks and adjustors are mounted horizontally, front to back on either side under the front lid, rather than vertically, and the similar rear units are also mounted horizontally, but laterally, from side to side. According to Ruf PR Marc-André Pfeifer, the benefit of having them horizontal rather than vertical is that 'the car doesn't bounce on bumps like it would with conventional vertical springs and dampers, so it doesn't lose contact with the road surface, and therefore it doesn't lose traction.' It also provides greater space for accommodating wider tyres and bigger brakes. The fuel tank occupies a large proportion of the front boot area, but you fill it up via a race-style funnel accessed through the cap in the front lid. This shorter filler pipe also enables a larger-capacity tank, currently 8 litres (1.8gal) more, and which will eventually be 105 litres (23gal).

Marc points out that this is, really, 'the prototype, the first driving car, where we can collect experiences and make notes as to how it's working, what we need to alter and adjust.' In which

This rear tracking shot of the CTR-4 shows its prominent rear wing, nicely colour-coded with the rest of the car, while the rear bumper corners have slatted vents to aid heat dispersal.

ANTONY FRASER

RIGHT: **The cabin of the Ruf CTR-4 Yellowbird is at once sophisticated yet retro, featuring state-of-the-art instrumentation and gauges, with drilled pedals and hound's tooth-upholstered bucket seats.** ANTONY FRASER

BELOW: **Everything about the Ruf CTR-4 driving experience is extraordinarily exact, with an uncanny smoothness to the steering and the smoothness of the ride.** ANTONY FRASER

case, we're privileged to be able to see how they're getting on, and even at this stage this is a truly incredible car. I buckle up, fire up the deep-throated flat-six, and ease out of Pfaffenhausen on the flat farmland blacktop to one of our photo locations, a wonderful sweeping B-road, which we have pretty much to ourselves.

The quicker I go, the more the steering lightens up. It's unfailingly very precise, and there's no drama moving the steering wheel, partly because the new suspension allows the road wheels to turn more freely. Frankly, it's almost unnerving how smooth and direct it is, and how silky the ride. It's all very acute, from the turbo-fused acceleration to the braking punch and tight turn-in. Everything about the driving experience is extraordinarily exact, there's an uncanny smoothness to the steering lock, and when I press the accelerator pedal there's a dramatic surge forward, accompanied by the whistling of the wastegate with each shift.

This is a distinctly macho car, requiring some 3,000rpm to actually get it going, and then every gearshift is a minor workout; it's certainly not a soft touch. I'm using mostly 4,000rpm before each shift, and it has seven speeds, and though I've engaged seventh it's not for long on this fast, serpentine B-road. Actually, there doesn't seem to be much difference between sixth and seventh, and I'm still accelerating hard in seventh. The rev-counter is zinging round to 5,000, 6,000rpm, and the boost gauge is equally agitated, going right round to 1.2 bar with each throttle thrust. Turn-in is hyper-sensitive and the steering is extremely sharp, and the surge of energy it delivers when I apply the accelerator literally pins me against the backrest. Conversely, the stoppers are so strong that, under braking, my torso lunges forwards into my belt.

This is a much more potent car than its Pfaffenhausen siblings, including even the mid-engined CTR-3. It's quite different in character to other Ruf models, which could be described as relatively placid by comparison. This Yellowbird you can't be soft with – you've got to grasp the controls and really go with it. The paradox is, its very lightness and delicacy of handling and steering is at odds with the massive power available. Marc says:

The more you get the feel of it the better you know how it's going to behave. It has a huge personality, and it asks what you'd like to do with it, very directly, and you are the driver, you decide what to do, and that means in a very tough way. A major factor with most modern sports cars is that you're not afraid because you have so many electronic aids inside that you know that, no matter what you do, it will save you. Here we are in the realm where you can go over these limits, but it's you that has to take care of it. Of course, we have standards and safety regulations, but the limit of this car is so much higher in performance and cornering that first you have to get used to it. Its light weight means you have much higher braking efficiency; you can brake later, you can accelerate earlier, you can go at higher speeds around the corners, so everything is one or two steps above the limits that you've been used to before.

The person responsible for achieving these standards is Alois himself. While Stefan Roser was the test pilot for the original Yellowbird, Alois has the most experience in the behaviour of rear-engined cars, so it is he who has raised the bar and set the parameters for the new Yellowbird. Marc explains the company philosophy:

We've tried to achieve a weight balance that matches the behaviour of the mid-engined CTR-3, and this new pushrod suspension, front and rear, provides many more possibilities for us to achieve that goal. Then, of course, you just need a lot of test driving, where you either hunt for performance limits like top speed or acceleration, or – what is more important from our point of view – ensure that the car gives you as much fun as possible when driving it, because that's what it's all about, the pleasure of driving. You can make a lot of calculations and theoretical concepts, but in the end, it always comes back to experience, and this is our strength.

ABOVE: **The author enjoying himself on the Bavarian blacktop, having discovered that the CTR-4 Yellowbird is a distinctly strong-willed car, requiring at least 3,000rpm to motivate it, with every subsequent gearshift a minor workout.** ANTONY FRASER

RIGHT: **On the flat farmland blacktop, one of our photo locations is a wonderful sweeping B-road, which we have pretty much to ourselves, and the quicker I go in the CTR-4, the more the steering lightens up.**
ANTONY FRASER

Next year we celebrate eighty years of Ruf, and that's what we've tried to put into this car.

Back at the Pfaffenhausen showroom there's a group of Brits enjoying a guided tour – hi there, readers – and after refreshments I head out again in the new Yellowbird, reflecting that life just doesn't get any better than this: it's such a thrill. The car's colossal power is instantly delivered, and the whole tactile experience of the new CTR-4 is above and beyond what you would normally expect, even in a Ruf. This is a very sophisticated sports car with racing connotations as well, in the way the power is delivered and the slight shudder accompanying each shift, almost like a hint of torque steer with each gear change as the power comes in. I don't have to be trying very hard to make that happen: squeeze the throttle pedal and we're off! Let's not talk about horse power: this CTR deploys elephant power – and of course that's partly down to its lightweight construction. So, it's a muscle car in the sense that it requires you to use your muscles to actually control it when you're accelerating hard. But as well as deploying brute power it will pootle with the meekest of them in an urban context. Its ride is amazing too, and that's mainly to do with the orientation of the springs and dampers. As Alois puts it:

You feel that the unsprung weight is really minimal, and you notice when you drive how nicely the wheels stick to the road; the suspension still delivers very good ride comfort too. At the front we've gone longitudinal, so we have more space for the fuel cell and for luggage capacity and the other ancillaries we have in there. We made a different fuel cell that's filled up from the aperture in the front lid, and by doing that we've gained 8 litres (1.8gal) more fuel capacity, because you don't have the filling pipes of a normal 911. Also, we wanted to have steering that is very direct and very precise, and it's hydraulically assisted but with an electric pump, which means we can keep the engine compartment cleaner and bring weight to the front for better weight distribution. We gave up on the rear seats for that reason too, so instead you've got a luggage box behind you.

Alois takes us the few kilometres to the Ruf skunkworks, where the chassis for Yellowbird CTR-4 number two is in the process of being created. The skeleton of the chassis sits on a dais in the workshop, looking for all the world like a racing module. Two technicians hold up a complete carbon side of the car for Antony to shoot, demonstrating the lightness

Walking around the car with the author, Alois Ruf highlights some of the CTR-4's evolutions compared with its Ruf forebears. ANTONY FRASER

of it by using just two fingers. Alois obliges by picking up the entire roof panel by himself. The front and rear sub-frames are crash structures, made of lightweight steel, and bolted to the carbon monocoque. 'The bonding happens only between the parts that are made in carbon fibre. The tub is made by a German firm, the same company that makes all the DTM tubs for the race series.' Some areas are solid and extremely rigid, while other box-sections are voids.

You probably felt when you drove the car how rigid it is; there is no squeaking, there is no flex, you don't have the feeling that something is moving around, like in a steel body; it's very solid. So, we are very proud that we have done something with the traditional 911 shape that didn't hurt it. Usually whatever people do to modify a 911 only makes it worse, not better, and here we have put something together that could have been an evolution of that iconic body.

There is no doubt that the new Yellowbird CTR-4 is a masterpiece. Hints of it were manifest in the air-cooled, carbon-bodied 'Ultimate', but the Yellowbird is nothing less than a quantum leap in Ruf's ever-evolving take on the 911. Come home to roost? Far from it: these flights of fancy are still very much on the wing.

RIGHT: **Two members of the Ruf chassis construction team hold up a complete carbon side of the CTR-4 in-build, demonstrating its lightness by using just two fingers. Much of the bodywork and the special DTM tub – or safety cell – which is the nucleus of the chassis, is carbon fibre, topped off with a steel roll-cage.** ANTONY FRASER

BELOW LEFT: **Holding up the CTR-4's roof panel with his bare hands, Alois Ruf shows just how lightweight the carbon-fibre bodywork is.** ANTONY FRASER

BELOW RIGHT: **The core of the Ruf CTR-4 platform consists of a cross-braced steel and carbon DTM (Deutsche Tourenwagen Meisterschaft) race car tub, including roll-cage, with rose-jointed wishbone suspension arms.** ANTONY FRASER

TAKE IT TO THE TOP: FVD'S 991 GTS

In 2015, Porsche applied turbos across the board to all its 991s bar the GT3, for the benefit of emissions as well as performance and economy. Whether that devalues the awesome status of the 911 Turbo – the 991 in chronological terms – is a moot point, though rather irrelevant because that's just how it is.

To evaluate a 991 GTS, Antony and I visited our old friends FVD, located at Umkirch near Freiburg in the glorious Black Forest region. We're greeted by the next generation of the Brombacher family, Franziska, Max and Theo, who are handling day-to-day business and tech whilst their father Willy tans in Florida. In amongst a cross-section of Porsches – 997, 968, 964, 993, 3.2 Carrera – I'm in the workshop chatting with the three

siblings, plus FVD sales manager Alex Ben-Mahmoud. From one to another they tell me variously about the GTS and ongoing FVD projects.

Hospitalities to one side for a moment, we focus on the firm's brand-new 991 GTS show car. The parts specialists and components suppliers have always had a project car on the back burner to assess the components they sell and demonstrate their tuning prowess – putting their money where their mouth is, in fact – and we've featured several over the past few years. The latest ex-factory GTS is capable of 312km/h (194mph) thanks to its new 3.0-litre twin-turbo flat-six, while the FVD car is tuned with uprated software and modified exhaust, hiking the model's normal output from 450bhp to 540bhp on the dyno. Finished in Achat Grey Metallic, picked out with lemon-yellow flashes on the front lid, roof, side skirts

FVD Brombacher's 991 GTS pauses at Holzschlägermatte restaurant, halfway house on the Schauinslandstrasse hillclimb route. Tuned with uprated software and modified exhaust, the GTS's normal output rises from standard 450bhp to 540bhp.

ANTONY FRASER

and engine lid, the GTS runs centre-lock BBS wheels whose rims are also picked out in matching yellow. External graphics include a yellow fvd logo and Brombacher side stripes on the doors. Carbon leather seats dominate the cabin, with special stitching highlighting the leather upholstery.

As well as providing a mechanical test-bed for evaluating products they'd happily endorse and offer for sale, FVD are in the process of trying out the Nankang tyre brand, not a make we would normally associate with high-performance sports cars. To be perfectly honest, till now it had simply never booted up on my rubber radar, focused as I currently am on Vredesteins, Falkens and Continentals. This is not intended to be a tyre review, nor a eulogy of any particular brand; save to say that FVD is mightily impressed with Nankang's AR-1 on-road semi-slick, and although it is not Porsche approved due to the lack of an N-rating, they feel it is an economical alternative to the brands that most of us conventionally fit on our Porsches. Their evaluation will continue for a while yet, with on-track excursions planned, because, as Max explains;

They're not conventional street tyres, as much of the tread surface is slick. You do get a lot of tyre noise on the road, so for long-distance drivers we would probably not recommend them. My first impression is that it's like glue on track and on street, but it's noisy so we have a plus and a minus at the moment.

Once FVD are happy with the tyres they'll add an appropriate wheel and tyre package to their web stocklist inventory. 'More customers are now using their cars on weekends for track days, so it makes sense to offer a cheap option for that.' The cost is likely to be about €400–€500 per 20in rim. 'We want to be sure this combination works on this car because it's not normal for us to associate with an economy brand like Nankang, so it's a project, and if we're happy with it, it's a new way for Porsche owners to have fun on track for less money.' So far so good, then:

In a track situation these tyres are retaining their temperature and not exceeding maximum working temperature, and not graining, and although they may have a 30 percent shorter working life compared with Michelin Pilot Sport Cups, they are less than half the price. And most of the track-day guys destroy their tyres in just one day. Depends how you drive, of course: if you're a little bit more conservative they'll last longer, but driving competitively they will be finished in a day.

Apart from their outrageous 997 Turbo Cabriolet, which was wilder than anything dreamed up by Stuttgart's bling merchants, FVD are generally not that extravagant in terms of visual embellishments. But, as far as fresh aero parts go for the GTS, it already has the side skirts mounted on its sills, which are more than 20mm (0.75in) wider than the original ones, while the front splitter, diffuser and rear spoiler Gurney flap are yet to be applied. The light strip spanning the rear of the car is normally unique to the four-wheel-drive C4 Carrera, but FVD think it looks great so they've installed it on their GTS. The aerodynamic profiling is also a work in progress. 'We have two versions of our project car's bodywork revisions,' reveals Franziska, indicating the blue 991 Turbo on the forecourt, complete with splitter, sill extensions, diffuser and extended rear wing.

The aerodynamic package on that is the old-style version, and we're developing the young fashion version on the GTS, which is Max's interpretation. So there's a little bit of competition between Max and Alex while they create two different kinds of look on the car. Max is more inclined towards a big wing area with a big spoiler up front and flaps on the side, more like a racing car, while Alex's version is more like a 993 RS without such big wings. There will be two virtually different cars in the end, the less dramatic RS style or GT3 Cup style with bigger aero.

It's not just about the look: the aerodynamic additions are checked in the wind tunnel to verify their efficacy. It will also be possible for customers to combine elements of the two 'looks', because all the parts are produced by the same supplier, Moshammer, who are based in Berlin.

We were impressed by the parts and the mountings we received from them, and they are easy to fit: you don't have to cut or glue because you're only mounting on the original existing mounting points. We like that, because we can send the parts all around the world and we don't need to explain to somebody in Hong Kong how to mount the part because it's obvious and straightforward.

The mechanical embellishments are equally evident – at least when the engine's fired up – by virtue of the modified exhaust system. The conversion starts by incorporating a 200-cell HD converted stainless steel sports catalytic converter (that's 200 cells per square inch). Max explains:

LEFT: **An FVD Brombacher-tuned 991 Turbo outside the firm's Umkirch premises. The splitter, sill extensions, diffuser and extended rear wing represent FVD's alternative aero set-up, avoiding the use of big wings.** ANTONY FRASER

BELOW: **Close-up view of the silencer, exhaust pipes and turbo on a Porsche 991 GTS. The silencer box bears an FVD plate. FVD's conversion of the 991 GTS begins with the installation of a 200-cell HD converted stainless-steel sports catalytic converter, the benefits of which are manifest in gains in horsepower and torque.** ANTONY FRASER

That's the newest generation of the sport catalytic converter, and it's a really expensive thing because there's a lot of cladding inside: one of these is around €400 even before we get into the exhaust system. We've made everything a little bit sportier, a little bit more aggressive. And this is something that the customer can already buy [he shows me the part number], but it is the first time that the complete system, including software and all the other modifications, is mounted on one car, so we have to test it to prove our initial horsepower and torque gains.

It goes on a Dyno before and after. 'The sound is incredible. It is loud – wake the neighbours loud – like a race car, though it is dimmed by the press of the Sport button, and this is our first experience with this range and volume of sound which this system produces, so we are excited about that.'

The FVD crew reckon their GTS's 3.0-litre engine had a head start in the power-hike stakes, being some 70bhp better off than the quoted standard figure out of the box.

We were lucky that we had a car with a little bit more power than it should have had as standard, so we tuned it to 70bhp on top of the existing power. So

that's 540bhp at 6,500rpm, and the torque figure is 651Nm (480lb ft) at 4,000rpm, which is conservative, and we've already pulled back because we felt we had too much for a rear-wheel-drive car. We've mostly achieved that increase in power by remapping the ECU. It's a nice power curve; it lowers at the end so it's manageable, it's not like it jumps at you, and it's good to drive.

By focusing on the 991 GTS as well as the 991 Turbo, FVD are on top of the game.

It's a little bit more complex to tune a normally aspirated car, and now every 911 has a turbo of course, that makes it easier to adjust the boost pressure. It's a whole lot of power that you need to change, and to match that so the car feels natural and not too excited, and especially that you don't risk something with the engine. Our target is to make it stronger, more reliable and a daily-drive car. The best solution would be to have a racing car at the push of a button, and that's not possible, but we're going in this direction, and that's only the start. It's a project car, and we're developing parts for it that we can sell later on.

Talking of parts, which is FVD's stock in trade, we do the guided tour. In the year since we last visited a great deal has changed. There's been plenty of expansion, and although the workshop and IT departments haven't changed, the reception has been reshuffled, but, more fundamentally, the purchasing office, stores and dispatch are now around the corner in a different building, with much greater capacity all round. They've painted the 964 hoarding as well – what was Mint is now Yellow. FVD also sells a few cars, more as a sideline, and we notice a couple of long-bonnet 911s and a trio of 996 Cabriolets imported from the USA.

Time for an outing. I spend a bit of time concentrating on getting my ear tuned in to the difference between the tyre noise and the exhaust noise, because at a certain resonance they're pretty similar. I alternate the GTS's energy mode switch from Normal to Sport and Sport Plus, where the bubbling noise abates, while the suspension stiffens and the shift actuates more quickly. I can have a comfy ride, a sporty drive or a track-day blast. 'In Sport mode it matches perfectly with our exhaust,' says Max. 'With the regular exhaust there wasn't much of a difference in the exhaust in the different modes. Now you can really hear the difference when you change the mode.'

The Schauinsland Hillclimb

We motor leisurely through Freiburg and head through the prosperous suburb of Günterstal, where the climb starts at a totally innocuous spot 400m (1,300ft) above sea level. There is a white marking on the road indicating the start of the Freiburg-Schauinsland hillclimb, but blink and you miss it. It's like that at the top too, with no obvious finish line, though the adjacent restaurant is quite busy so I'm watching out for vehicles at this point rather than signposts. In its day, this was one of the most spectacular hillclimbs on the European Hillclimb Championship calendar, and had a reputation for being one of the most difficult too. Comprising 127 corners, it runs for nearly 12km (7 miles), summiting at an altitude of 1,200m (4,000ft) in the Schauinsland highlands, which, once you're out of the trees, afford fabulous views into valleys and the distant hills.

To start with, the route is flanked by mature beech trees and scrub, but after a few corners it climbs into a dense forest of conifers, with single-section Armco barrier to one side and, more often than not, rock face on the other. I have to say, these Nankangs are gripping mightily impressively as I twirl the steering wheel. I glimpse forest tracks on some hairpins, daylight on others, but the blacktop is flanked by unremitting green till it emerges dramatically at the Holzschläger Matten-Kurve, where we pause to survey the most glorious view out over

Revelling in the FVD GTS's performance around Schauinsland's myriad hairpins, switching between Normal, Sport and Sport Plus modes, while the suspension stiffens and the shift actuates more quickly – and the exhaust gets louder.

ANTONY FRASER

A clear run across the top of Schauinsland allows the FVD 991 GTS to deploy its power, and the throttle response when the turbos come in is instantaneous.

ANTONY FRASER

the subalpine pastures – and return later to lunch at Die Kurve chalet restaurant. This is but half distance on the climb, where in its 1960s heyday, most of the 60,000 spectators gathered in the grandstands, long gone now, to catch a glimpse of the cars as they flashed by, one by one, before ducking back into the forested turns for the final half-dozen kilometres.

Back in 1957, the new FIA European Hillclimb Championship featured works teams from Porsche and Ferrari with drivers of the calibre of Ludovico Scarfiotti and Edgar Barth. Although the calendar varied, Mont Ventoux, Gaisberg and Freiburg-Schauinsland were included every season for fifteen years. Porsche drivers wore the Sports Car category crown from 1958 to 1968, while bagging the Gran Turismo title literally every year from 1960 right up to 1980. Perhaps Freiburg-Schauinsland's most important meetings were in 1963, 1964 and 1965, when the World Sports Car Championship included both rallies and hillclimbs, and Edgar Barth (Jürgen's father) was victorious in 1963 and 1964, though in 1965 Ludovico Scarfiotti led Gerhard Mitter home in the Ferrari Dino 206P. In 1963 Barth, driving a Porsche 718 RS, posted an average speed of more than 100km/h for the first time in the event's history, and in 1964 he won again in the 718 RS, taking 6min 36.4sec to cover the 11.2km (7 miles), followed in third place by Herbie Müller in a 904/8. Between 1957 and 1970, the list of Schauinsland winners is topped by Barth, with Jo Bonnier, Scarfiotti, Heini Walter, Gerhard Mitter, Peter Schetty and Rolf Stommelen also claiming the laurels for Porsche – and, just twice, Ferrari.

The factory teams' interest waned in the early 1970s, though Freiburg-Schauinsland staged one final meeting in 1972, when the DRM (Deutsche Rennsport-Meisterschaft) visited the hill-climb in its inaugural year. The 139-strong entry featured Reinhold Jöst in a 908/03, though the winner was Hans-Joachim Stuck in a Köln 2600 Capri. Would we cut the mustard in a 991 GTS? Undoubtedly, though the heroes of yesteryear wouldn't have had to contend with cyclists, hikers and bikers – who are banned on weekends for their own good.

After lunch there's more serious photoshooting to be done, and shooting means driving. Schauinsland is an amazing adrenaline rush as I sling-shot from one curve to the next, sweeping into the large, open radius of the Holzschläger Matten-Kurve: there's hardly a straight worth the name, just endless bends of varying degrees of arc and apex, sometimes open enough to see the exit, though sometimes that's obscured by foliage. All the time at the back of my mind is the historical perspective – that the titans of the sport once hurtled up here, putting life and machine on the line. There's never a sense that the GTS is going to get away from me; I feel you can trust it all the time, and that it's not going to bite me mid-turn. Maybe I lose a little in the way of emotion in a car that's so competent; imagine how raw the experience would be in a short-wheelbase 911! Then I would be living more literally on the edge.

Going quickly, FVD's GTS is a combination of driver intuition and co-ordinated controls. Steering is impeccable, and from bend to bend I aim it precisely where I want it to go and it complies with no drama. There's the omnipresent popping and banging on the overrun, and the throttle response when I press down and the turbos come in is instantaneous with that satisfying surge forward. No need for trepidation about grip: these Nankang

Panning shot of the **FVD 991 GTS** at speed on Schauinslandstrasse summit, revealing the stark lemon-yellow detailing on wheel rims and sills against the subtle Achat Grey Metallic hue of the car bodywork. ANTONY FRASER

The **FVD 991 Turbo's** aero kit is more modest than their **GTS** – comparable with a 993 RS with not such big wings, they claim. In any case, the aerodynamic additions are fine-tuned in the wind tunnel to ensure they **work.** ANTONY FRASER

Posed beside Schauinsland's Holzschläger Matten-Kurve, the **FVD 991 GTS** shows off its pert rear contours and lemon-yellow detailing.

ANTONY FRASER

semi-slicks really do *do* the business, heating up and holding their temperature well, considering this is a B-road at a relatively high altitude, where it's cold but sunny. They really do have a lot of purchase when they're leant on, and their road noise is something I could probably live with because they are so grippy.

What goes up must come down, and even though I prefer going up, it's still exciting zooming down, and of course you don't need to have so much power heading downhill because you have gradient and weight of car working for you. But on the ascent, you feel the engine working harder, and that's more thrilling because it's delivering the most power and the most torque. Going down doesn't require full throttle to attain optimum performance; it's about braking harder too, as well as judging turn-ins accurately. 'It's also a little bit safer to go up than down,' Max reckons, 'because if you miss a corner you really are going too fast, but if you're heading up you always have a little bit of gravity to fight against.' Whatever, this is the perfect environment for honing and appreciating an automotive work of art. It may be a project car but, frankly, it's hard to see how the GTS could be bettered as it is, though the additional aero might raise the stakes a little, on the autobahn as well as visually. Whatever they do, it won't be an uphill struggle.

NUCLEAR POWER: THE ATOMIC 991 TURBO SE

A 991 Turbo S is a very fast and capable car by any standards. But as a track-day weapon? When we hear the word 'Atomic', those of us of a musical persuasion inevitably conjure up images of Blondie. However, when applied to a Porsche Turbo in the Nürburgring neighbourhood, we find ourselves dallying in the workshops of Atomic Performance Parts and Motorsport Equipment, a nanosecond from the hallowed circuit.

I'd driven over from England with race photographer Carlie Thelwell, having hustled my 986 Boxster S through the Low Countries to Germany's Eifel region. It's Nürburgring 24-Hours weekend, and the district is rammed with performance cars, engendering a buzz all of its own. My particular goal, though, is Atomic, to have a drive in their specially tuned 991 Turbo S. Atomic have two premises locally: a showroom on the first floor of Nürburgring's full-on shopping Boulevard, in which they display a car they've tuned – such as this – as well as regular race wear and fan clothing. Their business nucleus is their workshop in Kelberg village, 5km (3 miles) from the Ring, and about the size of an aircraft hangar.

Full frontal of Atomic's 991 Turbo S, enhanced with a sports exhaust and racing catalytic converters as well as modified turbos with larger spinners, and larger intercoolers, raising power output to 650bhp. KOSTAS SIDIRAS

This cutaway of a Garrett turbocharger casing was on display in the showroom of Atomic Racing Performance and Tuning Parts in the Nürburgring Boulevard. Here's how it works: the engine's exhaust gases spin up the turbine wheel located at left – to some 150,000rpm – connecting with the compressor wheel in the centre, which receives air from the right-hand side of the unit. The cutaway circular tube supplies compressed air to the engine. JOHNNY TIPLER

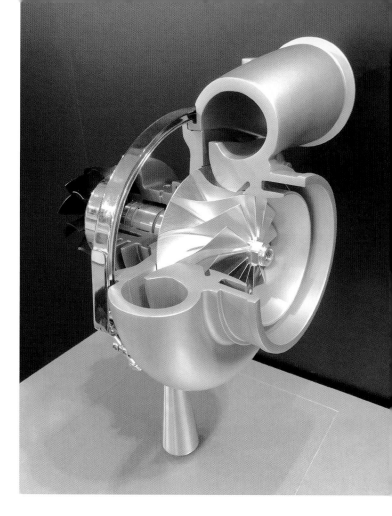

I'm chatting here with Atomic's principal, Dmitry Ryzhak: lean, personable and with a twinkle in his eye, he explains (in perfect Russian-accented English) that, initially, the building was planned just as a workshop but then split into two with a car-storage facility for their own cars and customer's cars – one of which happens to be a 996 GT2 from Japan in delectable Zanzibar Red. A couple of hunky Nissan GT-Rs are in the throes of competition preparation, but centre stage is my core objective: the white 991 Turbo S, liberally peppered with Atomic graphics.

Dmitry explains the thinking behind its transformation from continental cruiser to trackable tornado:

> We use it mostly here for Nürburgring laps, and at some other circuits such as Hockenheim, Spa, Zand-voort and Assen, also in the Netherlands, and the Lausitzring. We do multiple runs on the Nürburgring, track days and timed events, here or at Spa. On track days, the circuit's usually open for a full day, so you arrive in the morning and you can drive your session, which is like 30–45 minutes, depending on classes, or on certain days it's from morning until midday, and then after lunch it's open again all afternoon. You can calculate lap times yourself, and I use an on-board device to record videos and for lap timing.

Dmitry takes the wheel on circuits, and his business partner, Oleg, does drag racing events with it.

Dmitry describes the tuning enhancements:

> Obviously, even in stock condition, the 991 Turbo S is very good, but we decided to go a little bit further, so we installed a sports exhaust with racing catalytic converters – though from the rear it looks stock – and we have fitted modified turbochargers with larger spinners, and we also installed larger intercoolers, so output is now about 650bhp.

It's all very well upping the power output, but what about the handling? Dmitry explains:

> This year we upgraded the suspension to H&R competition coil-overs, which is perfect for circuit use. The normal suspension works well, and sometimes you feel that it is dancing on the road, but it is a bit too soft, especially at the Nordschleife when you have very long, fast turns and you want it to be glued to the track.

Atomic technicians installed the suspension and it was set up by a racing driver who did the fine-tuning and wheel alignment. Wide-rim 19in Advan Racing GT wheels enable fitment of slightly wider tyres, which are Michelin Cup 2, 265 instead of 245 at the front, and 325 instead of 305 on the rears. They elected to retain the standard Porsche brakes because they work well, they're lightweight, they don't fade, Dmitry likes their initial bite, which is powerful enough, and yet they can still employ standard pads. 'I have not had any issues with braking, on the Nordschleife or any other tracks,' he says.

However, the key factor in raising the 991 Turbo S's power was remapping the ECU. This was carried out by Dmitry's work

LEFT: **An under-car view of one of the turbos and exhaust pipe on the Atomic 991 S Turbo.** KOSTAS SIDIRAS

BELOW: **The hand-held remote Cobb ECU map and software module controls everything aboard the Atomic 991 Turbo S, from power stages to the speed of the PDK shift.** KOSTAS SIDIRAS

partner, Oleg, whose speciality is tuning cars for circuit and drag racing. 'We have several maps that we use to reprogram the ECU,' says Dmitry, 'and you can easily take it up to 550bhp, or even 750bhp, in the space of 5 minutes.' It might depend on the nature of the racetrack – Spa versus Nordschleife, for instance – the track surface, or weather conditions, or how much power you need, but you can change the ECU mapping by plugging in the Cobb handset into a socket located in the passenger footwell. 'When Oleg was doing some drag racing events he was using the most aggressive mapping in order to get the fastest time, so there are lots of things you can adjust with the ECU and the tools that come with it.'

It's simple enough to set up the ECU monitoring apparatus, though actuating the electronics on the handset throws up myriad possibilities. Dmitry elaborates:

Once you've connected the cables to the car you have several options. For example, you can adjust the air-fuel power ratio, review temperature, ignition timing, check performance calibration in km/h or mph. You can change the map of the engine, and you can remap the PDK as well. To do that, you go to the change map

menu. There are mild and aggressive versions of the map, and it has a trouble-shooting facility, which highlights errors such as tyre pressures so you can erase them, and a PDK channel so you can see what's happening with the transmission.

The cabin interior is a suave blend of Alcantara and blue leather. The magnificent seats are from a GT2, and they swapped the normal multi-function steering wheel for a sports wheel with paddle-shifts to actuate the PDK transmission, creating a perfect driving position. There's no roll-cage, contrary to what you might expect in a trackable car, but Dmitry believes that the chassis is already so stiff that the difference that a cage would make in raising torsional rigidity would provide little benefit for the handling, though in terms of safety a roll-cage could be beneficial.

With every successive generation – from 996 and 997 to 991 – the construction of the chassis is better, so as a safety device we could fit a full cage, but I don't think just a roll-over bar would have much benefit. We have been thinking of fitting one for next

Author Johnny Tipler gets the lowdown on their business from Atomic bosses Oleg Kucharov and Dmitry Ryzhak. KOSTAS SIDIRAS

season, but it will make the car a lot heavier. So, yeah, it will be more like race car, but at the moment it's really good street car and it's also very quick on the track.

As far as future developments are concerned, Dmitry and Oleg are more inclined to focus on the sophistications of the aero:

Last year it had the front bumper and front lid from a GT3 Cup Car, but we returned it back to a stock bumper because of ground clearance issues, but soon we shall probably fit a rear wing from a GT3 RS and put a small carbon lip on the rear spoiler, and we will fit a front bumper from a GT3. So, if we do go deeper with the exterior stuff we will probably fit a roll-cage as well.

Atomic's roots go back to 2005 in the Ukraine, where Dmitry hails from, the firm relocating to Russia in 2007 when he opened a company in Moscow. The name was already in use by Oleg's performance tuning workshop, and as well as being evocative of immense power and fundamental energy, it was also a convenient acronym of his employees' initials. Dmitry was then in the process of starting his performance parts sales and distribution operation, and since their respective businesses complemented each other, they joined forces. Today, they are affiliated to Southern California-based Ravi Dolwani, manager of CSF Racing & High Performance Radiators, whose decals appear on the car.

It was in Moscow that Dmitry was bitten by the Porsche bug. He acquired his first one in 2011, a Cayman 987 S with manual

gearbox. Then, in 2013, he participated in the Russian Porsche Sports Cup, now called the Porsche Challenge. The Cayman came to a sticky end, however.

I'd bought it with a friend, and we took it to several track days in Russia and Europe, including the Nürburgring, and on the first run with its all-new suspension set-up, my friend crashed it. Which was a bit disappointing! So, in 2013, I bought a 997 Turbo with manual gearbox. I still have that car, which is now in Moscow, being rebuilt in GT2 style with just rear-wheel drive and GT2 body-kit, and I shall bring it to the Nürburgring to try it out.

Atomic have enjoyed an inexorable expansion. In 2015, they started their Dubai branch, and in 2016 they set up at the Nürburgring, located initially in the automotive industrial estate at Meuspath, across the road from the long Döttinger Höhe straight, where many of the local race teams and tyre and suspension manufacturers are based. When the retail and display space became available on Nürburgring Boulevard, they took that and relocated the workshop to its present site. Each Atomic outlet has a different emphasis.

Here, at the Nürburgring, we sell race wear and tuning parts as well as brake pads, discs, race seats and harnesses. We have a race shop in Düsseldorf, and in Russia we sell more hardware, brakes, suspension and exhausts, while in Dubai they are doing more tuning because there the customers want lots of power. In Dubai there is quite a big UAE Porsche club, which is well organized, and they hold lots of events at Abu Dhabi and the Dubai Autodrome, where there's an artificial skidpan too.

For Atomic, storage and maintenance are also big business, and customers come from around the world – one shipped a Subaru from China for safekeeping and easy access to the Nürburgring. 'Many guys prefer to have special cars that they only drive on the Nordschleife, and they like to keep it close to the circuit, so they come here in their everyday car, and collect their track car from the garage.' We contemplate the Zanzibar Red 996 GT2 that's come from Georgia. It reminds Dmitry of a recent event he participated in at the Ring, and in a way it sums up exactly why they created the Atomic 991 Turbo S:

There was an event at Nürburgring called the Gran Turismo, a very good track day, organized by Swedes, not too crowded, and I drove part of the event with our 991 Turbo S and part with a 997 GT3. It showed up how these two cars are completely different in that context. You get very different pleasure from driving both of them, but in the 991 Turbo S you can be very fast and still feel safe, but with the 997 GT3 you are 30 seconds a lap slower, and you have to work much harder as well. So, after a couple of laps with the GT3 I climbed out of the car feeling completely wrecked, while in the 991 Turbo S you drive with air-conditioning and PDK, and it's so much faster – and you get out feeling totally relaxed. The GT3 provides drama and raw dynamics, though. So, it depends on what you want to get from the car, because each one has its own advantages.

The 991 Turbo S not only showcases what Atomic can do, it's what Dmitry himself prefers to use on track.

Many people are driving GT3s and GT3 RSs, but I wanted a car that could be comfortable on the street and also on the track. Even a 991 GT3 is not as hard work as a 997 GT3, and since the 991 Turbo S is easier to drive than 991 GT3, you can hardly compare it to a 996 or 997 GT2. And, whereas the GT2 is rear drive, the Turbo is four-wheel drive and much easier to handle on the track.

As borne out by my recent outing with RSR Nürburg's Cayman GTS, there's nothing like a spot of on-track tuition in a properly set-up car, and last year Dmitry in the 991 Turbo S joined several drivers with GT2 RSs at the Nürburgring driving school. 'On one wonderful lap I was following one quite quick guy in his GT2 RS, and back in the paddock after the lap he came over and asked, 'What car is this?' because he could not believe a regular Turbo could so closely follow his GT2 RS!'

Time to put it into practice. To start with, Dmitry takes me for a demo run to show just what this atom bomber is capable of. The first aspect to remark on is the gruff blare from the exhaust: normally turbocharged flat-sixes are somewhat muted, but this is one heck of a barker. When he started it up in the workshop I thought, 'This is the loudest Turbo I've ever heard!' On the move, the ride is subtle, the suspension finely damped. Dmitry comments:

It's quite different from stock Porsche; the suspension is nicely balanced, which is good for daily driving on normal roads when it feels quite soft, but once you go

The suspension of the Atomic Gen2-based 991 Turbo S has been upgraded with H&R competition coil-overs, ideal for use on the Nürburgring Nordschleife's long, fast corners.

KOSTAS SIDIRAS

RIGHT: **A rear tracking shot clearly demonstrates the Atomic 991 Turbo S's elevated rear wing, providing maximum downforce in a high-speed situation such as the Nürburgring.** KOSTAS SIDIRAS

BELOW: **The Atomic Turbo S's GT3 seats fit the author like a glove, while the acceleration picks up instantly and the car is totally planted and confidence-inspiring on the glorious Eifel hills.** KOSTAS SIDIRAS

into Sport mode it firms up aggressively and hugs the road surface. Also, the brakes are working better and responding quicker because the car doesn't have to change its attitude coming into a corner.

One slight drawback to this suspension and braking arrangement is the accompanying metallic noises, but that goes with the territory.

We head out of Kelberg and soon turn onto a narrow hill road. With deftly applied squirts of power, we zing along the straight bits, heavy braking hauling us up dramatically – and noisily – for the recurring corners that snake through the arable

upland, then plunge down into wooded gulches and hurtle sharply back uphill again. There's no question that this is an extremely fast and well set-up chassis, unfazed by the constricts of the chosen route. It's a glimpse of how it could be on the myriad swoops and cambers of the big-dipper Nordschleife, and yet it's perfectly civilized on the main road heading back to base. Dmitry sums up:

This car is perfectly balanced, because GT2s and GT3s are a bit too aggressive for normal road use, especially the 991 GT3 RS, but the stock 991 Turbo S is a bit too soft, so with these changes we have found the perfect balance. We can create a car exactly like this for our customers, all carefully calibrated and effectively hand-built. It's totally street-legal, and we can also see good results on the track or on the quarter mile.

We're not done yet, though. As I say, my visit happens to coincide with the 24-Hours of the Nürburgring, precluding an outing on the Nordschleife. However, on a recent visit to RSR Nürburg I discovered the Südschleife, an almost forgotten extension of the old Nürburgring circuit, parts of which are still accessible, and they provided a bit of an opportunity to spread the Atomic Booster's wings. It gives you an idea of what the original Nürburgring would have been like, a winding country road flanked by trees and ditches, and with no barriers till 1971. My snapper Kostas Sidiras knows the area, and I head out with him to record the action.

To start with, the Atomic Turbo S fits like a glove, thanks to those GT2 seats, and the regular steering wheel with its paddle shifts and lovely Alcantara rim feels just right. Driving it on my own terms, the level of control behind the wheel is perfect, the steering seems more sensitive than I would have expected. As I play myself in, I test the acceleration on a long straight: it picks up instantly and storms up and down through the PDK ratios as I tackle the wonderful open curves on these glorious Eifel hills, through which it is totally planted and confidence-inspiring. And then slowing down is a model of braking efficiency – if attended by scrape of pad on disc. It's a very seductive recipe: the ultimate in roadable speed, handling and braking, in perfect comfort, accompanied by a delightful aural soundtrack too. If this is what it's capable of on the road, then I'm signing up for a scud round the Nordschleife next time round.

Performance wise, Oleg says that it will go from 0–100km/h in 2.6sec, 'a little bit faster than the standard Porsche – we better that by two-tenths of a second – but from 100km/h to 200km/h (124mph) it's much faster: just 5.3sec, compared with standard, which is 7.10sec.' I am not surprised. This is an astonishing car, an accomplished example of what goes on at Atomic, and it can roost in my garage any time. In fact, I'm going nuclear: *Atomkraft? Ja, bitte*! I never thought I'd hear myself saying that!

It might just as well be climbing The Hill at Goodwood, because it is right next to the racecourse there: TechArt's 991 GTStreetRS storming the back roads in fine style. ANTONY FRASER

ART ATTACK: TECHART'S 991 GTSTREETRS

If you've got it, flaunt it! TechArt are past masters at that, and now they've hiked the horsepower and decked the ducting, everyone knows this rampant red roustabout is something a bit special. It's labelled the GTStreetRS: at first glance, a 911 on steroids, but precisely what sort of uppers we're dealing with isn't totally clear. And, of course, that's half the point. The reason you buy into any of the pumped-up Porsches put out there by the satellite tuners orbiting the Stuttgart solar system is that you wish to differentiate yourself as overtly as possible from the mainstream. And this beastie is the very latest manacled fist to emerge from TechArt's Leonberg lair.

It is 2019's Festival of Speed weekend, and I'm with TechArt's PR man, Marc Herdtle, discussing their latest GTStreetRS in the lee of Goodwood racecourse. First, the look of it. Those of a nervous disposition avert your gaze. The black detailing that highlights the various scoops and aero has a curious mottled effect, rather than the more conventional criss-cross weave normally manifest in carbon and Kevlar components. Marc explains:

We call it the Forged Design car. The black, random-mottled material is similar to the Lamborghini-Calloway composite; it's carbon fibre, with strands randomly aligned, so they're not like a mesh, and this gives

two things: stability to the components, but, more importantly, it provides another styling finish, which means that the bodykit is different from the GTStreetR.

And that particular vehicle is a livid lime-green machine with similar black detailing. Colour palette? There's nowhere to hide!

Starting with the 996, there have been three generations of GTStreet models.

We have a number of customers who prefer not to take their car to the racetrack, or just store it in their garage: we have those who like to drive it every day, simply because it's fun. And it's not like a race car, which, after a few kilometres will become too demanding.

The GTStreetR was no shrinking violet, but the RS model has gone a step further.

Another intention was to give the car a more aggressive look. This Forged Design composite material is fairly well known and it's been used in this market for the past three years or so. Lamborghini-Calloway actually invented it, and as far as I know Forged Composite is actually a brand name they gave to the material. But we wanted to give the car the optical appearance of this material because it really makes it a bit more radical, even more so than the GTStreetR, where one of the prominent features was the carbon-fibre mesh used for the bodykit.

As a further sophistication, the GTStreetRS is also fitted with high-tensile lightweight glass made by Corning Gorilla Glass.

Like its lurid lime-green stablemate, the GTStreetRS is also based on a Gen2 991 Turbo S, but in addition to the new

elements of bodykit, it also has a stronger TechArt power kit, incorporating new variable turbine geometry turbochargers, lifting power output in Sport mode to 770bhp and 920Nm (679lb ft) of torque, which is good enough to travel from standstill to 100km/h in a mere 2.5sec, and from 0–200km/h (124mph) in just 8.1sec. Top speed is (a governed) 340km/h (211mph) on road-legal tyres, while 360km/h (224mph) is doable with appropriate tyres on.

We do the walkaround. It's a lesson in the whys and wherefores of bodykit-enhanced aerodynamics. The front lid is unique to this model, while add-ons include the wheel-arch extensions, a profusion of air inlet and outlet ducts, as well as diffuser and trim on the rear wing. Each a piece of plastic sculpture in its own right, these pieces of bling bejewel every aspect of the car's extremities. Marc does the specifics:

If we start at the front, there are several air channels specially configured for this car, beginning with the front apron and active splitter that optimize airflow to the large ducts ventilating the water radiator and oil cooler. The front lid is in carbon fibre, which we call the TechArt aero lid because it has an aerodynamic shape that guides the air into the two NACA ducts that provide additional brake cooling. It's important to stress that these are not merely visual features; every air duct and every opening you can see in the car's body has a technical and practical purpose.

There's more ducting over the top of the front wheel arches in the shape of ventilation louvres that extract hot air from the brakes. These louvres are similar to those of the GT3 RS, but Marc stresses that they are TechArt parts, being slightly larger and angled differently, to improve the ventilation inside the wheel arches and assist with heat dissipation from the brakes. The ducts in the rear three-quarter panel ahead of the rear wheel arches feed air to the intercoolers, and are also a little bigger than the regular 991 Turbo S. There's also an intriguing air duct on the leading edge of the rear lid, which serves to guide additional air into the engine, necessary on account of the power hike. On both lower corners of the rear panel there are paired vents that release hot air and also act as venturii to augment rear downforce.

The black front lid is a hollow carbon-fibre shell, composed of upper and lower layers, and the underside is embossed with the TechArt logo. With the front lid lifted, the eye falls on the unusual orifices that link with the NACA ducts in the lid, channelling the cooling air downwards. 'Everything that TechArt does with a car body has a function,' declares Marc. 'It's there for a purpose; hardly anything is done just for ornamentation or special effect.' That said, you don't own a TechArt car if you're anything other than ostentatious.

Visually, of course it's making an extreme statement, but all such offerings have to be backed up by a set of equally rad wheels. In this case, they are 20in forged alloy TechArt Formula IV Race, in matching black, progeny of the company's five-spoke wheel design going back twenty years and now viewed as classic in some circles. Actually, these are double-fives – ten-spoke, if you like. Marc qualifies the designation: 'Our wheels evolved from Formula II to Formula III, which was TechArt's first forged wheel, and then Formula IV Race, which is a lightweight forged wheel with a central locking device, and that is basically how the Race wheels differ from the others.' They're shod with Michelin Pilot Cup Sport 2, which are 265/35 ZR20 at the front and 325/30 ZR20 at the rear. The brakes are original Porsche 991 Turbo ceramic composite discs, and although TechArt used to make their own brakes, they decided that the standard-issue stoppers were so good they might as well stick with them.

The rear wing is one of the more complex devices that I've seen: it's an active two-level bi-plane that can be raised and lowered at the press of a button on the centre console, cantilever-tilting by 15 degrees. The wing also activates automatically, so it deploys at certain speeds, and then in performance mode its angle self-adjusts by 15 degrees to generate more downforce on the rear axle. Its supports and upper level are in black carbon, with that deep red lower section and endplates. All TechArt aerodynamic bodykit passes through the wind tunnel during its development, and the shape of the top

Rear three-quarter static of the Gen2 911 Turbo-based TechArt GTStreetRS displays the adjustable two-tier wing and aerofoil. The curious mottled effect on the wheel-arch spats is inherent in the carbon-composite material.
ANTONY FRASER

wing profile is a case in point, being similar to the GTStreetR, though the RS version employs a little spoiler at the top of the car's rear window, which has a very slight angle – enough to deflect the airflow directly onto the wing profile. 'Overall, it's well balanced aerodynamically,' avers Marc, 'which means it has sufficient downforce, especially at higher speeds, but it still has a good drag coefficient, and that's one of the achievements of the engineering department, working with our designers in the wind tunnel.'

The underneath of the car is almost completely covered, so in effect it's flat, in the interests of generating ground-effect downforce, amplified by the diffuser at the bottom of the rear valance. It also has a more cosmetic effect of highlighting the centrally mounted exhaust tailpipes, which consist of four tips, the culmination of a full TechArt system. Marc again:

This exhaust generates a suitable sound for the car, and it's a controlled system that's operating without steps, so it's continuously adjusting the sound. Usually exhaust systems just have the valves open or closed, but this one has intermediate positions as well, so it's still possible to homologate it in terms of noise so it's road-legal, but on the other hand when you're in the mood you just switch to Sport mode and then you'll have the full sound experience as well.

The clue as to the car's persona is in the name – this is a road car, though, as Marc affirms, it can perform perfectly well in track-day mode too. 'It can be driven perfectly normally on the street, and then you can go to the racetrack and drive it in an impressive way because it's powerful enough to perform like a genuine sports-GT car.' As a package, you can see how it comes together, providing the security of the Turbo's all-wheel-drive powertrain, combined with the specially evolved aero. Suspension is enhanced by PDCC (Porsche Dynamic Chassis Control)-compatible Bilstein coil-over dampers. 'In that way, you have a car that is not only quick in a straight line, but can also drive winding roads quickly, and it still provides all the comfort you expect from a 991 Turbo S.'

True enough. The so-called Clubsport cabin is a sophisticated snug bar where creature comforts abound: 'It retains air conditioning, it has heated seats, regular sat-nav, and it has everything you need to drive in everyday mode,' Marc says; 'it's the best of both worlds – one which is pure performance, and the other which is comfort and individuality.' It's equipped with snug-fit TechArt-monogramed seats, with GTStreetRS embroidered in the backrests. Another new fabric to be incorporated in the seat upholstery is 'virgin wool', complementing the leather, said to be not merely comfortable (which the seats undoubtedly are) but also beneficial in cabin climate control as well as having flame retardant properties. There's also a feast of Alcantara going on,

The cabin of the TechArt GTStreetRS is equipped with monogrammed seats, upholstered in 'virgin wool' and four-point harnesses, with matching red detailing on the clock, rev-counter face and Sport Chrono dial.

ANTONY FRASER

The smell of leather: a rich welter of tanned hides hangs in TechArt's upholstery workshop, ready for cutting to clad the interiors of customer cars and the firm's own products. JOHNNY TIPLER

The upholstery workshop at TechArt's Leonberg premises, with sewing machines and numerous pattern templates for car seats and cabin upholstery as well as the in-house steering wheels.
JOHNNY TIPLER

and a GTStreetRS plaque on the glove locker declares this car is number two out of ten special editions. Occupants can select either the four-point harness or regular seatbelts, all in red to match the car's body colour, depending on the envisaged action. Instead of rear seats, the space is occupied by a cross-braced rollover bar, painted in red to match the bodywork. The PDK shift is nicely embossed with TechArt's logo, and elements of it are in matching red as well. The TechArt wheel is flat across the bottom to clear your thighs, and it's manufactured in-house – we've admired their workshops when visiting their Leonberg premises, revelling in a leathery welter of vertically suspended hides (sniff those skins!) and lines of skeleton wheels. There's a bespoke element to all TechArt offerings. As Marc affirms:

All our steering wheels are completely made in house; we have our own moulds on which the wheel is built up on the basic inner steel rim and arms, and all the features and functions are incorporated onto it. If the customer orders a heated steering wheel, for example, this element will be built into the TechArt wheel.

Another example of the company's personalizing service is the perforated Alcantara lining the central areas, through which the red body colour is visible. Other neat touches include the red clock, rev-counter face and the Sport Chrono dial. Even the electric seat adjuster levers are painted red. Every GTStreet-RS is delivered with a hand-stitched document wallet, a rather fetching handmade helmet bag – containing a red racing helmet with the number 2 painted on it, relevant to this particular car, of course – and a shoe bag to hold your driving shoes, also in the same colour and material as the cabin interior.

As far as Porsche are concerned, companies such as TechArt who hone and fettle their products are about as welcome at the Festival of Speed as a peregrine at a pigeon party. The GTStreetRS doesn't get a run up The Hill, but nevertheless, it is parked on a plinth among the supercars for the duration of the Festival weekend. So, we do at least get to grips with it in the hinterland surrounding Goodwood racecourse.

Even just sitting behind the wheel, let alone starting up, this is an awesome machine. I slot the PDK shift into D and off we go. I play myself in, feeling out the gutsy power delivery. That little red turn button on the steering wheel arm is just too tempting! I switch to Sport mode, and instantly the power kit comes on, manifest in a surge of revs and blast of exhaust volume – and an additional gobbet of power, should I wish to deploy it. Like a giant ladybird, the GTStreetRS prowls the Sussex back roads. It's firm, but not distressingly so, and though I can feel all the undulations in the road, the ride is fine.

The Sussex downs provide some hugely entertaining and – if you're pressing on – challenging enough hilly back roads, and I sling the GTStreetR through a series of agreeably banked S-bends, taking care with throttle pressure, and it steers perfectly and flows smoothly through the turns. I can easily induce as much drama and excitement as I wish just with a tweak on the accelerator. It's a delectable experience. On the straight, it's exhilarating, with acceleration suggestive of an Olympic

sprinter, bolting along the forested straights and pressing me back in my seat unless I'm circumspect with the throttle. Yet at no time did I feel it had the better of me, and, ultimately, it's a very civilized car.

Our photoshoot involves a succession of swiftly executed about-turns for the snapper's benefit, and as I approach some of the more uneven turnarounds I apply the on-board nose-lift mechanism so the front splitter doesn't catch on cobbles, elevating the nose by 60mm (2.5in). The on/off button is between the seats, roughly where you might expect the cigarette lighter to live, and the front drops to normal ride height once on the move again.

While some tuners might strip their subject car to the bare bones in a quest for lightness, in pursuit of speed and handling finesse, TechArt does not seek to save weight; rather the opposite, as they strive to provide the most comfortable and occupant-friendly environment within the cab as possible.

Our cars still have their navigation system, their air-conditioning, whatever it takes, and all TechArt cars, even if it's the GTStreetRS, which delivers the ultimate performance, can be individualized so it has everything you can possibly need for the perfect driving experience, and we should not be confused with tuners that are mainly focused on getting the best lap times, for example. Saving the last gramme is not really the point, because otherwise we wouldn't have all these creature-comfort features still on board. We are presenting a

ABOVE: **On the straight, the TechArt GTStreetRS is exhilarating, bolting along the forested roads, and yet, ultimately, it's a very civilized car.** ANTONY FRASER

RIGHT: **Driving through a series of S-bends, the helmsman finds that the TechArt GTStreetR steers perfectly smoothly, though drama can be provoked and corrected with a dab on the accelerator.** ANTONY FRASER

Fabulous painting of a 991 Turbo S by specialist Porsche artist Tanja Stadnic, who's presenting her artwork here at a company reception (www.tanjastadnic.com).

TANJA STADNIC

complete package, a car the customer can drive every day, or in racing mode if he likes.

Everything mentioned above, when applied to the GTStreetRS, would add €143,520 to the price of the standard 991 Turbo. But this is customizing at its finest, if most blatant.

We've only seen spy shots of a car that's purportedly the forthcoming 992 Turbo testing on the Nürburgring, though rumours suggest it's not far away from release, probably late 2019. TechArt are currently working on their own version of the 992 Turbo, and we shall no doubt be reviewing that in due course. Modern art has always been about pushing the boundaries of what's acceptable, sometimes assaulting the viewer's sensitivities, which doesn't please everyone, especially not the purists. But TechArt have done something fairly sensational with the 991 Turbo and gone that extra mile with the GTStreetRS. It grows on you. In fact, it is a work of art on its own terms.

THE LONGEST DAY: THE NÜRBURGRING 24-HOURS WITH JÖRG BERGMEISTER

Pounding the Nürburgring's combined F1 and Nordschleife circuits, the world's fastest GTs vie for track space with tin-tops and hot hatches during the extraordinary 24-Hours race. Following the fortunes of the Falken Racing Team's Porsche 991 GT3 R, I stay up all night, but do I get lucky?

With one accord, participating drivers regard the N-24 as simply the best race in the world, and it's easy to see why. The entry list comprises 202 assorted cars – models you might conceivably expect to see on the road. Turn them into racing cars and let them loose for a day and night on the most amazing racetrack in the world: that's the Nürburgring 24-Hours. It's staged on a combination of the Nordschleife and F1 circuit, totalling 24.38km (15.149 miles) per lap. There is nothing quite like it: the difference between this and other 24-hour events is the amazing variety of cars, the unique topography, and the challenges that those factors create.

June 2019 saw the forty-ninth running of the event, which, since the demise of world championship events on the Nordschleife, has become the most important meeting on the fabled circuit's calendar. The N-24 is a stand-alone race, though sharing rules and regulations with the ten-round German VLN Langstreckenmeisterschaft Nürburgring (VLN Endurance Racing Championship Nürburgring). It's significant enough to attract direct manufacturer support, with the leading Porsche teams vying with Mercedes-Benz, Audi and BMW, and crewed by a significant number of professional racing drivers. The 202-car entry list kicks off with an eye-watering melange of supercars, including the Audi R8 LMS, Mercedes-Benz SLS AMG GT3, Porsche 911 GT3 R and BMW M6 GT3, plus a smattering of Aston Martin Vantage AMR GT4s, the Chrysler Viper CC, Nissan GT-R GT3, Lexus RCF GT3, Ferrari 488

LEFT: **Jörg Bergmeister knows the Nürburgring really well, having driven his first lap aged twelve, and tackled his first 24-hour race here in 1999.** CARLIE THELWELL

BELOW: **The sun comes up over the Nordschleife as the Falken 991 GTR rushes through Schwalbenschwanz bend, with the race barely at half distance.**
CARLIE THELWELL

ABOVE: **The turbocharged 718 Cayman GTS features in the second phalanx of the N-24 grid, along with normally aspirated Cayman GT-4 CS. This is the H&R-sponsored Mühlner Motorsport Cayman rounding the Nordschleife's Karussel.** JOHNNY TIPLER

ABOVE RIGHT: **Martin Ragginger took the first stint in the Falken team's brand new 991 GTR for the 2019 Nürburgring 24-Hours. The biggest change in the car's controls was the absence of a clutch pedal, with every gear selection taking place electronically now.** JOHNNY TIPLER

GT3, KTM X-Bow GT4, Lamborghini Huracán and Glickenhaus SCG003C. That's just the quick ones; there are two more tranches, the second wave headed by Cayman GTR-4 and GTS, Audi TT and BMW M4, with the third wave a mix of Golf, Civic, WRX, Clio and Astra hot hatches. Of the 672 drivers present, top-line aces in the Porsche camp include Nick Tandy, Earl Bamber, Kevin Estre and Jörg Bergmeister, to name but four.

To get the stats in order, since 1970 the N-24 has been won twelve times by Porsches, and last year's winners Estre/Dumas/Vanthoor/Bamber qualified fourth fastest for the 2019 race. The entry includes forty-two Porsches – twenty-one GT3s and twenty-one Caymans – subdivided into 991 RS and Cup versions, and 718 GTS and GT4 versions. Fans certainly get value for money: as well as the N-24 the weekend kicks off with heats of the World Touring Car Championship and a race for historics, in which a broad array of Porsches past – 944 Turbo Cup, 964 Cup and 911 ST – vie with old- and young-timers of every persuasion.

In 2019, the Porsche factory is represented by seven cars – Manthey, IronForce, Frikadelli and Falken – crewed by four drivers apiece, most of whom are contracted to Porsche. It's the Falken Team's twentieth year at the N-24, so I'm monitoring their progress accordingly. This time they have a new 911

– a 991 GTR, helmed by Jörg Bergmeister, Dirk Werner, Klaus Bachler and Martin Ragginger. Team boss Sven Schnabl, who preps the car explains:

From the outside it looks mostly the same, but if you look beneath the bodywork it's different: for instance, everything is done by electronics, including the transmission, so there's no clutch pedal. The air intake is different, and we have new wishbones in the front, so quite a few changes. Things are developing very quickly in these GT3 cars and every step and stage means we'll go faster and faster and then the governing body will try to cut us on power and try to slow us down. It used to be that we would be a lot faster on the straight and slow in the corners, but now we're a lot slower on the straights, in fact slower than Porsche Cup Cars, even slower than GT4 cars, so they can overtake us, but then we have to dive-bomb them into the corners.

We discuss BoP: the balance of performance that's intended to make all the cars the same, more or less. 'The rule makers have different strategies: they can change the weight of the cars, restrict the size of the boost, and there's all kinds of things they can change on the cars to make them equal and thereby get closer lap times and better racing.' Though in previous years' N-24s, their success has been debatable, this year they seem to have got it about right.

Jörg Bergmeister is flush from a class win at Le Mans the previous weekend, and I quiz him about the specific challenges of the N-24.

Well, it's definitely a big challenge; it's very demanding on the driver and if you take the traffic into account, you definitely need a lot of luck to finish this race. There are many cars out there, and even if you think you have an understanding with another driver, you can't rely on that as a matter of trust, and you really have to be careful when passing.

With thirty-five named corners – and maybe 100 more unidentified curves – the Nordschleife is a hard circuit to really get the measure of. 'I did my first lap of the Nordschleife in my mum's womb,' declares Jörg

and because my dad used to race here, I know the track really well. I did my first lap in a car when I was twelve – it was not quite legal, but we did it anyway. And then I did my first 24-hour race here in 1999. The tracks couldn't be more different. Le Mans is all about high speed and low downforce, and here it's just complete craziness! You are managing the track here, especially on the Nordschleife, where there's very limited racing room, so getting through without too much risk and not being completely crazy as a driver is key if you really want to finish the race.

ABOVE: **The author chatting with Jörg Bergmeister in the Falken Team hospitality suite ahead of the 2019 Nürburgring 24-Hours.** CARLIE THELWELL

RIGHT: **At the 2019 Nürburgring 24-Hours, Jörg Bergmeister was flush from winning the GTE-AM class at Le Mans the previous weekend driving the quasi-works Team Project 1 991 RSR; in a career dotted with success, he also won the Carrera Cup in 2000, the GT class at Le Mans in 2004, and the ALMS GT2 title eight times.** PORSCHE PHOTO ARCHIVE

Porsches are in the blood: Jörg raced a 964 Cup Car twenty-five years ago, and he's been a factory driver since 2002, handling iterations of 996, 997 and 991. You'd imagine that, given the very different nature of the modern F1 circuit compared to the Nordschleife, drivers might take a bit of a breather on the GP track. Think again!

For sure, you know there is a bit more room for error on the Grand Prix circuit, which there is not on the Nordschleife, but in the end you always drive to a certain limit, and in qualifying especially, the driver really has to go to 100 per cent. Normally, in a race you try to be a bit more safe where you only drive to 98 per cent because you cannot afford to make a mistake. The track is unique, composed of two circuits very different in character, so for drivers it's a great challenge to be fast here, and it means taking a lot of risks and at the same time wanting to finish. Traffic is the main difficulty, and there are very few other races where there's such a big difference in speeds. The track is very unforgiving because there's no room for any mistakes out on the Nordschleife, where there's no gravel run-off, so it's difficult to push and try to maximize the performance, while making

sure the other cars know you're coming up behind them. That makes it really challenging, and different to any other 24-hour race. You have to find a rhythm, try to learn how the different competitors behave, to read them, to know which lines they take and which line to overtake them. This is where experience pays

ABOVE: **Jörg Bergmeister tells Johnny Tipler about Porsches he's raced previously, including a 964 Carrera Cup Car twenty-five years ago. He's been a factory driver since 2002, handling various iterations of 996, 997 and 991.**
CARLIE THELWELL

LEFT: **The Falken 991 GTR driven by Martin Ragginger exits the Mercedes Arena complex just after the start of the 24-Hours race.**
JOHNNY TIPLER

The Falken team's 991 GTR driven by Jörg Bergmeister, Dirk Werner, Klaus Bachler and Martin Ragginger in the 2019 Nürburgring 24-Hours race, here on the modern Grand Prix circuit. CARLIE THELWELL

LEFT: **Members of the Falken team's entourage following the N-24 out amongst hardcore fans in the environs of the Nordschleife.** CARLIE THELWELL

RIGHT: **As dusk falls over the Nürburgring Nordschleife the place enters a whole new mysterious dimension, where sounds, smells and light sources take on a fresh intensity.** CARLIE THELWELL

off a bit: you remember someone from before, and you know what kind of line you can take to overtake them. This is the toughest race, for sure.

Let battle commence, then. The forecast is dry – actually it's 28°C (82°F) – so slicks are anticipated for the whole race. Qualifying sessions have taken place over the previous couple of days, and at 2.00pm on Saturday the cars are wheeled out onto the grid, which is promptly swamped by race fans. As the 3.30pm kick-off approaches, I make my way to the Yokohama S-bends just after the start/finish straight. It's like the onset of a thunderstorm: the mighty rumble and then the deafening blast as the first tranche of fifty or so cars hurtle through the zig-zag, manifesting a colossal cacophony of shrieking engines and sequential shifts, headed by a couple of Mercs and a Frikadelli Porsche, and plummeting away down to the Dunlop hairpin. There's only one spinner – amazingly, a BMW M4.

Then the herd rushes behind me at Ravenol Curve and onto the outer section of the F1 circuit. While the big Mercs,

Porsches and BMWs are quickest initially, there are also some Italian exotics in the top ten, including a Lamborghini Huracán and a couple of Ferrari 488s – and a great-looking Glickenhaus. There's not long to wait before tranche two arrives, the medium-quick Group 4 brigade, led by a KTM X-Bow, and then, three minutes later, come the hot hatches. Such is the pace of GT3 machinery that before the tin-tops have done a complete circuit, the leaders are busy lapping them. It's truly frenetic and mesmerizing.

During the first few stints it becomes clear that the 911 GT3 R is the top car, keeping the Mercedes SLKs, R-80s and M6s honest. One of the Manthey Racing Porsches – lurid green – is out of contention early on with a flat tyre, while their other lemon-yellow 911 moves into the lead after five hours, Kévin Estre overtaking the lead Mercedes with two wheels on the grass at top speed on the long Antoniusbuche straight – as the Merc laps a backmarker. Crewed by Estre, Michael Christensen, Laurens Vanthoor and Earl Bamber, the #911 GT3 R retains the lead for the next seventeen hours – till Vanthoor

misses a yellow flag while overtaking backmarkers. They've been leading by over a lap, but are handed a 5-minute stop-and-hold penalty, compromising their scheduled fuel strategy in the process.

Twenty-four hours is a fair stretch of time to be concentrating on a race, and having logged the fortunes of the leading Porsche protagonists, it's time to venture out into the forested sections beside the deep Nordschleife to immerse ourselves briefly in the hedonistic maelstrom wrought by race fans, many of whom have been in situ for the whole week ahead of the race. Their presence is manifest in self-built viewing platforms, including scaffold towers and treehouses, and adapted vehicles, with tents, shelters, campers and trucks pitched in the lee of the circuit. Falken's PRs, Nick Bailey and Kerstin Schneider, gather a posse of us together and we shuttle up to Brünnchen for a nocturnal ramble – an encounter with Mad Max, Burning Man and Glastonbury rolled into one, with racing cars as backdrop.

It's midsummer, and, as twilight deepens into fleeting night, the circuit's only official light source is in the paddock and pit lane. The rest of the track is illuminated by the racing cars' headlights and the surrounding self-generated spectator enclaves, randomly interspersed by fireworks, thunder flashes and bonfires. The soundtrack is unremitting dub, techno and heavy metal – oh, and barely audible race engines. A concoction of aromas greets the senses too: race engines, cook-ups and barbies adjacent to the footpath, and fry-ups emanating from strategically placed bars and chuck wagons attracting groups of fans. From time to time I scramble through marshal's posts to photograph the action from behind the Armco, though for many fans the racing is inconsequential.

There's a crashed Cayman at Brünnchen and it takes a good hour to recover it, so there's a full yellow section through there. At Wippermann, though, the action is phenomenal as the fast cars plunge into the dip and hurtle through the right-hander, lights ablaze in the dusk, lapping slower cars in the process. Back on what passes for the footpath, a swing occupied by two young women and a man arcs in front of me, and I duck and scamper past. Suspended from a mighty oak,

Falken team drivers Klaus Bachler and Dirk Werner have a laugh with the author ahead of the Nürburgring 24-Hours race. CARLIE THELWELL

Dirk Werner has driven the Nürburgring 24-Hours eleven times, and he affirms that all the top drivers regard the N-24 as the best – though the most difficult – race on the calendar. CARLIE THELWELL

it's just one of myriad obstacles encountered on the trackside footpath, along with braziers, bonfires, wilfully scattered barbecues, deckchairs and scaffold towers – not to mention rocks and tree roots. This is all well and good for diehard fans, fortified by who knows what, but for those of a more delicate disposition – and don't get me wrong, I camped at Le Mans the previous year – it's a relief to get back to the more sanitized surroundings of the F1 circuit.

During their down time, I chat with Jörg Bergmeister's co-drivers, Dirk Werner and Klaus Bachler. Drivers get to be experts in one persuasion or another, and endurance events are no exception. Dirk has driven the N-24 eleven times, and Klaus has done it four times. It's not about personal glory; they're sharing details about the car with each other, down to how it's feeling through a particular turn. You sense that camaraderie behind the scenes. Dirk agrees:

> We share everything, and this is also the secret of a good team – that you help each other – because in the end we all drive the car. You cannot share too many things between the Porsche and the BMW guys because it's two different manufacturers, but it can also happen that you are in the car and there is something on the track, like oil or debris, so you radio this information back to the garage because the knowledge will help your team mates too. If you feel something is happening with the car, if it's just something small, maybe it's better to wait until the next planned pit stop, otherwise it would be inefficient to come in, because of the delay and loss of time.

Their team, Falken Racing, obviously has a more specific agenda than, say, Manthey, who are questing technical solutions, or (Sabine Schmitz's team) Frikadelli, who are chasing the win. For Falken, it's also about tyre development, and the programme is built around the team and the 24-Hour race. They're developing tyres specially for the Porsche and their BMW M6 GT3, just two cars, whereas other tyre manufacturers have several supported teams from whom they can derive feedback. Jörg Bergmeister elucidates:

> Falken can concentrate on this one car, but, just an example, we had three different slick compounds – soft, medium and hard – but we had very few opportunities to develop the hard tyre because of the weather conditions on the Nordschleife, and during the whole season we have only one or two months

where we can run hard tyres, and this is around the 24-Hour race, and maybe you won't need them again after the 24-Hour race.

For Falken, the new year starts on the Monday after the N-24, when they start testing new compounds based on what they've learned during the race. In the winter months they test in Spain (Ascari) and Portugal (Portimão), though it is still difficult to replicate likely conditions encountered at the Nürburgring. Experiences at other VLN rounds certainly add to the database.

With a couple of hours to go, I speak to Klaus Bachler in the Falken team's pit garage, just before his final stint. He reveals:

We had bad luck with a slow puncture early on – maybe we picked up debris somewhere on the Nordschleife – and then obviously it takes quite a long time to get back to the pits, so we lost a lot of time there. Then the tyre disintegrating destroyed the bodywork, so we lost 45 minutes changing that, and that put us down to sixty-fifth, but now we're just five laps down and we're back up to seventeenth.

He is quite optimistic. But, half a dozen laps into his stint, Klaus loses it in Pflanzgarten and glances off the barrier. The car spends the rest of the race in the garage as they try to sort out the damage to no avail, and they're classified seventeenth.

Meanwhile, Kévin Estre has taken over the second-placed Manthey car for the final two stints, and he recovers the car's

position to within just 30 seconds of the lead Phoenix Racing Audi R8, finally settling for second overall. Porsche haven't quite proved their point this year, but the number of surviving 991 GT3 Rs is testament to reliability over other marques… if that's any consolation. No question: Falken will be back next year. As will the crazies out in the forest. I may join them. Or probably not!

ABOVE: **At the 2019 N-24, Klaus Bachler drove for the Falken squad, though he is also on the driver roster of other Porsche works-supported teams such as Team Felbermayr-Proton.**
CARLIE THELWELL

LEFT: **There are thirty-five named corners on the Nürburgring and Nordschleife, with perhaps 100 unnamed: this is one of the latter, the turn between Brünnchen and Eiskurve, with the Falken 991 GTR getting two wheels over the kerbs.**
CARLIE THELWELL

CHAPTER FIVE

THE 718 CAYMAN AND BOXSTER

In 2017, the normally aspirated flat-six engines that previously powered the Cayman and Boxster models – from 986 through 987 and 981 evolutions – gave way to turbocharged flat-four powerplants in the 718 model open and closed two-seaters. I've sampled a cross-section of 718s, from standard Cayman to GTS and tuned Boxster, but here is the basic specification related to the GTS. The range-topping GT4 RS continues to use the naturally aspirated flat-six, now up to a staggering 4.0 litres!

The 718 GTS's 2.5-litre flat-four unit has a redeveloped intake duct and optimized single turbo with VTG and larger compressor, pushing the air into the combustion chambers at up to 1.3 bar pressure, enabling improved torque and faster acceleration. Power output rises to 365bhp, 35bhp more than its GTS predecessor running the naturally aspirated flat-six engine, plus 70Nm (52lb ft) more torque. Both GTS models are available with a manual six-speed or PDK transmission. The Sport Chrono package is standard, including dynamic gearbox mounts, and in PDK mode, the 718 Boxster and Cayman GTS

sprint from 0–100km/h in 4.1sec, with a top speed of 290km/h (180mph). The 718 GTS models are fitted with 20in Carrera S wheels in black satin finish. The front discs are 330mm diameter and the rears 299mm. The standard chassis with Porsche Active Suspension Management (PASM) lowers the ride height of the GTS models by 10mm (0.4in) compared to the S model. Porsche Torque Vectoring (PTV) with mechanical rear differential lock provides greater agility and stability.

Visually, the GTS differs from other 718 models with its Sport Design front apron, while at the rear, the tinted tail lights, black logos, black rear apron and black sports tailpipes give it its standout appearance. Being mid-engined chassis, the 718s are endowed with excellent lateral dynamics, evidenced by a 718 GTS lapping Nürburgring Nordschleife's 20km (12 miles) in 7min 40sec – on standard tyres. That makes it 16 seconds quicker than the previous Boxster GTS and 13 seconds quicker than the old Cayman GTS.

Sport mode, actuated by turning the button on the 360mm steering wheel, allows the driver to choose between Normal,

OPPOSITE PAGE:

The Cayman 718 and its crew are on a mission to rediscover the corners and crests that are evident in period photographs of the Gaisberg Hillclimb, and to do their best to match them.

ANTONY FRASER

THIS PAGE:

Stripped of its body chassis, the backbone skeleton of the 718 Boxster and Cayman reveals the driveline and running gear, including the exhaust system downstream of the turbocharged 2.5-litre flat-four.

PORSCHE PHOTO ARCHIVE

Being a flat-four unit powering the 718 Boxster and Cayman, the single turbocharger is a more prominent item than it might be on a flat-six, located on the lower right-hand corner of the engine.
PORSCHE PHOTO ARCHIVE

One you'd have blown up and pasted on your bedroom wall – a marvellous cutaway illustration detailing the internal mechanicals of the 718 Boxster GTS. Ideal for whiling away those sleepless nights...
PORSCHE PHOTO ARCHIVE

Sport and Sport Plus driving programmes. In Sport mode the engine responds even more directly, as the PDK is set up for shorter response times and optimum shifting points to provide maximum acceleration. The transmission shifts down earlier and holds the revs to maximize performance. When downshifting, throttle blip is automatically activated to optimize the engine revs. In Sport Plus mode these characteristics are even more pronounced, and tailored to deliver maximum performance. This mode also features Launch Control for a racing start. For vehicles equipped with PDK, the button can also be used to activate the Sport Response function, which primes the engine and transmission for the fastest possible unleashing of power, so the turbocharger builds up the pressure faster. This guarantees maximum responsiveness for a period of around 20 seconds.

The Porsche Active Suspension Management (PASM) system, integrated as standard, provides even better traction and thus enhanced driving performance. The PASM sports chassis,

ABOVE: **The 718 Boxster GTS shares its 2.5-litre flat-four powertrain and running gear with the 718 Cayman.**
PORSCHE PHOTO ARCHIVE

RIGHT: **The cockpit of this 718 Boxster is equipped with manual shift and the latest switchgear and instrumentation.**
PORSCHE PHOTO ARCHIVE

which is lowered by 20mm (0.75in), is also available as an option, being an additional 10mm (0.4in) lower than the GTS standard chassis. Porsche Stability Management (PSM), which provides automatic stabilization control of the vehicle when on the limit, permanently monitors the direction of travel, speed, yaw and lateral movement. PSM Sport mode is included in the standard Sport Chrono package, enabling push-on drivers to explore its limits on the race circuit. Porsche Ceramic Composite Brakes (PCCB) are optional fitment, consisting of six-piston fixed calipers, painted yellow, acting on 350 × 34mm discs at the front in conjunction with four-piston fixed calipers and 350 × 28mm discs at the rear. The 20in Carrera S wheels are shod with 235/35 ZR20 tyres at the front and 265/35 ZR20 tyres at the rear.

718 BOXSTER AND CAYMAN GTS (2017–2019)

Layout and chassis

Two-seat roadster and GT coupé, unit construction steel body/chassis

Engine

Type	Horizontally-opposed mid-mounted flat-four, rear-wheel drive
Block material	Aluminium alloy
Head material	Aluminium alloy
Cylinders	4
Cooling	Water-cooled
Bore and stroke	102.0 × 76.4
Capacity	2497cc
Valves	16 valves dohc VarioCam Plus
Compression ratio	9.5:1
Carburettor	Direct injection, single turbocharger and intercooler
Max. power (DIN)	365bhp at 6,500rpm
Max. torque	420lb ft at 5,500rpm
Fuel capacity	64ltr (14gal)

Transmission

Gearbox: 6-speed manual or 7-speed PDK
Clutch: Single dry plate or twin plate PDK

Ratios	Manual	PDK
1st	3.31	3.91
2nd	1.95	2.29
3rd	1.41	1.65
4th	1.13	1.3
5th	0.95	1.08
6th	0.81	0.88
7th	n/a	0.62
Reverse:	3.55	3.55
Final drive	3.89	3.62

Suspension and Steering

Front	Independent suspension with MacPherson struts, coil springs, electronically controlled dampers, anti-roll bar
Rear	Independent suspension with MacPherson strut, coil springs, electronically controlled dampers, anti-roll bar
Steering	Electromechanical with variable steering ratio and steering pulse
Tyres	235/35 ZR20 front, 265/35 ZR20 rear
Wheels	8 J × 20 ET 57 front, 10 J × 20 ET 45 rear
Rim width	8in front, 10in rear

Brakes

Type	Four-piston monobloc calipers front and rear, discs vented and cross-drilled
Size	330mm front, 299mm rear

Dimensions

Track	1,527mm (60.1in) front, 1,535mm (60.4in) rear
Wheelbase	2,475mm (97.4in)
Overall length	4,379mm (172.4in)
Overall width	1,801mm (70.9in)
Overall height	1,272mm (50in)
Unladen weight	1,450kg (3,197lb)

Performance

Top speed	290km/h (180mph)
0–60mph	4.9sec

OPPOSITE PAGE:

Against a stunning mountainous backdrop, the 718 Cayman heads up the Gaisberg hill from the Zistelalm Hotel, situated in one of a couple of hamlets that flank the route.

ANTONY FRASER

CLIMB EVERY MOUNTAIN

For two decades in the 1960s and 1970s, Porsche ruled the European Hillclimb Championship and, in 1958, Wolfgang von Trips clinched the Hillclimb title, having stormed the 718 RSK up the 8km (5-mile) Gaisberg mountain road to win the Grosser Bergpreis von Österreich (Great Mountain Prize of Austria). Back in the 1950s and 1960s, the Hillclimb Championship was a significant series on the international motorsport calendar, and ranked highly on Porsche's aspirational must-win list. In this, it succeeded for an incredible twenty-two years running, from 1958 to 1980. So, what better way to celebrate Taffy von

Trips' achievement from five decades ago than to reprise his run up Gaisberg – in the latest 718 Cayman.

Gaisberg is close to Salzburg, and the drive to Austria has the makings of a decent road trip, so my snapping colleague and I rendezvous at Harwich to board Stena Line's marvellous SS *Hollandica* for the overnight voyage to the Hook of Holland. It's a trip we make annually, and the ship's metropolitan restaurant staff welcome us like long lost friends. Disembarked the following morning, we motor the Cayman 718 blithely through the Netherlands, Belgium, Luxembourg and France, hanging a left at Strasbourg into Germany to attend the Ruf track day at Hockenheim, where we overnight before the six-hour push down to Salzburg. Rather than risk a citation, my colleague stumps up for an Austrian carnet entitling us to use their motorways, and Fräulein Sat-nav guides us by a precipitous single-track route winding up the backside of the Gaisberg mountain. It's dark, but I am aware of unfenced drop-offs of unknown depths and we proceed gingerly. We emerge at a more established road, which we discover with some relief next morning to be halfway up the actual hillclimb route, rather than the back lane we ascended the night before.

There's an annual revival of the Gaisberg hillclimb, as there often is at such venues, but today we're in competition for space on the blacktop with cyclists, bikers, hikers and local pensioners. It's warm and dry, even under the tree canopy, and it's clear that, back in the day, this would have been one heck of a drive – 8.652km (5.376 miles) from bottom to top. We rediscover corners and crests that are evident in period photographs of the hillclimb, and do our best to emulate them, me posing mid-road with appropriate mountain topography in the background, while a substantial palace of a building at the start of the climb provides a fine reference point as well – though it's a shame it's since lapsed into dereliction. The hubbub surrounding the assembled runners and riders appears in the photos to be much the same back then as it would be at a modern event.

The European Hillclimb Championship dates back to 1930, instituted as an FIA-sanctioned series in 1957, when runs were staged at six different venues across Europe. The series carried on as such up to the present day, with twelve rounds now, of which at least two of the original runs survive (Trento-Bondone and St Ursanne-les-Rangiers) from the halcyon days of the early 1960s when works entries from Porsche, Ferrari, Abarth and Alfa Romeo vied for supremacy on the slopes. The Europa-Bergmeisterschaft was Porsche's happy hunting ground; while outright victory for the marque was rare on the big-time international stage until the late 1960s, due to constraints of engine

With beautiful mid-engined balance, the 718 Cayman handles impeccably around the twists and turns of Gaisberg's scenic ascent.
ANTONY FRASER

capacity as much as anything, the nimble sports racing cars and GTs like the 718 RSK and 904 GTS had the measure of all-comers on the serpentine mountain climbs. Porsche drivers were the hillclimb specialists, and by 1965 the 904-based Kanga-ruh Spyder, the following year's 910 Bergspyder and its successor the Type 909 from 1968 were as specialized as they came.

Not to put too fine a point on it, Porsche drivers von Trips, Edgar Barth (Jürgen's father), Heini Walter, Herbie Müller and Gerhard Mitter wore the Sports Car category crown from 1958 all the way up to 1968, while in the Gran Turismo class, Huschke von Hanstein, Heinz Schiller, Hans Kuhnis, Eberhard Mahle, Anton Fischaber, Rudi Lins, Sepp Greger, Claude Haldi, Wilhelm Bartels, and brothers Jean-Marie and Jacques Alméras claimed

ABOVE: **The 718 Cayman GTS at the startline assembly area of the Gaisberg Hillclimb – an event where the original 718 RSK enjoyed some success six decades ago.** ANTONY FRASER

LEFT: **Rounding one of the numerous hairpins on the way up Gaisberg Hillclimb in the 718 Cayman, to the staccato accompaniment of its guttural flat-four turbo soundtrack.** ANTONY FRASER

The 718 Cayman's sat-nav plots the route of the Gaisberg Hillclimb; perversely, the chequered flag indicates the location of the start rather than the finish. ANTONY FRASER

the GT title literally every year from 1960 right up to 1980 – an amazing success record by any standards.

So, to return to the season we're celebrating, 1958, there were six rounds, held at Mount Parnassus (Athens), Mont Ventoux (France), Trento-Bondone (Italy), Freiburg-Schauinsland (Germany), Gaisberg (Austria) and Ollon-Villars (Switzerland). Von Trips won three of them – Athens, Trento and Gaisberg – with Barth, Bonnier and Behra winning the others. That year the 718 also won the 1958 Targa Florio outright in the hands of Barth and Wolfgang Seidel, and won its class at Le Mans – third overall – with Jean Behra and Hans Herrmann at the wheel. Von Trips' Gaisberg-winning 718 RSK was followed in the timing department by a pair of Borgward H1500 Spyders – helmed by Bonnier and Herrmann, no less – with Taffy's Porsche team mates Barth, Behra and Walter next up in three more 718s.

And here we are at the Gaisbergrennen, armed with a state-of-the-art Cayman 718. Could I beat von Trips' fifty-year-old time of 9min 24.1sec recorded on 15 August 1958? You would think so in a modern Porsche, but by how much is a moot point, the Cayman being heavier (if more powerful – 142bhp versus 296bhp) than an RSK. Tempting as it might have been to give it a go, in deference to other road users, I refrain from attempting a complete run at full chat. Besides, my colleague is frequently urging me to stop so he can capture a particular moment on camera.

Cayman 718 and 718 RSK

It's not so much 'what's in a name' as 'what's in a number', and it's no coincidence that Porsche elected to endow the newest Boxster and Cayman models with the 718 numerals, mainly on account of the return to the flat-four engine configuration, albeit in turbocharged format. Our press car is the very latest Cayman 718, powered by the twin-turbo, 2.0-litre flat-four that yields 300bhp and rushes from 0 to 100km/h in 5.1sec; we had a manual six-speed, but the PDK does the dash in 4.9sec. On the autobahn my colleague managed 225km/h (140mph) on one de-restricted section, thwarted not by traffic, which dutifully pulls over smartly to the inside lane, but by the omnipresent roadworks that bedevil much of the autobahn network. However, between Munich and Salzburg, when he was asleep, I wound it up to 249km/h (155mph), and it's up at those sorts of speeds that Porsches come into their own and really feel invincible. The downside, of course, is the soaring fuel consumption at these velocities, though we do cover the clicks quicker. And when it comes to motorway service areas, the Germans have the French autoroutes licked in terms of refreshment and snack quality.

This is not the 'S' model, but nevertheless the base 718 Cayman is a lovely cabin to inhabit. The largely nocturnal run we do from Salzburg to Vesoul in Haute-Saône, eastern France, takes six hours, passing through Germany, Switzerland and blink-and-you-miss-it Liechtenstein, and we emerge at our hostelry none the worse for wear. The seats are half leather and the backrest bits incorporate leather here and there with rather coarse canvas-like inserts. There are three gilt inserts on the steering wheel arms, which suggests something's been left out, which of course isn't the case, but they somehow don't work aesthetically. So, it matches up on the comfort factor, and we fitted a week's worth of gear on board plus all the snapper's equipment, including lights and so on. Even with some stuff stowed on the rear shelf in the corners behind the steeply-sloping C-pillars the rear view is not compromised.

Our only gripe is the Cayman exhaust noise. Perhaps this is unavoidable with a flat-four; it is what it is, and it doubtless beats the flat-six on the emissions count. Nevertheless, we couldn't help but compare it to the noise of a big motorbike when accelerating hard: either a Ducati or perhaps a Subaru, a horizontally opposed engine without enough cylinders. Yet, here we are, on the staggeringly gorgeous Gaisberg subalpine slopes, following the distant tyre tracks of the flat-fours that powered the original 718 RSKs. We have been accustomed to the sublime aural clarity of the flat-six for so long that a return to the harsher,

This aptly numbered 718 Cayman placed 123rd in the 2019 Nürburgring 24-Hours, piloted by Ralf Zensen, Fabien Peitsmeier, Michael Küke and Edgar Salewsky, captured here in a panning shot on the F1 part of the circuit. CARLIE THELWELL

The 718 Cayman offers a perfect driving position, with appropriate seat angle and distance from pedals and manual six-speed shift lever all harmoniously co-ordinated. ANTONY FRASER

guttural four-pot soundtrack seems somehow regressive. Want your 718 to sound like a six? Our friends at Cargraphic exhausts can make a diesel six sound like a petrol V8, so maybe there's an answer there. Otherwise, you still have the Cayman GT4 RS, endowed with 414bhp 4.0-litre flat-six!

In terms of performance it pulls jolly well, and it's certainly as fast as the 6-cylinder car. It's got plenty of go, and it does everything well except sound nice. As my colleague remarked, 'if you were deaf it would be the perfect car'. There is a lot of road noise from the tyres, and it reverberates inside the cabin in a way that Caymans have always done, though you don't notice it until you realize how loud the radio is. But I'm splitting hairs: all told, this is a superb car. And I'm loving the colour, Graphite Blue Metallic, with black wheels. We get a lot of admiring looks, too.

As for the original 718 RSK, it's a rare car, with just thirty-two made. It superseded the 550 Spyder in 1958, and was built on an aluminium-panelled spaceframe chassis rather than a backbone chassis like the 550's. The 718 weighed a skimpy 530kg (1,146lb), and was powered by the 1498cc four-cam 'Carrera' flat-four, developing 142bhp at 7,500rpm, deployed via transaxle and five-speed gearbox that had synchromesh on second through fifth gears. That recipe explains why it was so effective on a twisty circuit or hillclimb. It evolved into the RS60 in 1960, when rule changes called for a taller windscreen and, in essence, the RSK gave birth to the better-known Porsche sports racing cars such as the 904, 906, 910, 907, 908 and 917: in just over ten years they went from the 718 RSK to the 917.

On the international stage, the 718 RSK Spyder's record was impressive, frequently scoring high places through reliability and fewer pit stops, when the big Jags, Astons, Ferraris and Masers faltered. Unleashed in 1957, the 718 RSK came into its own in

The original 718 RSK was an open-top Spyder racing car, better emulated by the Boxster, though the Cayman is prefigured by a cavalcade of 1960s Porsche competition coupes, ranging from 904 through 906, 907 and 908 to 917. ANTONY FRASER

1958, placing third in the hands of Harry Schell and Wolfgang Seidel at the Sebring 12-Hours. Behra and Scarlatti were second in the Targa Florio, and 718 RSKs claimed third and fourth positions overall at Le Mans that year with Behra/Herrmann and Barth/Frère heading the action, which was Porsche's best-ever result at La Sarthe up till then. Behra and Barth rounded off the season with fourth in the Tourist Trophy at Goodwood. Sometimes fitted with a pair of tail fins, the RSK also appeared in single-seater guise as an F2 car when central-seat all-enveloping bodywork was permitted, and also as the open-wheeled 718/2.

Thirty-two 718 RSKs were produced in total, and in 1959 the works cars carried on where they left off, taking third, fourth and fifth at Sebring, a win for Barth/Seidel at the Targa Florio, fourth, sixth and seventh at the Nürburgring 1,000km, and second for the dream team of von Trips and Bonnier, beating works Astons, D-type Jags and Testarossas, at the Tourist Trophy. For 1960, the 718 RSK was superseded by the RS60, and by 1961 it was also built as a coupé, while the 718 chassis numbering continued into 1963. After that, Porsche's front-line competition car was the 904.

As for Wolfgang von Trips – the man with seven Christian names and an aristocrat to boot – he was an ad hoc member of the Ferrari race team from 1956 till 1960 and 1961, winning the Dutch and British GPs – at Zandvoort and Aintree. Von Trips drove the 718 RSK for Porsche in 1958 and 1959, handling the 718 F2 car as well, but reverted to the Scuderia Ferrari for 1960 and 1961. He was killed at Monza in 1961 and was posthumously ranked second in the World Championship as runner up to team mate Phil Hill (rather like Ronnie Peterson, also killed at Monza and placed second to Mario Andretti in the 1978 F1 title race).

Now for our own runs up the Gaisberg course. We've spent the night at the Zistelalm Hotel, Gaisberg, right beside the road in one of a couple of hamlets that flank the route. It's a substantial old building of the creaking floorboards and lederhosen persuasion, open log fire in the lobby, and must have been extremely popular on race days. The scenery is absolutely stunning, with beautiful alpine pastures above and below, and pinnacled mountain ranges folding mistily into one another. We wash the Cayman and ease out onto the hillclimb, where the panoramas are absolutely staggering: beautiful wooded slopes with a

The inaugural Gaisberg Hillclimb was held in 1929, featuring names that would become legendary on the international Grand Prix racing stage, including Rudi Caracciola, Manfred von Brauchitsch and Hans Stuck Snr. ANTONY FRASER

jagged backdrop receding into the distance. Cows and goats dot the meadows, autumnal yellows and oranges vie with deeper pine green, while dwellings have typical chalet-style roofs.

As well as sweeping corners, there are fairly long straights to get up a bit of velocity before coming to a hairpin, full-locking and powering round the turn and firing the 718 up yet another

Approaching the summit of the Gaisberg Hillclimb in the 718 Cayman before the final plateau where it's signed as being 1,288m (4,226ft) above sea level. ANTONY FRASER

gradient, another incline. To get the best time, clearly, I'm clipping all the apexes where possible, which we can't necessarily do on every corner because it's two-way traffic, but that's what the guys back in the day would have been aiming to do, hugging the cliffs on the inside and avoiding the verges on the other. I wouldn't say there's anything particularly demanding about the Gaisberg run, though it's fast and there are indeed some tricky bends that require full concentration and technique. The sobering thought is the drop-offs into the forest as well as the void, all the way up, because where there's no meadow it's dense woods, and if you go off that's where you're going. I log thirty corners on the way up, not counting innumerable squiggles, and including the two really serious hairpins.

Once the road finally sweeps right into the circular summit plateau it's an opportunity to ease back and contemplate what's here. There's parking for maybe fifty vehicles, so it would have made a handy assembly area for competing cars that had done the climb. Surprisingly, there is no monumental reference to the eponymous hillclimb, just to an aeroplane flyer from the mid-1930s. The inaugural hillclimb was in 1929, so even back then it was used regularly as a motor sport venue, with the likes of Rudi Caracciola, Manfred von Brauchitsch and Hans Stuck Snr in action, but the only other stone is the trig point that says it's 1,288m (4,226ft) above sea level. The café-bar grabs our attention, where my colleague observes that, 'it may be worth pointing out to the reader that he should ignore all the historical interest for a while and get out of the car and just admire the magnificent view'!

We turn tail and glide down to the bottom of the hill for the nth time. We've a couple of appointments on our return schedule, both in the general direction of the Hook of Holland for the return crossing aboard the SS *Stena Britannica*, but that's three days on the road, nevertheless, mostly comprising autobahn and autoroute. A jetwash and a pause to snap the car on quay, and soon enough we're snug on board the leviathan for the night on the North Sea. There's the remains of hurricane Irma blowing, and now it's the waves that are mountainous, though mercifully the Cayman is not obliged to tackle these and the ship sails blithely on through the tempest. From one extreme to another, we've travelled through nine European countries and clocked 3,200km (2,000 miles). We'll be dreaming of those glorious Alpine passes for a long time yet, though.

Our 718 Cayman poised at the summit of Gaisberg Hillclimb as we contemplate the breathtaking Austrian Alpine scenery. The S-bend sign beside the road is something of an understatement.

ANTONY FRASER

HANS-JOACHIM
STUCK INTERVIEW

'What's he doing in my dad's car?' asks Hans Stuck. I'm show-ing him an interview I did with Allan McNish, where the Scot-tish ace is pictured in the Auto Union Grand Prix car that Hans Stuck senior grappled with in the 1930s. That car means a great deal to Hans Jnr. 'I was actually the first one to take it out after it was restored, at the Avus racetrack in Berlin in 1990. When I sat in this car, knowing that my dad was once driving it, I shed some tears. It was a precious moment.'

So, did he see his father racing?

Yes, I accompanied him in 1957–58 when I was six or seven years old. He was driving a BMW 507 sportscar at various hillclimbs, and in 1960 he was German cham-pion in a BMW 700. I was waiting at the finish line for him at the Freiberg-Schauinsland race, and he'd set the fastest time. I heard the other drivers, who didn't realize who I was, say: 'Oh shit, we can't catch the old fart,' and that made me very proud of him. Many times I was allowed to sit in the driver's seat to go down the hill afterwards and steer the car when the engine wasn't running. That was amazing for a nine-year-old.

Antony and I joined Hans-Joachim for lunch on the terrace opposite Frankfurt's baroque opera house. He's unusually tall for a professional racer, fast-talking, cheerful and unfailingly enthusiastic. Nicknamed Strietzel, after the German honey cake, by a besotted aunt, he began racing in 1969, aged eigh-teen. His BMW 2002 saloon was entered by Kopchen Rac-ing, followed in 1971 by a similar Alpina-built car. Hired by Ford works team boss Jochen Neerpasch to race Capris in the 1972 European Touring Car and German Touring Car series, 'Stucky' was reunited with BMW in 1973 when Neerpasch became BMW Motor Sport supremo.

The Munich firm provided March Racing with champion-ship-winning F2 engines, which was Hans's route into For-mula 2 and thence Formula 1 in 1975. Forays with Shadow, Brabham and ATS followed, totalling seventy-four Grand Prix starts and just a couple of podiums, but for the time being his reputation was based on regular successes in BMW tin-tops. That, and the fact that he was one of the sport's wild boys, a devil-may-care prankster with long hair and a ready grin, somewhere between James Hunt and Gerhard Berger.

There had been a flirtation with Porsche: 'My first outing in a Porsche 911 S was in the Nürburgring 1,000km race in 1970

ABOVE: **As a boy, Hans-Joachim Stuck watched his father in action on the hillclimbs where he had made his name in the 1930s, and gained a taste for racing when he was allowed to steer the car back down the hill.**
ANTONY FRASER

RIGHT: **Strawberry fields forever: an invigorating conversation with Hans Stuck over lunch in Frankfurt's flamboyant Parisian-style Operncafé Restaurant beside the main Opera Square.**
ANTONY FRASER

with Clemens Schickentanz, and we won the Nürburgring 24-Hours in a BMW, as well.' Then there was a fourteen-year hiatus with no Porsches at all until he joined the Swiss entrant Walter Brun when he bought a Porsche 956 in 1984.

My first race was the Spa 1,000km with Harald Gröhs, and we came third. That was the start of my third career in motor sport. Walter Brun gave me the chance to drive the customer Porsche and I won at Imola with Stefan Bellof. I thought that Porsche was a cool car and I knew Stefan was on the way to a full-time contract with Tyrrell, so I called Professor Bott (head of development at Porsche) and said: 'I am free for the next year, so maybe I can drive for Porsche,' and he said, 'I thought you had a lifetime BMW contract!' So I went to see him and within ten minutes we made a handshake agreement for racing.

Hans speaks warmly of his 'third career'.

I learned so much in my years with Peter Falk, and having Derek Bell as team mate was like heaven on earth. Nobody could beat Porsche as they were so perfect with their preparation, with their development and on-track race strategy. Absolutely fantastic. Peter Falk calculated that I was the driver who'd clocked up the most kilometres in track time with the Porsche 956 and 962 because I did almost all the testing in Weissach. I did so many kilometres. Sometimes I was asked to do a 500km (300-mile) test, and at 3 o'clock the mechanics would fill up my car with 90 minutes left and then go home, and then it would be just me and the ambulance and the fire tender there, and I would finish the test, put the car in the workshop, close the door and drive home! They just left me to it!

With a few exceptions, every 962 produced after 1984 was signed off at Weissach by Hans.

No customer car left the premises without having a shakedown, which was my job as I was the only driver living close to Stuttgart. I was living in Garmisch at the time, which was two hours away, but Jochen Mass was in South Africa, Derek was in England and Bob Wollek was in France, so I was the closest one available. For the amount of kilometres I was doing I was very lucky. I had some big crashes, too, but always to the back of the car. Crashing with the front meant you were history. Gartner, Bellof, Winkelhock – they were unlucky.

Hans highlights the difference between the 956 and 962: 'In the 956 the pedals were ahead of the front axle line, and for safety reasons they had to move the pedals behind the axle line. This is why the 962 was 100mm (4in) longer. That was it.' The IMSA

version of the 962 used a single turbocharger. 'There was much longer throttle lag and then an explosion of power like the BMW 320tc touring car. The sound was nicer, though. Power output was a little higher in the single-turbo version, as it used a bigger turbocharger and could handle a bit more boost.'

In 1984, there were one-off outings in a Porsche 944 Turbo and a 935.

Jürgen Barth, who was Porsche customer sports representative, called and said that Bob Akin was looking for a driver in IMSA, and this was my first race for him. And the 935 is like swinging a hammer, as it has a very light front end with only the gas tank, and the engine's at the far back. It was such a difference between empty and full tank: when the tank was full the handling was nice, but when it was empty it was terrible. It was a fantastic car – the engine, the brakes and so on – but it was a bugger to drive, I tell you!

It's a generation thing, but most racers who've experienced them cite either the 917 or the 962 as their favourite Porsche. Hans is no exception:

The 962 was a good configuration and the combination of downforce, tyre width and power was the best I had ever driven. Those things had so much to give. The faster you made a corner, the more downforce you got. That was due to Norbert Singer's design. Underneath the front of the car was a bubble, and this created the suction. This bubble accelerated the air

Hans-Joachim Stuck illustrates a racing manoeuvre with an opposite lock motion.
ANTONY FRASER

beneath the car and the diffuser in the back sucked the car onto the ground. One of the greatest moments was having a Porsche 962 in 750bhp qualifying set-up, with qualifying tyres and full wing. The only car that had more downforce in 1979 was in Formula 1, when we had the ATS wing car, but this was more like a cannonball as nobody knew whether the sliding skirts would work or whether they would jam.

Hans drove a 911 GT2 S and Turbo S for Brumos in IMSA in the early 1990s, and he once drove a 964 Carrera Cup car at Spa as the celebrity driver. 'I tried to go too fast at Eau Rouge and I crashed it. The mechanics said, "Normally we wouldn't repair it, but as it's you, we will try to repair it overnight on the condition that you win next day." I didn't let them down!'

Despite placing second overall and winning the GT1 class at Le Mans in 1996, Hans feels the GT1 was at the end of the Porsche performance ladder. It was a 911 chassis with a 962 back end bolted on, and it never felt connected. It didn't have the stiff structure that the 962 had.

Hans-Joachim Stuck was overall winner of the 1993 IMSA Supercar Race Series in the Brumos 964 Turbo 3.6, winning the rounds at Lime Rock, Watkins Glen, Cleveland, Laguna Seca, Portland, Phoenix and Sebring. PORSCHE PHOTO ARCHIVE

Despite lots of testing with Norbert Singer and Thierry Boutsen and myself, we never got the car to where we wanted it. By 1998, when Uwe Alzen was driving, it was better, but when I drove it with Bob Wollek in 1996 and 1997 it never was perfect. Sometimes you felt that the rear did not belong to the front, and vice versa. Boutsen and Wollek felt the same. Thierry Boutsen was at my place three weeks ago and we came to this issue again. We remembered the GT1 at Spa, going through the double left-hander down to Stavelot, and he said it was terrible, he never could get on the power as it would never hold one line. On the throttle, it was open, close, open, close. Normally we set a race car up on the throttle, but this one always needed some correction. We tried automatic differentials, but it never really worked.

Over the years, Hans shared touring and sports car drives with top-line stars including Chris Amon, Jacky Ickx and Thierry Boutsen. 'Niki Lauda and I lived very close by one another. We did eight years in F1 together. I used to see him most weekends and we'd have breakfast together.' He also holds another of his contemporaries from BMW saloons in high regard:

I admired Ronnie Peterson very much. Not only because he was fast, but one thing I learned from Ronnie was that you get in the car, do fifteen laps, drive the shit

Hans-Joachim Stuck, Walter Röhrl and Hurley Haywood shared this 993 Turbo S GT in the GT class at Le Mans in 1993. This car was a road-legal Turbo S, stripped down for racing and powered by a smaller 3.2-litre twin-turbo flat-six, producing 475bhp, and was the prototype for the 993 GT2. It failed to finish at Le Mans in 1993, but placed second in the Daytona 24-Hours in 1994. PORSCHE PHOTO ARCHIVE

out of it, and then say what is wrong with it – and that is a good way. Don't moan, just drive it to the max – and then complain!

My best team mate was Derek Bell, and we are still good friends. When we came together it clicked. Everyone knew his part. Derek accepted I was a little bit younger, but maybe a bit faster. When it came to the crunch, I knew I could rely on Derek one million per cent and he knew he could rely on me one million per cent. Best team mate you could have. You knew he'd be fast and he'd fight and be good in the wet, and he wouldn't destroy the car. Derek knew how to drive a car with problems and still make it to the finish. He was much more successful than I was, and when Professor Bott suggested that I drive with Derek I said thank you for the Christmas present!

It's no surprise that the Nürburgring Nordschleife is Hans's favourite European circuit. He explains his next choice is because it's not been 'Tilkered' (that's to say, rendered modern and characterless):

My second favourite is Sebring, in Florida, because it is fast and has not been destroyed by punishing chicanes and tarmac run-offs. The new circuits like Malaysia, Shanghai or Dubai (where he won a 24-hour race) are so boring. It's different times – you cannot land a jumbo jet on a grass strip, and you cannot do F1 at the Nordschleife, but the tracks that Hermann Tilke is building do not require big balls any more. Same with the modernising of classic circuits like Spa: if you do something wrong and go onto the 50m tarmac run-off area like at Eau Rouge and Raidillon, if your turn-in doesn't work, you open up the throttle a bit more and go straight. When you speak to guys like Montoya or Hamilton, they say it is nice, but the sheer driving pleasure was different when it was not like this.

As for historic events, he's ambivalent.

I was at Laguna Seca in 1989 with the 917/30, the legendary Mark Donohue car – 1,000 horsepower, and you know what, I was shitting my pants! You go flat out with this car and there is no safety. Tyres have much more grip than ever before, so you go faster, with nothing but that little aluminium tube frame around you. I did this race and I said: 'From now on,

if I do something like this I will only do it at a moderate speed, like a parade.' You would not have a 100-year-old man do the 100m hurdles. These cars are priceless pieces of history, so you have a lot of money riding under your butt. You should show these cars to the public, make some noise, maybe have some spinning wheels on the startline, but no racing. The Festival of Speed at Goodwood is fine. Perfect. You drive up the hill on your own terms and the speed is under your own control. But as for the Revival, I told Charles (Lord March), I would do it, but only at my kind of speed.

Stucky's garage does house a couple of classics, however. 'I have a BMW 700 like the one from my father's last race. And a BMW 2002ti, which is totally restored – I take those out regularly, but never use more than 7,000rpm. But I would never race them. It's nice just to polish them and drive the passes in Austria when the sun is shining.' There was also a classic Porsche. 'I had a 356, but I sold it because in 2002 I bought a house in Florida and I sold the Porsche to buy a speedboat, which now I think was a bad idea. I am desperately looking for a 356B or C, and if one comes up for a decent price I will buy one again.' With half his career spent in front-engined cars, Porsches thus configured also work for him.

I had a 944 3.0-litre company car, which was fantastic. Good efficiency, lots of torque, the biggest normally aspirated 4-cylinder engine at the time. But my preference was a 928 Club Sport as a company car as it had such a nice ride. Fantastic! In fifth gear it pulled 3,000 revs, 250 clicks. The air conditioning was also really good. When I won Le Mans in 1987 I drove it home after the race, as it was so relaxing. It was a seven- or eight-hour drive, but I wasn't tired – it was a great car.

As for that particular car, we met up with Hans for lunch subsequently at the Nürburgring in the Porsche hospitality tent. He was here for the Porsche Driving Experience training day, just ahead of the fabulous Old Timer meeting, and we had a surprise for him. We'd spotted the very 928 CS he was given in 1987 in the private collection of OPC Gelderland at Leiden, belonging to proprietor Mark Wegh, and Mark kindly agreed to have Hans's 928 trailered to the Ring for this rendezvous. Hans was overjoyed to be reunited with 'his' 928. In point of fact, he received a succession of 928s during his tenure as a works driver, and the first one he inherited from Stefan Bellof.

Here in the Nordschleife car park, Hans-Joachim Stuck is overjoyed to be reunited with the 928 given to him by the factory when he was a works driver. The car is currently in the collection of Mark Wegh at Porsche Center Gelderland, and kindly dispatched to the Nürburgring specially for this reunion: it coincided with the model's fortieth anniversary, in celebration of which Antony Fraser and the writer drove another 928 there from Silverstone, coincidentally logging 928 miles (1,493km) on the round trip. JOHNNY TIPLER

As a works Porsche driver, Hans Stuck was given a 928 as his personal transport, which he used to commute between the testing at the Nürburgring and his home, as well as European circuits where he happened to be racing. ANTONY FRASER

I knew when I joined the Porsche factory team in 1985 that all the drivers were allocated these cars, and Professor Bott said, 'Hans, we want to give you a car, and Stefan (Bellof) just gave his car back yesterday,' so I

took Stefan's 928. He'd brought it up to Weissach the day before, it was washed, and they put some fresh tyres on it, but there were still loads of things in the car belonging to Stefan. I found a pair of shoes, some tickets for the racetrack, all sorts; he must have lived in that car. I'd never driven a 928 before, but in the first 10km (6 miles) going from Weissach to the motorway, I discovered the power, the sound – that V8 is a jewel – and you have this long hood in front of your nose and perfect seating position. It was just great.

Hans had five 928s in total.

Year by year we regularly got new cars, and this was the second one. I loved it from the first day I got it. It's in mint condition, still perfect. Look at the quality of the leather – even the steering wheel. Maybe a hundred people have touched it, but it's still like new! So cool, my little baby.

An original number plate amongst the toolkit under the hatchback confirms it's his car from 1987.

I had two white ones when the 962s were in Rothman's livery, and then when we had the Super Cup I had a dark blue one, then another white one, and the last one was a red 928 GTS, which was a real flyer: it had 350 horsepower, and for me the great thing was that it was a perfect car for driving long distances between the tracks for races and testing, but also you could go onto a track with it and it was a perfect track car as well. Don't forget this was a Club Sport and the Club Sport is set up precisely for that.

He waxes starry-eyed.

This was a fantastic car to drive really fast, but it was still a relaxed drive. In 1986 I drove my 928 to Le Mans and then I did the 24-Hours, and after the race I was still so fired up with adrenaline that I started to drive back home, but then I felt so tired I drove into a parking lot and fell asleep – and suddenly there was a policeman knocking on the window to see if I'm still alive! The longest journeys I did in the 928s were from Austria to Le Mans and Nardo in southern Italy. I live in the south of France now, which is about nine hours from my home in Austria, and I do it regularly, and I like that. I never have any problems getting tired. If I do sometimes, I stop, I run around the car five times this way and five times the other way, and it restores the blood circulation. What really makes me crazy is traffic jams; I hate that, and the German motorways at the moment have so many roadworks.

Having viable back seats, the 928 could also serve as Stuck family transport:

My son Johannes was carried around in there as a baby, so it brings back really precious memories. Now I really regret I didn't buy it for a good price after I was supposed to hand it back, and now I probably couldn't afford it! Still, I'm happy to see it in such great condition here.

His personal 'old timer' collection includes a BMW 700 from the years that his dad was driving. 'I also have a BMW 2002 Turbo, a 1951 Beetle, which is my year of birth, and a 1979 convertible Beetle; I have an M3 CS, the one with the carbon roof, and my wife has an 1983 Turbo-Look 3.2 Carrera Cabriolet. And I also have a 1936 Porsche tractor!' Is there room for a 928? Who knows! Hans takes 'his' 928 CS up the road to Dottinger Höhe:

Do I really have to give it back? It runs perfectly, the gearbox is fine, there is no rattling, the steering is great steering, the power good – it's a big day for me. If Mr

Wegh ever wants to run the car in a classic event and he needs a driver he should call me and we'll do it.

Hans still regards his two Le Mans wins (1986 and 1987 with Bell and Holbert) and two Sebring wins (1986, 1988, Gartner, Akin and Ludwig) in a Porsche 962 as his greatest achievements.

I'm still looking for one important thing, though. I want to race with my two sons. Johan is well established with BMW Z4 touring cars and Ferdinand did his ADAC Formel Masters (Dallara chassis, VW engine for junior drivers) in 2014. We want to do the Nürburgring 24-Hours and I want to finish this race in a decent way and then say to my boys, here is the steering wheel, now go do it yourselves!

Former BMW sparring partner Dieter Quester called him recently with a proposition. 'Dieter is 67, and he wants his last race to be the Daytona 24-Hours.' Could Stucky be tempted? 'It all depends on your physical condition. I have a personal trainer and I am in pretty good shape for long-distance races.' As ever, there's a twinkle in his eye: something tells me Strietzel will stick around for some time yet. For now, we usher him into the driving seat of our 997 Turbo Cabriolet for a tour of Frankfurt city centre – the steering-wheel is on the wrong side as it's a UK press car, but he just laps it up, regardless.

Unfazed by the right-hand-drive 997 Turbo Cabriolet we've presented him with, Hans-Joachim Stuck takes it for a tour of the streets of Frankfurt. ANTONY FRASER

THE TECHART BOXSTER 718

Teutonic tuners TechArt have embellished the turbocharged 718 Boxster S, and invited us to take a ride in it in the Black Forest. TechArt is possibly the most prolific of the cluster of specialist Porsche tuners and decorators orbiting the Stuttgart mecca, and their Leonberg HQ is just a few kilometres from Weissach. Judging by past form, it's no surprise that they've already laid hands on the latest, most radical incarnation of the Boxster and wrought some of their magic on it.

In 2017, my photographic colleague and I show up at the firm's art deco-style split-level buildings on the outskirts of medieval timbered Leonberg to rendezvous with erstwhile in-house PR man Tobias Sokoll. We revisit the tannery where hides are prepared for upholstering customer cars and TechArt's own products, including the intricately wrought steering wheels. The aroma of leather is deeply soporific, redolent of childhood backseat journeys in the parental limo (if not my dad's eccentric foray into Beetles). We see half-a-dozen TechArt-tweaked vehicles – based on Cayennes and 997s and 991s – up on hoists as mechanicals and peripheral trim panels are attended to. The showroom rotunda displays a further six vehicles, including a black Cayenne, Macan and 991 cab and coupé. Among the line-up in the steeply sloping external compound is the 991 C2 S

with its subtle air-force grey and black striped livery that we'll be test driving shortly, while on pole position is the gleaming white 718 Boxster S.

The car's exterior is distinguished by its permanently raised TechArt rear wing and front spoiler with splitter in body colour. It's fitted with the firm's own 'Racing' exhaust system, culminating in a pair of central titanium tailpipes with matt carbon-fibre tips. Running gear includes in-house branded sport springs and their own Formula IV 21in aluminium wheels – 9 × 21 OT 50 and 9.5 × 21 OT 58 – which here are finished in matt black with lemon yellow rim lips. Tyres are Vredestein Ultrac Vorti R, 245/30 ZR21 on the front and 265/60 ZR21 on the rear.

In the cockpit that striking acidic hue is picked up in the ornate stitching of the trim in the leather and Alcantara-clad cockpit upholstery, comprising the monogrammed seats, door cards, door-pulls and dashboard. Carpets and luggage mat are leather edged and sewn with matching yellow stitching. The show-off decorative parts are lacquered or highlighted in carbon fibre, including the seat backs, centre console inlay, anodized sport pedals and illuminated door entry guards, Sport Chrono clock, steering column casing, glovebox, sun visors, airbag panels, storage compartment lid and PDK selector. The whole ensemble is set off by the TechArt three-spoke PDK sports steering wheel, featuring the red mode button – Sport and Super-sport control; the three-segment wheel rim is clad in a combination of Alcantara and perforated leather, with PDK shift paddles lacquered in matt black with Alcantara on the reverse, which is a tactile thing and also warm in winter. Detailing like this turns a good car into a real work of art.

OPPOSITE PAGE:

TechArt's 718 Boxster S is distinguished by its permanently raised rear wing and front spoiler with splitter in body colour, plus the firm's own Formula IV 21in aluminium wheels – finished in matt black with lemon-yellow rims. ANTONY FRASER

THIS PAGE:

ABOVE: **The TechArt 718 Boxster S outside the company's art deco-style split-level Leonberg headquarters.** JOHNNY TIPLER

RIGHT: **In the clearing stands a Boxster: here, the rotund rump of the TechArt 718 S has the pert aerofoil permanently erect.** ANTONY FRASER

The running gear is tweaked too. The suspension is lowered with sports springs by about 35mm (1.4in), and with PASM in operation about 25mm (1in), and wheel spacers are fitted on the rear axle. The brake calipers are painted in high-temperature-resistant custom colours and feature the brand logo. Tobias elaborates:

> It's fitted with the TechArt sport brake kit, but the dampers are the normal ones that come fitted on the 718 Boxster. The TechArt car has 21in wheels whereas the maximum diameter fitted by the factory is 20in and I think you feel that it rides quite well. People often think, 'Oh, bigger wheels, handling will be rubbish,' but we tried to figure out a good set-up with camber and toe-in, and the car handles very well and the cornering is great.

True enough; at the time of writing, both Tobias and I own Boxsters of our own – though mine is a 986 S and his is a 987 S – so we are connoisseurs of the model, and we both endorse Boxster handling as characterizing quintessential Porsche. It's when we hit the high road that the startling performance is unleashed. The company's own Techtronic power kit, branded TA082/S1, is configured for the 2.5-litre turbocharged flat-four 718 Boxster S engine, and delivers 350bhp and 420Nm (310lb ft) – a hike of 50bhp and 60Nm (44lb ft). I get Tobias to tell me about the mechanical specification and what has been done to the engine, and what the power kit consists of:

> The Techtronic application is an additional ECU, but it's not one of the inferior ones that only have two places where they kick in, delivering boost before and behind. Our Techtronic kit is integrated in the management system of the car, and it takes into account oil temperature, water temperature, rpm, how the driver floors the pedal, what mode you are in – it monitors all those factors, so it's multi-dimensional. The Techtronic is also only active in Sport and Sport Plus. In normal mode we'd have to do serious engine remapping.

Extremely subtle and sophisticated, then. And, it seems, safe, too.

> When a new engine comes in from Porsche our guys fit the Techtronic and they go on the dyno and do the mapping for the 718 engine, and then test drive it, and of course they take care not to compromise the safety parameters of the engine that were originally built in. And anyway, our TechArt warranties cover engine and timing chain up to €75,000 so you can be confident there will be no problems.

In this case the gearing stays the same as the standard 718's, though the company also has other power kits involving bigger turbochargers, where the gearing is changed. So, is it any quicker than the standard 718? The official figures give 0–100km/h acceleration as 4.4sec in PDK and 4.2sec in Launch mode, maxing at 277km/h (172mph). The TechArt 718 S does the 0–100km/h sprint in 4.0sec and goes up to 296km/h (183.9mph), so there you have it.

Bearing in mind that the 718 Boxster was launched in March 2016, it hasn't taken TechArt that long to release its own take on the new model. Tobias clarifies:

> It's been under development for about four months. Techtronic development takes time. There's a lot of research behind it that's specific to the new 4-cylinder turbo engine, and also our aerodynamic fix for the bumpers and rear wing, made out of carbon fibre, which has to be evaluated for strength and efficiency before we can release it.

Well, that's the data taken care of, now for the open-air driving bit.

Let's count them: twenty, thirty – we lose track of all the Porsches whizzing past, all modern ones. They must be company cars; of course they are, because we're beside the L1177 back road between Leonberg and Weissach, and they're almost certainly connected with the factory. Like schoolboys collecting car registration numbers, we spot a few oddballs among the Boxsters, Cayennes, Macans, Caymans and 991s: prototypes disguised with loosely veiled silhouettes. They regard us and our TechArt 718 Boxster S with equal curiosity, probably realizing it isn't one of theirs, but nevertheless nosy about the yellow-banded wheel detail and distinctive aftermarket front spoiler that tags it as an outsider. But it is a wonderfully undulating road, plenty of ups and downs, which we like to use for photography when we visit the Leonberg-based firm, and we are perfectly entitled to be here.

Like in all modern Porsches, the TechArt 718 cockpit is a superbly comfortable environment, and as I snuggle into the driving seat, it's the work of seconds to shift and tilt it to arrange my ideal driving position. The four-pot motor fires up and thrums a feisty staccato beat. From urban to rustic, we motor into surroundings where I can open up the Boxster and my colleague can take pictures of it. Hopefully he's remembered the film this time.

I choose my moment. Acceleration is pretty instantaneous – I floor it at 3,600rpm and take it to 5,000rpm, and it charges off like a berserk bull, and at that point I lose the sensation that it's a 4-cylinder engine. Impressively, the PDK pops it into top at 7,200rpm. I'm allowing the PDK free rein so I can focus on the road ahead, given the velocity I'm now travelling at. I'm surprised by the guttural squawk of the flat-four exhaust; it's not a mellifluous blare, more a craven bellow. Tobias reassures me that TechArt are currently working on a system that will provide a more melodic aural effect. While I hanker for the superior classiness and aural delight of a flat-six I can't help be astonished at the earthy, full-on zest of the blown flat-four. It even makes me question my reserve regarding water-cooled in-line fours too.

RIGHT: **The candy-coloured lemon-yellow detailing is prominent in the TechArt 718 Boxster S cockpit, picked up in the seat and wheel-rim stitching, sport knob, dial faces, air vents and PDK shift and housing.** ANTONY FRASER

BELOW LEFT: **When bidden, the TechArt 718 Boxster S can oblige with a violent take-off, while braking is equally formidable, even in the wet, as here during front tracking.** ANTONY FRASER

BELOW RIGHT: **The writer glories in the dramatic punch and dynamics of the TechArt 718 Boxster S as it tucks into the chosen line through a series of bends as if on rails.** ANTONY FRASER

As more opportunities unfold for exploiting its forcefulness I revel in its dramatic punch and dynamics. Like with all Boxsters, cornering is utterly blissful at any velocity, tucking into the chosen line through a series of bends as if on rails as the mid-engined chassis lies flat and roll-free. Then, when bidden, its take-off is violent, and in each ratio I'm now seeing around 7,000rpm, while braking is equally neck-strainingly formidable. On a smooth road it is sublime, on any blacktop that's less even it rides perfectly pleasantly. A tourist town looms – Neuenbürg – and suddenly we're immersed in holiday traffic: the Boxster's the centre of attention as folk crane their necks to see just what it is that's crawling by, attracted by the fancy wheel detail and purposeful white charger styling. We loop around a series of hairpins up to a lofty *Schloss* and take a break on the gastro-terrace overlooking the town and its deep valley floor. The trek resumes, and we're quickly away from the honeypot and onto clear country roads again. Of course, I'm only cannonballing to see what it's made of; as I trawl to and fro for Antony's panning shots it's as placid as a lamb (though ready to frolic whenever you say).

So far so good. But ominous clouds are gathering over the Black Forest, our luck changes and the rain squalls in – horizontally. Luckily the Boxster roof is one of the best-designed and most reliable canopies in the world, and with the press of the switch it's performing the overarm overhead arc to nuzzle comfortably onto the windscreen header rail, and I sit out the shower, munching a cheese pretzel. We've come 50km (30 miles) or so from Leonberg by now so we've no alternative but to go for it, rain or not – the issue being that Antony's lenses won't stay dry in the tracking shoots. I wind the Boxster up and dash past him as he crouches beside a soggy corner. Again, handling is perfectly flat and controllable, and the Vredestein rubber deals with the standing water perfectly adequately.

We pause in a forest glade where pines provide a modicum of shelter, and take stock. My lasting impression is of the wonderfully precise Boxster handling and turn-in, and a very lively chassis despite the big wheels and tyres. TechArt have done a great job on a car that's already a proper goer. Is it necessary? We are all wilful victims of temptation and inclined to tune and modify our cars. And if that's you, you'll understand what they've been up to. Craving ever greater performance from my own cars, I have considered having a turbocharger – or perhaps supercharger – fitted on my 986 Boxster S. But instead of messing around oneself, TechArt do the job for you. That's their forte, a tuning niche for owners craving just a bit more aesthetically and dynamically from their Porsches.

THE 718 CAYMAN GTS

What if you really want to exploit the performance of your Porsche to the full? Who better to show you the ropes than Ron Simons and his RS Nürburg and RSRSpa track driving operations. In spring 2019, he very kindly provided a 718 Cayman GTS for me to test my skills for a few laps on both Nürburgring Nordschleife and Spa circuits. His itinerary included a tour of the spectacular Mosel wine-growing region.

Driving along the Mosel valley, you cannot help but be immersed in vineyards. They line the flanks of every hillside, horizontal terraces clawed out of the rock face, and long, staked lines of vertical planting sometimes tumbling right down to the roadside. Every charming riverside town and village is replete with hostelries and wineries offering tastings and wines for sale. So, Tipler by name, tippler by nature, how could I refuse an invitation from RSR principal Ron Simons to join him on a mosey along the Mosel, halting at some of the spectacular viewpoints and vineyards en route? The deal was sealed by the promise of a few laps in one of his track cars around the hallowed asphalt of the Nürburgring Nordschleife and Spa-Francorchamps circuits.

That car turned out to be a scarlet Cayman GTS, and for a few days my constant companion was this roustabout road hog. I travelled to our Ring-side rendezvous with shutter-boy Fraser and his fiancée, Ingrid, and found ourselves billeted virtually trackside at Breidscheid in apartments belonging to Hotel Landhaus Sonnenhof. It is the place to be if you want to watch the action as well as savour trackside vibes. Sure, there other spots such as Brünnchen where you get an overspill of both, but at Breidscheid you have the eateries of timber-framed Adenau nearby too.

Ron Simons' RS Nürburgring HQ is 300m from the Nordschleife access and the same distance from Nürburg village Schloss in the other, and the maintenance facility and offices are surrounded by parked Porsches and Mégane hot hatches – at least a dozen of each. He even still holds on to a similar number of Alfa 75s, his start-up track-driving tuition cars from when I first met him a dozen or more years ago. We togged up, me in trusty Peltor and Sparco gloves, and eased down to the Nordschleife assembly area. It was a public day, so heaving with hotheads and wannabe racers in a plethora of Porkers, Beemers and hatchbacks. I've done the Ring a few times, also courtesy of Ron, as well as stood behind the Armco snapping away at the N-24 and Old Timer. But unless you do it every weekend you forget the running order of the turns, and you find yourself unexpectedly in corners that are actually familiar,

Tackling the Eau Rouge and Raidillon section at Spa-Francorchamps in the RSR Nürburg 718 Cayman GTS: it is such a thrill to get it right.

ANTONY FRASER

once you're in them. So, I was glad of Ron's inimitable exhortations to brake – or not – turn in, power on, and was not surprised when the 'hand of God' eased the wheel in the appropriate direction on my behalf from time to time.

The first thing Ron observes is that I am too close to the steering wheel when I need to opposite lock. 'That's a personal thing,' he says, 'but I think give yourself a little bit more space by moving the seat back a notch and then the wheel's also clearing your knees when you need to operate the pedals.' Our car is well known to the officials, so we breeze through the gate and I flash my RSR card at the barrier, and we are swiftly out on track. The road ducks right onto the Nordschleife, ignoring the modern F1 circuit. I need to play myself in, so to start with I let everything else go past. 'Keep it over to the right,' shouts Ron.

'There's more traffic coming. Indicate right, and then people know that you've seen them.' And that's how it goes: there's such a disparity between speeds, with no shortage of GT3s versus doddering sightseers as counterpoint, so I'm having to gauge who to pass where and who to keep out of the way of.

I act on what Ron tells me, and this is a typical directive for most corners:

> *…Little bit of brakes, and turn in, try to keep your hands on the wheel, use all the track on the right here, keep on going, speed is fine, no brakes, and you're fully on the left here at the turn in, and… wait, and we turn in, keep your speed, don't brake, go to*

the left, still on the throttle, fully right, a little bit of brakes and turn in, and keep your line…

We begin the plunge down to Breidscheid: 'Wait, and now you go – Antony must be taking pictures here – turn in, on the brakes, wait, and on the throttle, and use the road on the right … this is the Lauda corner…'. Which is kind of poignant now.

Imagine that, for a full lap and then another one, with this focused, non-stop torrent of instruction coming at you! I loved it, and it was literally laugh-out-loud thrilling. Ron had my voice recorder on, so I could quote you his whole commentary – but you'd need to be in the driving seat. It's easy to be intimidated by the Nordschleife: the never-ending succession of tricky corners, all subtlety different, some radically different, and it would be well worth paying for a tutored session on the uncluttered circuit. And that Cayman GTS with PDK is nothing short of phenomenal. No turbo lag, just instant power allied to the PDK, masses of grip and taut handling, a beautifully balanced chassis, and steering nicely weighted. It feels like a glove, and what seemed at first like an unknown car is now a close friend.

Ring done, we head out onto the region's fast A- and B-roads, and Ron leads in his GT3 RS. To start with we're on the 257, winding its way via some quite demanding bends through a few villages towards Bonn. The traffic is predominantly Ring-bound, and every other vehicle is some sort of sports car or racing motorbike. Soon enough, we're revelling in rolling Eifel mountain scenery, cloaked in different patches of green, deciduous versus pine, and all now lusciously blooming, as the hillsides fold into one another. This is beautiful high country with craggy spurs, and the villages sporting trompe l'oeil stonework around the

LEFT: **The Mosel is one of Germany's most prolific wine producing regions, with spectacular views over the Mosel valley, enhanced by RSR Nürburg's 718 Cayman GTS posed on a hill road beside a vineyard terrace.** KOSTAS SIDIRAS

BELOW: **Our route with the 718 Cayman GTS takes us into high arable fields of yellow rape, where the rural road surfaces are remarkably smooth.** ANTONY FRASER

windows, a lot of timber-frame buildings and Gothic script identifying shops, hotels and wineries. One such town is Altenahr, where there's a ruined medieval castle atop the wooded hill, all craggy turrets and ancient walls, with the river flowing through the middle of it. This is the most northerly on our trip.

Under acceleration, I don't think we'll be staying with Ron very long, but on the open downhill sweepers the Cayman holds onto him; I'm under no illusions that he's hanging back for us, of course, but it is thrilling nonetheless. The PDK thinks for you and does all the work if left to its own devices, and it's quite uncanny how it's always in the right gear, blipping the throttle to get the revs right for the downshift – and all the time I'm accompanied by the guttural stuttering of the flat-four sound track.

Before long, I'm seeing grape vines, a mixture of terraces and vertical planting with the vines extending up the rocky hillsides, as the Mosel tumbles over a rocky bed to my right. All wine-growing regions are punctuated by chateaux, and the Mosel domains are similarly headquartered with equally substantial edifices. One such is Marienthal, a former nunnery where wine has been made sporadically since the twelfth century, and we pause for lunch in the congenial courtyard of Weingut Kloster Marienthal. The bottled wares of the chateau shop – the Brogsitter Riesling in particular – prove irresistible to my companions.

The Mosel is Germany's third most prolific wine producing region, which borders the river from Koblenz upstream to Trier. Ron wants to show us some more spectacular views looking out over the Mosel valley, so we drive the cars up hill roads and metalled tracks, scarcely a car's width, to the disgruntlement of a few walkers, but we enjoy some astonishing views from the vineyard terraces at these higher elevations. Back on the regular

road system, our route takes us into the hills, past yellow rape fields, looking down at forest across lots of other hills. As the surfaces are remarkably smooth, the Cayman's now in Sport mode, and if you're an inveterate boy racer there are few things more amusing. More to the point, these back roads winding over the hillsides are almost as thrilling as being on the Nürburgring itself, and in Sport it really romps away.

We dine that evening at Kobern-Gondorf, in the Alte Mühle, a truly amazing restaurant run by the ebullient Thomas Höreth and his wife. It's housed in a former chapel and water mill, festooned with trinkets, *objets trouvés* discovered on site over the establishment's 1,000-year history. Thomas makes his own wine – and fabulous it is – and we dine in the shadow of enormous wooden grape presses. Certainly, one for the record books.

A second comfy night at Hotel Landhaus Sonnenhof's Breidscheid annexe, and we rendezvous with Ron and his photographer Kostas again. Our ultimate destination is Spa-Francorchamps, taking in another swathe of Mosel scenery and highpoints along the way. To begin with, we drive around part of the Südschleife, which gives an idea of what the original Nürburgring circuit would have been like without any barriers – Jackie Stewart's 'Green Hell' seems pretty apt on this narrow road, with ditch and trees on either side. Then it opens out. If this Cayman GTS belonged to me I would be running it all the time in Sport mode: it's so much tauter, the steering seems more acute and turn-in sharper. The quality of these German roads is phenomenal, with bend after long, arching bend, winding up and down hill, and a joy to be driving on in a car like this.

The Mosel road trip took the 718 Cayman GTS through an endless succession of vineyards, including Altenahr, with medieval castle atop craggy landscape.

KOSTAS SIDIRAS

We're following the Mosel, though at this point I couldn't say whether it's upstream or downstream, but we're in the broad valley, high above Cochem castle with its quayside town where the river cruisers are moored up. The river must be 100m (300ft) wide, flanked by a towpath and chestnuts in bloom, with very steep terracing either side. The vines extend two-thirds of the way up the hillsides, which are covered in scrub and woodland on the top. We're on the A49 going towards Trier, enjoying some thrilling sweeps and swoops. Every few kilometres we pass through a riverside village composed of picturesque, timber-framed buildings with window boxes and wall painting decorations. It's kind of Riviera, with plenty of hotels and a few campsites. Wine is definitely the theme, and in each village there are several establishments – bars, restaurants and wineries – advertising wine tasting. The vines were introduced by the Romans, and the wine trade has been established ever since.

Still tracking the Mosel, the terraces on my right-hand side are coming right down to the road, with the cheeky vines actually tumbling over the stonework onto the kerb. Looking across the river, there's another village, predominantly white buildings with grey or terracotta roofs, a church spire, with immaculately terraced vineyards going up behind. We pass a big lock just as one of the commercial mega-barges that ply these waterways filters into the chamber. In some places, the terracing is like a patchwork quilt, and the producers' names are writ large on the hillsides. The grapevines are mostly arranged in vertical planting, lines of vines and stakes running down to the roadside, with people between the vines tending them. Elsewhere, the terracing is carved out of the rock face, with some of the cliff actually netted and then surmounted by vineyard, which must be quite daunting to work on if you were a picker.

We pause at Bremm, and Ron leads us up to an amazing vantage point accessed on a farm track and through woodland, where an escarpment overlooks an astonishing meander in the river – a hairpin bend, if you'll accept the motoring simile – hundreds of feet below. Apparently, people hang-glide from here, and it's popular with hikers. Far below, a train makes its way across a bridge on one side of the land, passes through a tunnel and emerges like a worm on the other. You do get a sense of the expanse of the country from up here, with all the different valleys and mountains folding in on each other, forested on the tops and with vineyards on the flanks. The local winery is Bremmer-Calmont. Ron says it's called 'the hot mountain', because it gets the sun all day, and at a 65-degree incline, it's the steepest vineyard gradient in the Mosel. The roofs of the houses way down below are a bizarre agglomeration of triangular pitches, something that is only evident from above. And

Ferry cross the Mosel, with RSR Nürburg's 718 Cayman GTS in transit, mid-river, against a backdrop of Riesling vineyards and *Schloss*-crowned village.

JOHNNY TIPLER

you can also trace the roads snaking their way up the hillside, and the farm tracks that bisect the vineyards.

'There's so much else to see,' says Ron, 'like the military bunker for the government, left over from the Cold War, where they were going to run the country from if the bomb went off. We're relatively near Bonn, which was the capital, that's why. Really, you need a week to see everything properly.' We make a detour to Burg Eltz, another jaw-droppingly picturesque *Schloss*, all turrets and pinnacles, and perched on an impregnable bluff. Unsurprisingly, it's a honeypot for sightseers.

For an amusing diversion we make a river crossing aboard a little ferry: the kind that's harnessed to a cable so the current can't sweep it downstream – though it seems to have a plenty powerful engine. We carefully ease both Porsches on board – there's a bit of a lip to the drawbridges at either end – and enjoy the prospect of yet another achingly picturesque riverside haunt, a row of enticing hostelries overlooked by the looming carcass of a medieval castle. The ferry times its runs so as not

to impede the commercial barges and river cruisers – the only mystery is why they need to be so large!

The furthest south we get – in the direction of Trier and Luxembourg – is Bernkastel-Kues, where one of the vintners, J. J. Prüm, will sell you an exquisite bottle of Riesling for… €1,500. This is also the location of Zylinderhaus, a small motor museum housed in a newly constructed 1930s-style municipal building. It harbours an eclectic selection of BMWs and Mercedes-Benz automobiles, mostly from the 1950s, and there's a single Porsche 356C cabriolet. They're especially big on Borgwards, but my favourite is the brown-and-cream Steyr 220 from 1937, a 2.3-litre straight-six with its Streamline Moderne bodywork. We pause beside the river for a quick photo-op, the GT3 and GTS set against a backdrop of grand, late nineteenth-century Jugendstil buildings.

We enjoy a late lunch at another former monastery, Brauhaus Kloster Machern, a wonderful ecclesiastical establishment that's a stone's throw from what's reputedly the tallest river viaduct in the world. The institution was founded by Cistercian nuns in 1084, and they started making wine in 1238. In 1969 they switched over to brewing beer, and, for once, the beverage on offer is *Weissbier* (wheat beer) rather than wine.

We're done here, and it's time to turn tail and head northwest for Stavelot, where we have a dinner reservation at the Val d'Amblève, another fabulous gourmet treat. It transpires that Ron is also a connoisseur par excellence of fine wines and champagnes. He's brought a number of bottles from his cellar for us to sample, and frankly, I have never counted so many wine glasses on a restaurant table. Star attraction is the new 'Rare' champagne from Piper-Heidsieck; what can I say? Salut!

Our road trip culminates with two hours lapping Spa-Francorchamps. Ron's brand-new RSR Spa facilities are located just inside the gate into the track at Blanchimont. His techies take the Cayman for a check-over and inflate the tyres. I attend the driver briefing, and it seems that only three out of ten of us have driven at Spa before – I last attended an RSR session here in 2012. But still, there'll only be a couple of Caymans and a pair of shared Elises, so no pressure like there was back at the Ring.

I'm allocated Freddy Mayeur as my instructor and, suitably helmeted, we take to the track. We do a couple of laps and come in. 'You're gripping the wheel too tight, and being too aggressive turning in to the corners,' he advises me. We switch over, and he demonstrates what he means by holding the wheel between two fingers on each hand. 'It's like playing the piano,' he says. 'And braking and going back on the gas, it's the same: you must be smoother.' On several corners I've evidently been turning in far too soon, and at the entry to

ABOVE: **A castellated riverside house straddles the road at Bernkastel-Kues, as the 718 Cayman GTS takes off to investigate yet another Mosel beauty spot.** KOSTAS SIDIRAS

LEFT: **Johnny Tipler tracks Raidillon curve at the summit of Spa's Eau Rouge dash in the RSR Nürburg 718 Cayman GTS.** KOSTAS SIDIRAS

At the apex, rounding La Source hairpin at Spa-Francorchamps in the RSR Nürburg 718 Cayman GTS, as thrilling a circuit to drive – in its own way – as the Nordschleife.

KOSTAS SIDIRA

Fagnes we wait unfeasibly long before turning. The double-left sweeps of Blanchimont were difficult to get consistently right, as was the Bus Stop chicane for some reason, slow as it is.

Just free your mind and imagine you are on a Sunday drive. Your car is the cello and the track is your musical score. When you are relaxed behind the steering wheel, your driving will be much more serene. So, you don't have to think, 'maybe I should be faster', you don't have to fight with your steering wheel, just relax, breathe sometimes, stop racing in the corners. Of course, you have to deal with traffic, but before running you have to walk, to do lap after lap and then it will come by itself. Even on your last lap you beat your speed of the one before, and it was easier.

Sure, and at least twice I got Eau Rouge and Raidillon absolutely right, mostly by backing off earlier than anticipated on the downhill run on the old pits straight, and few things are more satisfying than that.

The superbly sorted chassis and power delivery of the Cayman GTS plays a significant part, of course. For the time being, the 718 Cayman GT4 retains the normally aspirated 4.0-litre flat-six shared with the 991 GT3. In any case, Porsche have done a superb job with their basic Turbo models, from air-cooled 930 to 991, and now that every car they produce – bar the GT3 – is turbocharged, perhaps forced induction will be better understood and more accepted as a route to better economy and emissions control as well as generating high performance. The cachet and charisma of an out-and-out 911 Turbo will never wane, though.

Explosive artwork of a 991 Turbo S by Sonja Verducci (www.saatchiart.com/sonjaverducci). SONJA VERDUCCI

INDEX